Aspen College Series

Women and Criminal Justice

Marilyn D. McShane
University of Houston

Ming-Li Hsieh
Washington State University

Published by Wolters Kluwer Law & Business in New York.

Wolters Kluwer Law & Business serves customers worldwide with CCH, Aspen Publishers, and Kluwer Law International products. (www.wolterskluwerlb.com)

To contact Customer Service, e-mail customer.service@wolterskluwer.com, call 1-800-234-1660, fax 1-800-901-9075, or mail correspondence to:

> Wolters Kluwer Law & Business
> Attn: Order Department
> PO Box 990
> Frederick, MD 21705

Printed in the United States of America.

1 2 3 4 5 6 7 8 9 0

ISBN 978-1-4548-2809-9

Library of Congress Cataloging-in-Publication Data

McShane, Marilyn D., 1956-
Women and criminal justice/Marilyn D. McShane, University of Houston; Ming-Li Hsieh, Washington State University.
    pages cm. — (Aspen College series)
  Includes bibliographical references and index.
  ISBN 978-1-4548-2809-9 (alk. paper) — ISBN 1-4548-2809-9 (alk. paper)
    1. Women — Legal status, laws, etc. — United States. 2. Women — Violence against — United States. 3. Female offenders — United States. 4. Women prisoners — United States. 5. Women criminal justice personnel — United States. 6. Sex discrimination in criminal justice administration — United States. 7. Sex discrimination in criminal justice administration. I. Hsieh, Ming-Li, author. II. Title.

  KF478.M37 2014
  364.3'740973 — dc23
                          2014003723

About Wolters Kluwer Law & Business

Wolters Kluwer Law & Business is a leading global provider of intelligent information and digital solutions for legal and business professionals in key specialty areas, and respected educational resources for professors and law students. Wolters Kluwer Law & Business connects legal and business professionals as well as those in the education market with timely, specialized authoritative content and information-enabled solutions to support success through productivity, accuracy and mobility.

Serving customers worldwide, Wolters Kluwer Law & Business products include those under the Aspen Publishers, CCH, Kluwer Law International, Loislaw, Best Case, ftwilliam.com and MediRegs family of products.

CCH products have been a trusted resource since 1913, and are highly regarded resources for legal, securities, antitrust and trade regulation, government contracting, banking, pension, payroll, employment and labor, and healthcare reimbursement and compliance professionals.

Aspen Publishers products provide essential information to attorneys, business professionals and law students. Written by preeminent authorities, the product line offers analytical and practical information in a range of specialty practice areas from securities law and intellectual property to mergers and acquisitions and pension/benefits. Aspen's trusted legal education resources provide professors and students with high-quality, up-to-date and effective resources for successful instruction and study in all areas of the law.

Kluwer Law International products provide the global business community with reliable international legal information in English. Legal practitioners, corporate counsel and business executives around the world rely on Kluwer Law journals, looseleafs, books, and electronic products for comprehensive information in many areas of international legal practice.

Loislaw is a comprehensive online legal research product providing legal content to law firm practitioners of various specializations. Loislaw provides attorneys with the ability to quickly and efficiently find the necessary legal information they need, when and where they need it, by facilitating access to primary law as well as state-specific law, records, forms and treatises.

ftwilliam.com offers employee benefits professionals the highest quality plan documents (retirement, welfare and non-qualified) and government forms (5500/PBGC, 1099 and IRS) software at highly competitive prices.

MediRegs products provide integrated health care compliance content and software solutions for professionals in healthcare, higher education and life sciences, including professionals in accounting, law and consulting.

Wolters Kluwer Law & Business, a division of Wolters Kluwer, is headquartered in New York. Wolters Kluwer is a market-leading global information services company focused on professionals.

To Helena Angelica DeFina (1963-2014), who was always a compassionate advocate for women.

MMC

To my grandmother, Mei-Yuan Ou-Yang, a woman of immense courage who escaped from a Communist state to a free society, and to all the other women who joined her in that dramatic journey.

MLH

Summary of Contents

Contents

3   The Female Victim and the Criminal Justice System 39

4   Prostitution and Sex Crimes 59

5   Women and Domestic Violence 81

6   Other Domestic Offenses 101

7   Female Drug Offending 121

8   Women and Corrections 141

9   Issues in Female Delinquency 163

Although it is important to integrate women's issues into all courses across the criminal justice curriculum, a focus class such as Women and Criminal Justice provides the depth and discussion necessary to access the nuances involved in the evolution of gender equality. Allowing students to view the chronology of legislation, judicial intervention, law enforcement, and punitive corrections practices provides a clearer picture of the progress made but also points out continuing struggles and imbalances in the justice system. Thus this text informs a course that includes history, economics, law, political science, sociology, psychology, and of course criminal justice.

As authors, we are sensitive to the criticisms that have been raised about gender-based courses, particularly in a field as traditionally male-dominated as criminal justice. In *A Room of One's Own*, Virginia Woolf wrote about the difference between writing in the "red light of emotion" rather than the "white light of truth." While reading emotionally tinged work often helps to ignite us to critique and condemn, it prevents us from perhaps more constructively and objectively working within reality. Anyone teaching in this field has experienced the potential for spirited if not volatile discourse when issues of crime and gender are combined. In balancing the emotional and the factual, we attempt to spark our students into creative thinking and effective problem solving. Sensitizing is a delicate process, with the goal of building not only local and national, but global awareness of the barriers to gender equity that still remain.

As always, we welcome feedback and suggestions for future work in this area. We would like to thank the faculty of both our respective departments for their support and the opportunities to teach Women and Criminal Justice. We are grateful for the publishing efforts of Wolters Kluwer, particularly Kaesmene Harrison Banks, as well as our kind and gentle project manager, Christine Becker. And finally, we would like to express heartfelt appreciation to our female mentors in the field of criminology and criminal justice who have paved the way for the careers we enjoy today.

Women and Criminal Justice

The Study of Women and Crime

Introduction

In January 1930, a night watchman in Chandler, Arizona, lost his life in a gun battle with a small band of outlaws led by Irene "The Animal" Schroeder. Captured after a long chase across the desert, Schroeder was returned to Pennsylvania to be tried for an earlier murder of a lawman there (Wagner, 1999). Her moniker came from her own assessment that "I am not a woman. I'm nothing but an animal . . . full of nothing but animal instinct and self-preservation" (Shipman, 2002, p. 212). Newspaper coverage of her trial also referred to her as "Irene of the six-shooters" and "the chunky little trigger girl." Reports also suggested that Schroeder had been a "canned heat addict" or sterno abuser, something alcoholics at the time often resorted to.

> Schroeder testified that she had an irresistible impulse to steal and that the holdups . . . thrilled her. She said the impulses began at age ten, when she fell and injured her head. She testified that she had attempted suicide on three or four occasions. . . . Special Prosecutor Charles J. Margiotti told the jury in his closing arguments that Schroeder had masterminded a crime organization, and that she and her accomplices had been "carrion birds swooping into Pennsylvania to prey on fellow humans" (Shipman, 2002, p. 213).

Schroeder was convicted, and one year later she was executed. She was the only woman ever strapped into Pennsylvania's electric chair.

Images of the female offender have ranged over time: from witches in the early American colonies to Wild West folk heroes to vixens in city brothels and ruthless axe murderers in country cabins. From the Bible referring to woman as responsible for the fall from grace, to the fingers pointed at single mothers in city ghettos, we have long found ways to separate issues of crime into issues of gender. The public and the media have historically been captivated by the statistically rare, and therefore perhaps more intriguing, notion of women — wives, mothers, and sweet, young daughters who are capable of committing crimes.

It is the goal of any course of study on women and criminal justice to help students explore the realities of gender differences in issues of criminality, victimization, and employment in the justice system. One of the key tasks, then, is to separate real differences from those merely perceived as true or those with no evidence behind them. Data, research, and theory will guide us on this quest. Historical and contemporary accounts of women's experiences help illustrate points and sensitize us to gender's impact on personal interpretations of events. These lived accounts also suggest possible explanations for behavior, but they are, at best, anecdotal and should be weighed as such.

Historical Criminology

In the earliest of criminological analyses, Dr. Cesare Lombroso wrote that although there were far fewer "born criminal" women than men, women were far more ferocious, revengeful, jealous, and inclined toward cruelty (1895, p. 150). He argued that because women are less sensitive to pain, they would also lack compassion. Because prostitution was not considered a "crime" at the time he wrote, such women were more likely to be viewed as impure, immoral, and weak. He distinguished this group from the truly criminal woman:

> What terrific criminals would children be if they had strong passions, muscular strength, and sufficient intelligences; and if, moreover, their evil tendencies were exasperated by a morbid physical activity. And women are big children; their evil tendencies are more numerous and more varied than men's but generally remain latent. When they are awakened and excited they produce results proportionately greater.
>
> . . . the criminal woman is consequently a monster. Her normal sister is kept in the paths of virtue by many causes, such as maternity, piety, weakness and when these counter influences fail, and a woman commits a crime, we may conclude that her wickedness must have been enormous before it could triumph over so many obstacles (Lombroso, 1895, p. 150).

It is no wonder that feminist criminologists have reviled the work of Lombroso over the years. Still, his theorizing represents common thinking of his time; it also illustrates the influence that his medical training must have had on his ideas and allows us to see how much our views have evolved in this area as well.

As Dorie Klein writes (1973, p. 6), early researchers like Lombroso did not credit women with the intellect of a master criminal, they were thought to be "inherently inferior to men at masculine tasks such as thought and production. . . . " Still, there are many examples of the criminal ingenuity and deviant talents of women, even in the early American colonial period. In the National Women's History Project (http://www.nwhp.org/resourcecenter/pathbreakers.php), the following biography appears:

Mary Peck Butterworth (July 27, 1686, o.s.-February 7, 1775) was born in Rehoboth, Massachusetts, when it was part of the Plymouth Colony. This was during the conflict known as King Phillip's War, which was one of America's bloodiest wars. It was a time of resistance and great bravery on the part of the Massachusetts Indians and the settlers. In 1711, she married John Butterworth, Jr. This was a time of mixed political loyalty and by the time of her marriage, she along with other members of her family were counterfeiting money. She used her fine needlework skills, attention to detail and organization acumen to counterfeit at least eight types of bills. By 1716 she had perfected a method of counterfeiting the 5-pound bills of Rhode Island. Her new money was made by placing fine muslin on a genuine bill, transferring the image using a very hot iron to clean paper. The muslin was then quickly destroyed. One of her brothers made the pens from crow feathers for lettering the bills. Other brothers and their wives were part of the kitchen workshop industry. Friends in Rehoboth, including the town clerk and members of the county court bought her bills for half the face value. When one of the accomplices confessed to the governor, Mary's house was searched but nothing was found. The confessions of the accomplice were impugned and charges were dropped (Zierdt, 2007).

As one of the first female superintendents of a women's prison facility, Katherine Bement Davis (1860-1935) could not help but be influenced by the work of theorists like Lombroso. As a criminologist, Davis was a proponent of criminal theories that presented offenders as being of subnormal intelligence and biologically defective. Nonetheless, as an advocate of the medical model, she was concerned about the number of prostitutes, their lack of education and skills, and their high rates of disease. Fines for prostitution, she argued, usually placed the female offender further in debt to her male pimp and were therefore counterproductive. However, Davis was also not immune from the concerns of her day, particularly those about cultural adaptation to life in the melting pot of America. She pointed out the many Italian names on the rosters of incarcerated women and speculated that they emigrated with "their own primitive ideas of vengeance." She lamented that some of the women murderers at her Bedford institution were caught up in the conflicts of their culture when their own codes make them "victims of the racial custom of revenge."

While others at this time were staunch proponents of eugenics principles such as the labeling of moral defectives and the feebleminded, Davis was more cautious. As a staunch advocate for the scientific study of crime, particularly the clinical assessment of the offender, Davis persuaded John D. Rockefeller, Jr., to donate $50,000 to establish a Laboratory of Social Hygiene directly across from the reformatory. This was one of the first institutes dedicated to the study of female criminality. Lombroso's perspectives on criminality may have been narrowed by his training as a physician, but others, like Katherine Bement Davis, came to see the broader array of social, cultural, political, and economic forces that influenced criminal behavior, including the behavior of female offenders.

Progress Toward Women's Rights

There are many reasons why women were slow to advance in gaining access to the rights and privileges that men enjoyed in the colonies. The role of military service, Browder (2006) explains, was crucial in defining citizenship during the Civil War era in this country. Being armed and defending your country were considered essential qualifications for those participating in the governance of the states. The idea that "patriotism is armed" is an enduring feature of our culture but also represents, ironically, a symbol of the barriers to be overcome by women.

One of the most important foundations for understanding progress toward legal recognition of women's rights is the work of the suffragist movement.[1] From the first women's rights convention in 1848 in Seneca Falls, New York, until the passage of the Nineteenth Amendment in 1920, the road to citizenship privileges was hard fought by a large group of dedicated activists. Some rights were acquired piecemeal, like in Massachusetts in 1854 when the legislature granted property rights to women. And, as we see, even though the Fifteenth Amendment was ratified in 1870, that amendment was not the means by which voting rights would reach women in this country. Though the wording of the amendment may seem gender neutral, thus opening the polls to women, those who tested its intent were all denied access to the voting booths.

Western territories like Wyoming, Idaho, and Utah, followed by California and Alaska, were the earliest to ratify enfranchisement for women. Unlike the established states of the eastern United States, the need for voters and stable property ownership, as well as the need to attract settlers and "grow" a population that would lead to statehood, probably explains the progressive policies. There were opportunities for women in the settlements of the west as restrictive stereotypes were necessarily shed and some adventure-seeking and perhaps less-traditional women became accomplished hunters and legendary pioneers. Success in this realm meant demonstrating that one could protect and provide for oneself, as well as for the family, often by farming, ranching, and, on occasion, shouldering a weapon and shooting to kill. Obviously, as suited the needs of our expanding young country, certain more aggressive and masculinized traits were tolerated in women, even extolled where circumstances demanded. Where deviant women were identified and stigmatized, they tended to be distinguished

---

[1] Critical events and accomplishments can be found at http://www.suffragist.com/timeline.htm.

by the racially mixed and sexually compromised status of the early female offender.

By 1893, men voting in Colorado made their state only the second one in which women had full voting rights. Unfortunately, in eastern states, women's rights issues had become entangled with support for prohibition, which all but destroyed any hope of passage. Despite advances made in the suffragist movement and through the passage of the Nineteenth Amendment in 1920, the status of women declined after World War I. Criminologist Dorie Klein argues that the simplistic images of women by authors like Sigmund Freud, Kingsley Davis, and Otto Pollak negatively impacted the social status of women:

> One can mark the decline in the position of women after the 1920s through the use of various indices: by noting the progressively earlier age of marriage of women in the United States and the steady rise in the number of children born to them, culminating in the birth explosion of the late forties and fifties; by looking at the relative decline in the number of women scholars; . . . Freudianism has had an unparalleled influence in the United States (and came at a key point to help swing the tide against the women's movement) to facilitate the return of women during the depression and postwar years to the home, out of an economy which had no room for them. Healthy women would now be seen as masochistic, passive and sexually indifferent. Criminal women would be seen as *sexual misfits*. Most importantly, psychological factors would be used to explain criminal activity, and social, economic and political factors would be ignored. Explanations would seek to be universal, and historical possibilities of change would be refuted (Klein, 1973, p. 338).

Even Adolph Hitler would proclaim that the woman's world was "her husband, her family, her children, and her home."

If you were reading a criminology book written in the 1940s, you would have come across this, or a similar, passage:

> Men steal for women or to bask in their ingratiating smile; women kill for men so that they may rid themselves of unwanted mates; both men and women kill each other because of sexual jealousy. While it is dangerous to generalize, it is almost proverbial that most offenses committed by women involve men, directly or indirectly. Women are often used by their male friends as decoys to put victims on the spot. In the days of the notorious Dillinger gang, several women made the front pages by being identified with the gang-killers as their "molls." In gang warfare, women play an important part. Though it is often said that they are dupes of the male gangsters, this is seldom the case. Often they furnish the brains in predatory crime. Regardless of their participation, they usually retain their feminine attributes, albeit with a certain acquisition of coarseness (Barnes & Teeters, 1943, p. 569).

Some of the more notorious female offenders were more correctly seen as created both by popular media images and by literary figures of the times. FBI Director (from 1924 to 1972) J. Edgar Hoover and the detective magazine genre contributed to the glorified images of gangster girls. The new image was as well-dressed armed bandits who were no longer ethnically diverse foreigners but, instead, were all-American ruthless and dangerous women. Browder (2006) assesses that Hoover had his work cut out for him attempting to disabuse the public of the romantic aura surrounding these characters. He went so far as to blame the creation of gangster men on gangster women, citing as an example the wayward parenting of the infamous "Ma" Barker.

Women, Crime, and Blame

For as long as we have been studying crime, people have simplified its context and blamed one thing or another for perceived increases in crime rates, even when actual crime rates were not increasing. The family has been a constant focus in this process, particularly the role of the mother. From morally weak mothers to working mothers, attempts have been made to link delinquency, drugs, and assorted other crime trends to various maternal deficits.

Data over the last decade appear to indicate that roughly 40% of White and 75% of African American children will experience family disruption through separation and divorce. Roughly 40% of births nationwide are registered to single women (Lee, 2012). Current estimates would indicate that there are more than 12 million single-parent homes, of which 85% would be female headed (Patchin, 2006). Research also suggests that youth in families where a single parent has a significant other on the premises are more likely to join gangs (Hill et al., 1999) and to have more unsupervised time in which to engage in delinquent activities. Data also indicate that in this country, over 40% of single-mother households with children are living in poverty (Lee, 2012).

Even though there is little, if any, evidence of an actual direct relationship between working mothers and delinquency, Vander ven (2003, p. 2) explains, "widespread maternal employment stimulates much public debate in magazine and newspaper editorials . . . talk radio, and prime-time news specials. Recently, the potential negative effects of maternal employment were debated in a Long Island newspaper following the tragic shootings at a Colorado high school, with a letter to the editor suggesting that the Littleton massacre was directly related to the absence and neglect of working mothers."

The Indirect Effects of the Law on Women

For feminists, legal barriers to the designation of certain offenses as serious crimes are a critical area of study and point to a need for political action. Areas of concern also include the prosecution of women or the creation of women victims when women are singled out for harsher treatment in incidents that involve pregnancy, parenting, and parental liability. Critics argue that aggressive prosecution of pregnant female drug addicts under fetal abuse statutes only seems to drive women further from view and keeps them from using social and medical services that would address not only their health but that of the baby as well. Laws that hold a parent legally and financially accountable for the offenses of their children, such as truancy and gang activity, have a disproportionate impact on women as they are more likely to be single mothers, the primary caregiver, and the custodial parent.

The use of the law to further penalize and thus perhaps victimize women (as we will see in coming sections) is a central tenet of both conflict and feminist theories of crime. For example, when first hearing the term *menopause defense*, one might think that it is a justification or explanation for some type of conduct that might help mitigate the culpability of a woman accused of some violent crime. However, legal scholars explain, that was hardly the case. In fact, it was

> . . . a creation of a civil defense bar that seized upon a cultural stereotype of aging women and prevailing sexist norms. The defense predominantly was asserted by men, in male dominated courtrooms, to devalue female plaintiffs, cast blame upon them, and attempt to deny women compensation or other remedies. . . . The essential premise of this defense was that a woman approaching mid-life was either mentally ill, physically ill or both (Bookspan & Kline, 1999, pp. 1271-1272).

In a study of cases appealed between 1900 and the mid-1980s, Bookspan and Kline (1999) found that when a menopause defense had been used, the result was mostly to the disadvantage of the women who were labeled with it. Insurance companies, husbands seeking a divorce, and employers used the claim in an attempt to deny benefits and compensation to women. For example, the authors note, "In a case documenting that a rusty, used, razor blade was in a bottle of soda the plaintiff ingested, defendant, Pepsi-Cola Co., unabashedly claimed that plaintiff's digestive problems and vomiting were due to her menopause rather than to the contaminated Pepsi that she drank" (p. 1272).

According to another study by Proano-Raps and Meyer (2007), the perception that a woman who was menopausal was not, at the moment, capable of being a wife was linked to the American Psychiatric Association's *Diagnostic and Statistics Manual*. The *Manual*, which is used to establish legitimate psychiatric disorders, associated menopause with involutional melancholia. When this diagnosis disappeared from the text in 1980, its use in the courts also ended.

Though the most blatant barriers to gender equality in society have been removed, many indirect and less obvious problems remain. Within the law, what may appear as a rational or neutral mechanism to accomplish some alternative goal, may really, in its effects, have a negative and disparate impact on women. For example, the *California Street Terrorism Enforcement and Prevention Act* seems to offer law enforcement officials a powerful tool in combating the activities of street gangs. Broad enforcement, however, and the legislation's often vague terminology and provisions may mean that a mother can forfeit her home if any portion of her child's gang activity takes place there, even unknowingly. This could happen despite the fact that she and her other children, who are not involved in gangs, reside there. In cases like this, the term *parent* is often inserted as a prosecutorial attempt to establish responsibility for financial liability or criminal acts when, in fact, the likelihood that the parent will be a single mother is overwhelmingly high. Thus, a seemingly neutral law providing "punishment" for parents with gang-affiliated children overwhelmingly affected females.

With California's street gang law in mind, it is instructive to consider the potential impact of other, similar laws (you should also consider that in cases of divorce, a woman is more likely to retain physical custody of any children). In every state in this country, parents can be held strictly liable for property damage caused by their children. Laws vary among the states on the types of claims that can be made, whether those claims are civil or criminal in nature, the range of possible fines, and the range of allowable punishments. In Utah, parents can be sued civilly for damage caused by a child driving without a license while being charged criminally for furnishing a vehicle to an unlicensed driver. Civil liability can also be incurred for a child's shoplifting. Many states have social hosting laws to hold a parent responsible for any accidents that might occur following liquor accessed in their home by underage drinkers.

Although many citizens applaud these efforts to hold parents more accountable for delinquency, it should be obvious that they have the potential to disproportionately affect more single mothers. Gang abatement laws in particular seem purposely constructed to appeal to a gang member's loyalty to his or her mother by providing avenues to charge women who receive any money or goods from their gang-member children.

Truancy laws also have the potential to disparately impact single mothers. In California, for instance, a parent may be required to attend hearings and parenting classes, submit to home visits, pay fines, serve jail sentences up to one year, or serve terms of probation and community service for violations of Penal Code section 272 (Stroman, 2000).

In yet another example of law that negatively impacts women, communities have begun to deal harsh penalties to "parents" who are found to violate the law in order to enroll their children in better schools in districts in which they do not legally reside. In Akron, Ohio, Kelley Williams-Bolar's motive for this crime was trying to protect her two daughters. Because her home had been broken into, Williams-Bolar did not want her children arriving there after school before she did. By registering them in a district near her father, the girls would be supervised. Using his suburban address instead of her own, she believed their safety would be insured. But Williams-Bolar was convicted of felony records tampering and sentenced to a short jail term, and her children were transferred back to the city schools. With that conviction, she is now facing the loss of not only her teacher's aid job but her future as a licensed teacher (Franko, 2011).

Although districts across the country seem to handle the problem differently, all legal interventions are costly and damaging to single mothers. After losing her job in a nursing home and her apartment in a good school district, Pennsylvania mother Latoni Crowder used a cousin's address to enroll her daughter in a school she trusted. Despite her defense that she just did not want to see her child fall behind while she was unemployed, Crowder was ordered to pay $1,359 in reimbursements over a 12-month period (Franko, 2001).

Women and Violence

Data and research on female offenders tell us much about the complex dynamics of their criminal activity. One of the more controversial areas of research involves whether women have the same capacity for violence as men. If, as many believe, violence is a sociological or psychological phenomenon enhanced by environmental rewards and interactions (which some feminists call *gender education*), then we must pay attention to the way we raise, instruct, and reinforce behaviors in both girls and boys.

On the other hand, if biological or physiological processes are responsible for violent behavior, then physical differences between men and women might explain differences in rates of violent offending. In a variety of recent books (*The Female Brain; Brain Sex; Sex on the Brain; Brain Gender*), researchers explore the way brain structure and hormones produce gender-specific behaviors. And according to one author, "the female brain is so deeply affected by hormones that their influence can be said to create a woman's reality" (Brizendine, 2006). Only over the last few decades have we introduced the concept of a "woman's reality" into law. The test for "reasonableness" often proffered to juries who are gauging the intent of a defendant's actions has been revised to include what a "reasonable woman" would believe. In this way, a battered woman or a very petite woman might believe that she had no other recourse but to shoot a potential attacker. In the past, the "reasonable man" test in law often precluded the necessity to think outside one's gender to understand how an attacker might be perceived.

Women clearly do not engage in violent behavior as frequently as do men. According to the Bureau of Justice Statistics, women make up only 10% of all convictions for violent crime. In examining data from the 1990s, Barbara Koons-Witt and Pamela Schram (2006) found that victims of violent crimes were six times more likely to report that the perpetrator was a male rather than a female. And, in instances where females committed violent crimes, they acted alone only about half the time. In cases where they had a co-offender, it was most often another female rather than a male (Koons-Witt & Schram, 2006). Retired Judge Patricia Wald from the U.S. Court of Appeals commented on the need to develop gender-specific sentencing strategies:

> No one disputes that women offenders as a group simply do not present the same degree of danger to the community that male offenders do as a group. Indeed, the Bureau of Prisons has instituted a separate classification category for women offenders based on their predominantly nonviolent character (Sherman, 2001, p. 1).

Even though what we call anecdotal accounts of some violent women can be found in crime literature, these narratives are not representative of female offenders or even female offenders convicted of violent acts. In a study of women who had been incarcerated in Texas for murder, Sorensen and Cunningham (2007) found that these prisoners were subsequently unlikely to engage in serious assaults. Their findings were similar to other studies that found that, overall, women in the federal system were unlikely to engage in assaults that led to any serious injury. That research indicated that women in federal custody engaged in serious assaults at "one-twelfth the rate of men" and that "there was no record of a female ever committing a homicide while in federal custody." Moreover, other studies of female offenders in state prisons have also documented that women have lower rates of serious violent misconduct than men (Sorensen & Cunningham, 2007, p. 552).

Women and the Death Penalty

In the period of time from 1632 to the execution of Velma Barfield in 1984, Strieb and Sametz (1988) calculated that 389 women had been put to death in this country. During that time, 32 different states executed at least one woman, although some engaged in the practice more frequently. Virginia had the most executions with 93 women killed, more than twice that of the state with the next highest number. Although most were executed for murder or attempted murder, Strieb and Sametz indicate that "a very high percentage of those convicted of murders killed their child, husband or lover, and almost all of them killed someone well-known to them. If not a family member, their victim was typically an employer, a neighbor, or, in the cases of slaves, a member of their master's family" (1988, p. 43). Twenty-seven cases documented that the woman was accused of witchcraft, primarily in and around Salem, Massachusetts.

The Strieb and Sametz (1988) data distribute executions of women across American history as follows:

- 1600s: 46
- 1700s: 101
- 1800s: 197
- 1900-1984: 39

Because these numbers do not account for increases in population, the figure of 39 executions in the twentieth century is even comparatively smaller than it appears. From 1900 to 1984, there almost seems to be a cultural reluctance to execute females.

As with males, there is a racial component to executions of females. Across the entire dataset, two thirds of those executed were Black and about 31% were listed as White. This profile reflects what was also found in relation to the execution of female juveniles in early America, although only a handful of these cases could be found. In those records, only one of ten offenders was designated as White, the rest being Black, American Indian, or of mixed race. Eight of the girls had committed murder, all of the victims were White, and most were children.

Streib (2012) reported that, as of year-end 2011, there were 58 women awaiting execution in 18 U.S. states. According to recent figures, women represent only 2% of the 3,146 total sentenced to death row in this country, although they also represent about 10% of homicide offenders (Graczyk, 2013). In Texas alone there are nine women currently on death row, compared to approximately 340 men. Records from the Texas Department of Criminal Justice indicate that five of those women are White, three are Black, and one is Hispanic.[2] In January 2013, Kimberly McCarthy, an African American and the only one of the group with an execution date, was the 13th woman in this country and the fourth woman in the state to be put to death in Texas since the courts approved revised capital punishment statutes in 1976. In that same period of time, Graczyk (2013) reports that, nationwide, more than 1,300 men were executed.

The Status of Women in the United States Today

The lists of achievements for women in government and industry have increased tremendously since one of the authors used to look through the employment ads in the newspaper with two separate sections: "Help Wanted — Male" and "Help Wanted — Female." We have had women run for vice president of the United States and for the nomination for president. Under the Obama administration, six cabinet positions are held by women, the number of women on the Supreme Court has increased to three, and 15 women are listed as chief executive officers (CEOs) on a recent Fortune 500 list. Still, as Sixel (2011) explains, the progress women have made in leadership roles in this country is not evenly distributed.

> While 90 percent of companies on the S&P 500 have at least one female director, only 49 percent of Houston's companies do. . . . While 56 percent of the S&P 500 boards have two or more female directors, only 15 percent of the boards in Houston can claim that. (Sixel, 2011, p. D5).

There are many who argue that a firm legal mechanism in our judicial system to enforce gender equality will not exist until a federal Equal Rights Amendment (ERA) is passed. Initially introduced almost 100 years ago in Congress, the ERA Bill has continually stalled because it has not had the required support of enough states, even though it would take only the affirmative votes of three more states to be ratified. As of now, Alabama, Arizona, Arkansas, Florida, Georgia, Illinois, Louisiana, Mississippi, Missouri, Nevada, North Carolina, Oklahoma,

---

[2] More information about these prisoners can be found on the department's website at http://www.tdcj.state.tx.us/stat/dr_women_on_dr.html.

South Carolina, Utah, and Virginia are the states that have not officially recognized gender equality.

There are many reasons why a gender-diverse criminal justice workplace is of benefit to the agencies and to society in general. An employee population that best mirrors the citizenry served (those processed by the justice system) can better address common issues and problems arising in the field. For example, agencies must follow strict staffing regulations requiring female officers to oversee the administration of urine testing for female offenders or accompany female juveniles in transit between facilities or court hearings. Without a sufficient number of female officers, the logistics of normal day-to-day activity can become a nightmare for administrators. There are other more general concerns as well. As the technology of law enforcement and corrections makes physical contact and raw physical strength less necessary, a wider range of people and skills can be utilized in the maintenance of order.

The Female Offender Today

In Harris County's Pretrial Services, defendants are interviewed following an arrest to determine their status and to make appropriate decisions about disposition. In the 2008 Pretrial Services Annual Report, the department indicated that about 21% of both felony and misdemeanor cases involved female defendants. The fact that there are fewer detention facilities available for women often means that all classifications of female offenders are housed together, including women who may be sick, mentally ill, violent, or elderly.

In general, the research literature on women offenders in the courts is fairly consistent in finding differences in sentences between males and females that are best explained by gender. As Doerner and Demuth explain, a number of studies have found that

> . . . female defendants are treated more leniently than male defendants (Bickle & Peterson, 1991; Daly & Bordt, 1995; Spohn, 2000, 2002; Steffensmeier, Kramer, & Streifel, 1993); however, there are some researchers who report no differences (Kruttschnitt & Green, 1984). Spohn (2002) shows that the odds of receiving a prison sentence are 2.5 times greater for male offenders than for female offenders after controlling for legally relevant factors. Research on sentencing in Pennsylvania courts by Steffensmeier and colleagues (1993, 2000) indicates that gender, net of other factors, has an effect on sentencing outcomes with female defendants sentenced less harshly than male defendants. Similarly, Griffin and Wooldredge (2006) find that women are sentenced more leniently than men in Ohio courts both before and after recent sentencing reforms (2010, p. 4).

Overall, female offenders are more likely than their male counterparts to have past, present, or both past and present victimization and experiences including physical, emotional, and sexual abuse. They are more likely to have grown up in a single-parent home and to have physical disabilities. These offenders are more likely to be minority women, unmarried mothers in their late twenties to mid-thirties. It has also been documented that women are more likely than men to commit crimes in order to obtain drugs (Peters, 2007). Thus, they are also more likely to be convicted of drug offenses and nonviolent drug crimes, which explains the significant increase in female incarceration. A substantial number of women processed through the criminal justice system have had some type of mental health diagnoses, specifically post-traumatic stress disorders and depression, and also have family members who have been through the criminal justice system. In addition, a majority of these women were unemployed at the time of their offending, and they have shorter work histories than male offenders as well as more limited vocational training (Davidson, 2009).

The profile of the typical female offender as described above indicates that there are many challenges to developing successful strategies for reintegration into the community. Though they generally have shorter criminal histories than their male counterparts, they are less likely to receive access to treatment programs (Peters, 2007). Treatment professionals frequently talk about the "additive effects" of each of the life problems these women face and the way the issues seem to interact to cause complex disabilities and disadvantages. To complicate the picture, you could add the problems related to the effects of crime, poverty, and substance abuse on the minor children that women are more likely to be caring for and the subsequent risk of delinquency in those children (Figure 1-1).

We have all heard people who argue that each offender, male or female, makes choices that result in his or her involvement in the criminal justice system. To many, this position is simple, as well as a black and white issue: "If only the person hadn't done this or that, her life would be fine. If the offender had not chosen to take those drugs or stolen that credit card, then they would be just like you or me, a law-abiding citizen." However, the reality, and what we learn through studying social problems is that life choices are much more complicated than the average person perceives them as being.

Challenges with housing, safety, discrimination, addiction, low levels of work skills or education, all affect us differently. Our childhood and family history, many theories tell us, play a significant role in shaping the way we view our environment, how we handle its deficiencies, and the choices we make. And, even though our choices place us at risk for exposure to victimization and criminal opportunities, unless we also encounter the means to change our circumstances, those risks can lead to incarceration, death, continued poverty, and health crises. The fact that many women are also single parents adds the risk of exposing children to this same cycle of deficiencies, risks, and consequences.

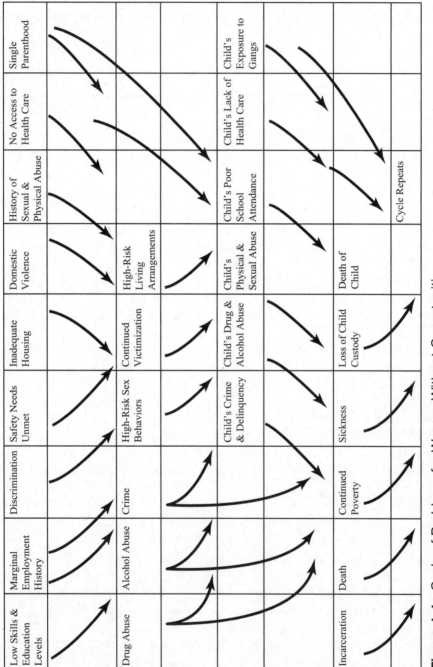

Figure 1-1. Cycle of Problems for Women Without Opportunities

Gender Effects on Perceptions of Crime Risk and Victimization

In truth, we can never really say that crimes against women have increased or decreased; all we are able to reflect on is the number of crimes and victimizations that are actually reported. Whether through law enforcement or some survey mechanism, the official tracking of the number of female victims is likely to greatly underestimate what may actually be occurring. We also know that some crimes are more likely to be reported than others, and so the difference between the real but unknown number of crimes and those that come to the attention of authorities vary by type of incident as well as by time and place. For example, when O.J. Simpson was arrested for the murder of his former wife, Nicole, calls to domestic violence hotlines and cases reported to police spiked dramatically. When former Miss America Marilyn van Derbur publicly shared her story of incest abuse, many women felt encouraged enough to report incidents they had once secretly suppressed. These media effects often give the appearance that a particular type of crime has increased, when in fact, it is simply the notoriety of famous cases that serves as a catalyst to current and future reporting.

The existence of large research databases such as the National Crime Victims Survey and the FBI's National Incident-Based Reporting System tells us much about the risks that women face for both stranger and domestic violence. Many of the data collection systems were developed by grants that were funded more than a decade ago as part of legislation to prevent violence against women. As government priorities change to issues such as immigration and homeland security, you will see fewer studies funded to research issues related to women and the criminal justice system. Still, those data collection systems, such as the homicide statistics published by the Bureau of Justice Statistics (BJS), are in place and can be accessed online. For example, the BJS homicide statistics website tells us that, between 2003 and 2005 in Texas, about one-quarter of all homicide victims were women, and those were predominantly White women.[3] And an earlier report by Ronet Bachman (1994) summarizes the trends we see in violent crimes against women:

> Although women were significantly less likely to become victims of violent crime, they were more vulnerable to particular types of perpetrators. Whereas men were more likely to be victimized by acquaintances or strangers, women were just as likely to be victimized by intimates, such as husbands or boyfriends, as they were to be victimized by acquaintances or strangers. The rate of violence committed by intimates was nearly 10 times greater for females than for males. Women who were the most vulnerable to becoming the victims of violent crime

---

[3] This website allows you to construct your own tables to answer questions about victimization. See what your own state's homicide victims look like (http://bjs.ojp.usdoj.gov/dataonline/Search/Homicide/State/StatebyState.cfm).

were Black, Hispanic, in younger age groups, never married, with lower family income and lower education levels, and in central cities.

Bachman (1994) also found that, except for when the crime was rape, women were more likely to be injured and require medical care when their attackers were intimates rather than strangers. White women with some college were more likely to be victims of theft, while Black and Hispanic women had higher rates of robbery victimization.

Risks may also vary across race, age, and economic groupings as well as by certain types of offenses, but fear of crime appears to be more correlated with gender. Studies seem to consistently indicate that although women are in one of the lower risk groups for crime victimization, they still exhibit higher levels of worry, concern, or fear of crime and seem to be more influenced in that fear by the media (Dowler, 2003). Still others argue that when the discrepancy between fear and actual victimization risk is better researched, there is less of a gender gap than originally thought. For example, it has been suggested that women only appear to be at less risk for crime victimization when, in fact, a large percentage of their victim experiences go unreported, particularly in cases of domestic violence and acquaintance rape. And, when the methods by which survey information relative to fear of crime is collected are carefully controlled, men are more likely to come forward and report higher levels of fear, concern, and worry about victimization than previously documented (Callanan, 2005).

Existing research also tells us that punitive orientations and attitudes toward punishment also seem to be influenced, to some degree, by gender. According to Callanan (2005), a review of the literature in the past several decades reveals that women appear more supportive of rehabilitation and less supportive of the death penalty than men; but, women favor longer sentences for certain type of crimes such as homicide and sexual assault.

Sophisticated studies of juror behavior also contribute to our understanding of how both men and women view women victims. For example, studies have found that women are as likely as men to let an alleged rape victim's lifestyle or prior relationships influence their perceptions of whether consent to sexual intercourse occurred. In fact, a study by Batchelder, Koski, and Byxbe (2004) found that women jurors often acted as a lightning rod or catalyst for increases or decreases in the alleged rape victim's credibility. In testing their thesis of intra-female gender hostility, they found that the women jurors were not only as likely as males to engage in victim blaming, but often were the ones in group interactions to initiate such criticism.

Women in the Workforce Today

Ironically, while the second half of the twentieth century saw women gain strides in virtually every occupational arena, the early twenty-first century has evidenced that they will still suffer similarly to men in times of economic recession and unemployment, which has distinct implications for crime. Although we have seen declines in fields such as seamstress work and clerical and office jobs, experts agree that women may have distinct advantages in the new marketplace. As one report indicates, "On average, there has been a shift away from traditionally male-dominated sectors like manufacturing to the service sector, . . . women now receive almost 60% of bachelors and masters degrees and dominate the health care sector, which is one of the fastest growing categories" (Goudreau, 2011).

Today, traditional criminal justice programs across the United States tend to enroll as many female majors as male, but the percent of females in criminology and criminal justice bachelor degree programs appears to vary by type of school (private versus public) and geographical location. According to a study of students enrolling in three University of Texas campuses (Dickson, 2010), White women tend to be more undecided about their majors than Black and Hispanic women who are more likely to enroll in the social sciences. In that study, gender explained more of the differences in major selection than did race or ethnicity. Given that almost 30% of students are likely to change majors at least once, and that social science programs tend to benefit from that shift, it may be inferred that the job market in criminal justice pushes upper division students toward that degree. University graduate programs in criminal justice report that women are now earning master's and doctorate degrees in criminal justice at much higher rates than ever before.

In 2007, Bjerregaard and Lord published a study indicating that criminal justice students on the whole, and in particular those interested in law enforcement careers, appeared to be more trusting of people than students from other disciplines. They also found that those oriented toward a law enforcement career were more intent on avoiding potentially unethical behaviors. Examining a wide range of studies produced over the last two decades, they noted their findings were consistent with those of other researchers examining the issue: female officers expressed higher ethical standards than male officers. As Bjerregaard and Lord (2007, p. 276) summarized from their research, "women are less likely to follow the group norm; women are more likely to be outside the informal rule system and culture." Like earlier studies, they found that "gender is consistently related to a lower perceived likelihood of engaging in unethical behavior and a perception of these behaviors as more serious" (2007, p. 276).

The Scope of the Text

Those who study the role of women in society will argue that the concept of gender is not a biological state, but a complex system of cultural, social, historical, political, and economic meanings influencing the way we view and incorporate others or isolate them. Beginning with the Suffragist Movement through the Civil Rights Era and the women's liberation movement, there has been an emphasis on providing equal opportunities in all facets of the home, the workplace, and the community. The popular media, magazines, journals, television news shows, and various commentaries all devoted substantial time to this topic. At the same time, criticism of government policies and emergent radical discussions served to highlight an overall sense of who is in power and who is being dominated. As minority groups began to get their discrimination message across, feminist concerns were added to the quest for equality. And, as noted earlier, a constitutional amendment guaranteeing equal rights (ERA) was passed by Congress but has yet to be ratified by the necessary number of states. By the beginning of the 1990s, female themes had become so prevalent that catering to "the female vote" was intrinsic to national political campaigns.

Despite the tendencies for courses on "Women and the Criminal Justice System" to focus primarily on female offending, our discussions will more broadly cover the victimization of women in society and how these experiences may bring them to the system both as offenders and as employees trying to make a difference through their contributions to justice in America. In the chapters to follow, we will look specifically at theories of crime and victimization and the way they can be used to explain and understand women in contact with the criminal justice system today.

Critical Thinking Questions

1. Is an Equal Rights Amendment still necessary? Look for general information about the states that have not passed the ERA. Is there some strategy that could be used to ensure passage of this legislation?

2. In trying to make parents of juveniles more accountable, have new laws disproportionately had a negative impact on single mothers? What can be done to assure parents take responsibility for their children without creating serious disadvantages for single mothers?

3. Examine homicide data on women from your state. How are trends moving and what factors could be influencing female homicide rates?

Books, Websites, and Media Resources

Walls, E., & Pulitzer, L. (2012). *Stolen innocence: My story of growing up in a polygamous sect, becoming a teenage bride, and breaking free of Warren Jeffs.* New York: William Morrow.

Women's Rights Movement Timeline: http://www.infoplease.com/spot/womenstimeline1.html

Women in American History Timeline: http://www.nytimes.com/library/magazine/millennium/m2/wolf-timeline.html

Mary Surratt's role in President Lincoln's assassination: http://law2.umkc.edu/faculty/projects/ftrials/lincolnconspiracy/surrattm.html

http://www.aroundthecapitol.com/code/getcode.html?file=./pen/00001-01000/270-273.75

http://www.nwhp.org/resourcecenter/pathbreakers.php

http://www.suffragist.com/timeline.htm

http://www.tdcj.state.tx.us/stat/dr_women_on_dr.html

http://bjs.ojp.usdoj.gov/dataonline/Search/Homicide/State/StatebyState.cfm

Films

I *Want to Live* (1958), Susan Hayward
The Brave One (2007), Jodie Foster
Bonnie and Clyde (1967), Faye Dunaway

References

Bachman, R. (1994). *Violence against women: A National Crime Victimization Survey Report.* Washington, DC: Bureau of Justice Statistics, Department of Justice.

Barnes, H. E., & Teeters, N. K. (1943). *New horizons in criminology.* New York: Prentice Hall.

Batchelder, J., Koski, D., & Byxbe, F. (2004). Women's hostility toward women in rape trials: Testing the intra-female gender hostility thesis. *American Journal of Criminal Justice, 28,* 181-198.

Bjerregaard, B., & Lord, V. (2007). An examination of the ethical and value orientation of criminal justice students. *Police Quarterly, 7,* 262-284.

Bookspan, P. T., & Kline, M. (1999). On mirrors and gavels: A chronicle of how menopause was used as a legal defense against women. *Indiana Law Review, 32,* 1267.

Brizendine, L. (2006). *The female brain.* New York: Broadway.

Browder, L. (2006). *Her best shot: Women and guns in America.* Chapel Hill, NC: University of North Carolina Press.

Callanan, V. J. (2005). *Feeding the fear of crime.* New York: LFB Scholarly Publishing.

Davidson, J. T. (2009). *Female offenders and risk assessment.* New York: LFB Scholarly Publishing.

Dickson, L. (2010). Race and gender differences in college major choice. *The ANNALS of the American Academy of Political and Social Science, 627,* 108-124.

Doerner, J., & Demuth, S. (2010). The independent and joint effects of race/ethnicity, gender and age on sentencing outcomes in U.S. Federal Courts. *Justice Quarterly, 27,* 1-27.

Dowler, K. (2003). Media consumption and public attitudes toward crime and justice: The relationship between fear of crime, punitive attitudes, and perceived police effectiveness. *Journal of Criminal Justice and Popular Culture, 10*(2), 109-126.

Franko, K. (2011, February 26). Some school districts trying to keep students out. *Houston Chronicle,* A3.

Goudreau, J. (2011, February 18). Jobs outlook: Careers headed for the trash pile. *Forbes.* Retrieved from http://finance.yahoo.com/career-work/article/111881/careers-headed-for-the-trash-pile.

Graczyk, M. (2013, January 29). First execution of woman since 2010 set in Texas. *Houston Chronicle.* Retrieved from http://www.chron.com/news/texas/article/1st-execution-of-woman-since-2010-set-in-Texas-4230862.php.

Hill, K., Howell, J., Hawkins, J., & Battin-Pearson, S. (1999). Childhood risk factors for adolescent gang membership: Results from the Seattle Social Development Project. *Journal of Research in Crime and Delinquency, 36,* 300-322.

Klein, D. (1973). The etiology of female crime. *Issues in Criminology, 8*(2), 3-30.

Koons-Witt, B., & Schram, P. (2006). Does race matter? Examining the relationship between co-offending and victim characteristics for violent incidents involving female offenders. *Feminist Criminology, 1*(2), 125-146.

Lee, R. (2012, September 5). Still getting by, but just barely. *Houston Chronicle,* A1, A11.

Lombroso, C. (1895). *The female offender.* (English version with Introduction by W. Douglas Morrison). New York: Appleton & Co.

Patchin, J. (2006). *The family context of childhood delinquency.* New York: LFB Scholarly Publishing.

Peters, K. (2007, May). *Female absconders on parole.* Graduate thesis, University of Houston-Downtown. Houston, Texas.

Proano-Raps, T., & Meyer, C. (2007). Postpartum syndrome and the legal system. In R. Muraskin (Ed.), *It's a crime: Women and justice* (pp. 103-126). Upper Saddle River, NJ: Prentice Hall.

Sherman, M. (2001). Women offenders and their children. *Special Needs Offenders Bulletin, Federal Judicial Center, 7,* 1-19.

Shipman, M. (2002). *The penalty is death: U.S. newspaper coverage of women's executions.* Columbia, MO: University of Missouri Press.

Sixel, L. M. (2011, February 24). Women work way onto boards. *Houston Chronicle,* D1, 5.

Sorensen, J., & Cunningham, M. D. (2007). Operationalizing risk: The influence of measurement choice on the prevalence and correlates of prison violence among incarcerated murderers. *Journal of Criminal Justice, 35,* 546-555.

Streib, V. (2012). Death penalty for female offenders, January 1, 1973, through December 31, 2011. Report Issue #66. Retrieved from http://www.deathpenaltyinfo.org/women-and-death-penalty.

Streib, V., & Sametz, L. (1988). Capital punishment of female juveniles. Paper presented at the annual meeting of the American Society of Criminology, Chicago.

Stroman, J. (2000). Holding parents liable for their childrens' truancy. *UC Davis J. of Law & Policy, 5,* 47-66.

Vander Ven, T. (2003). *Working mothers and juvenile delinquency.* New York: LFB Scholarly Publishing.

Wagner, D. (1999, May 22). 1930 gunbattle in Chandler. *Arizona Republic,* B3.

Zierdt, M. (2007). *Path breakers.* Resource Center, The National Women's History Project. Retrieved from http://www.nwhp.org/resourcecenter/pathbreakers.php.

Theories of Female Criminality

Introduction

Studies of women and crime tend to focus on why rates and types of offending differ from those of men. Throughout the research literature and based on data collected systematically from a variety of sources, evidence consistently shows that women have much lower rates of offending with less serious offenses that are less financially productive. In addition, the arrest, prosecution, and incarceration rates of females are also lower than those of males (Becker & McCorkel, 2011). This distinction is commonly referred to as "the gender gap," modeled after socioeconomic uses of similar terms in the labor market when discussing differences in wages (the wage gap) and in occupations and status. One of the more predominant features of the gender gap is the stability of women's lower rates of convictions for violent crimes. This trend is evident not only across the diverse cultures of the U.S. population but worldwide (Fishbein, 1992).

Tracy, Kempf-Leonard, and Abramoske-James (2009) comment that the lack of theoretical emphasis on the role of gender in criminology is somewhat ironic. They say this because "gender may have the best ability to distinguish crime, at least better than age, race and social class, which are far more common in scientific inquiries about offending" (Tracy et al., 2009, p. 178). In this chapter we will look at two groups of theoretical perspectives and how they view female criminality. The first group contains traditional criminological theories such as labeling, conflict theories, social learning, and social control. These theories were mostly proposed by male criminologists and focus primarily on either male criminality or criminality in general, with no specific reference to female offenders. However, they offer us meaningful ways to interpret not only criminal behavior but also society's reactions to that behavior.

The second group contains theories about female criminality that specify gender as a critical variable in understanding behavior. On the whole, these feminist theories are designed to sensitize us to the relative "invisibility" of women in the field (as offenders, workers, victims, scholars, and criminal justice policy makers). The work of many feminists is viewed as reactionary, because it critiques the idea of a patriarchal (male-based) society that empowers males in virtually all social interaction that matters. Males seem to control government, make rules, define gender roles, and set the patterns for power in society. In short, males are dominant, and females are subordinate.

Traditional Criminological Theories and Female Crime

As a rule, traditional criminological theories either assumed males and females were similar in their motives and behaviors or were expressly oriented toward explaining male criminality, particularly young male delinquency. Subculture theory was, in its design, an explanation for development of young male gangs. It was not really until the early 1960s that theorizing about crime became more gender neutral, but even then, the majority of theorizing was still male based. In fact, almost 20 years after his original presentation of a gang-based subculture theory, Walter Miller mentioned the presence of female gangs and more violent female behavior but cautioned that they posed far less of a threat than males (Williams & McShane, 2010).

Labeling Theory

About the time of the Civil Rights Era and the beginning of the Women's Liberation Movement, sociologists focused their attention on why certain people and behaviors came to the attention of society, and consequently law enforcement, and others did not. Also referred to as the "societal reaction" perspective, labeling theorists began with the assumption that no behavior is inherently deviant or illegal; it is our interpretation and reactions that bestow those traits on actions and activities. The stigmatization or condemnation of certain people and their traits is a product of group consensus about the undesirability of those features. Labeling theorists study the way we tag or judge others by the use of symbolically meaningful terms that convey disapproval. As an example, think of terms you have heard used in a negative way, such as calling a woman "butch," "sleezy," or "airhead."

Throughout our study of women in the criminal justice system, we will see how value-laden terms are applied to the behavior of girls and women. Images are created through the use of this symbolic vocabulary. The concept of a "double standard," such as boys being labeled "adventuresome" or "spirited" when they engage in delinquent behavior while girls are tagged as "troublesome" and "wanton" for the same behaviors, is the kind of value-laden concept a labeling theorist would explore.

Labeling theorists argue that even behavior that is not criminal can be stigmatizing. Prior to the 1980s, pregnant teens were removed from school and, often, even from their communities. They were "sent away," perhaps because of a fear that their "indiscretion" would set a bad example for others. The rejection and condemnation of others because of one's rule-breaking behavior (primary deviance), may lead an individual to view him- or herself as inferior or as an outcast. This self-perception can then lead to further and more serious delinquent conduct (secondary deviance). A study of youth in San Bernardino, California, who were put under the jurisdiction of the court found that girls were most often there at the request of their parents for less-serious offenses. It was as if parents found it more difficult to deal with the idea of a girl acting out, and had more fears about the consequences, if formal authorities did not step in and assist in the control of their child (McShane & Krause, 1992).

An example of labeling theory might be viewed in events surrounding rape charges against Duke University's lacrosse team by a woman who was hired to appear at one of their late-night parties. Media accounts ranged from portrayals of the accuser as a poor but hard-working dancer brutally attacked by drunken, sexually depraved, hooligan athletes from elite families to a mentally ill gold-digging stripper or prostitute making false claims against innocent boys. The selection and use of specific terms to refer to events and people, labeling theory reminds us, reflect the values, attitudes, and sentiments we intend to convey. In this example, events played out in political circles, courtrooms, television shows, and university administrative offices, each relying on the opinions and interpretations of social observers to create a media "image" of truth.

> With its overtones of race, sex and privilege, the Duke case instantly drew national news media attention. The accuser was a poor, black, local, single mother working at an escort service while enrolled at the predominantly black North Carolina Central University in Durham; the Duke students were relatively well-off, white, out-of-staters — members of a storied lacrosse team at one of the nation's most prestigious universities. The accuser's vivid account of racist and misogynistic taunts also fueled a simmering debate about the off-field behavior of elite athletes and the proper role of big-time sports on America's college campuses (Wilson & Barstow, 2007).

In just this short paragraph, you can see many value-laden terms that evoke emotional responses and might introduce bias into any attempt to legally interpret what actually happened.

Conflict Theory

One of the central concepts of conflict theories is power and the way it is used in society. These perspectives assume that conflict emerges between groups who are competing to control particular situations or events. The possession of resources (money, land, or political power) provides the advantage in situations of conflict.

Women often believe that they do not have the resources that men do to successfully influence the making and enforcement of laws concerning major social issues. That is, women have fewer of the "good old boy" networks that seem to grease the wheels of change or garner the votes necessary for passage of favorable legislation. With less experience or time in positions that traditionally result in political or economic power, women tend not to have the support of vested interests that would resolve conflicts in their behalf. The power to affect decisions is, therefore, synonymous with having resources.

In a high-profile case where female employees brought sexual abuse charges against a U.S. District Judge, the *Houston Chronicle* published the following comments in an editorial.

> Accused of multiple sexual assaults on female employees, U.S. District Judge Samuel Kent received a slap on the wrist and a four-month paid vacation. To date, his case represents the complete failure of the criminal justice system and the ability of the federal courts to protect their employees from harm at the hands of a powerful judge (*Houston Chronicle*, 2007).

Although Kent was eventually convicted of obstruction of justice and sentenced to 33 months in prison, it was not before several attempts were made to discourage the many different female employees from bringing any formal charges against the judge who had abused them. Considerable pressure from women's groups, and the media's uncovering of a long history of illegal conduct by Kent, was needed in order for the system to finally take action against a male member of its own elite body.

Because power can be equated with resources, it seems evident that those who are higher up in the social class structure will be the more powerful members of society. Their influence in the making of social decisions, and their ability to impose values, will also be greater than those of the lower social classes where there are a disproportionate number of women and women of color.

Conflict theorists also recognize that law itself represents a resource. If a group's values, such as not allowing women into combat or not providing maternity-leave job protection, are embodied in law, the group can use that law and its enforcement to its benefit. The agents of law with their enforcement efforts perpetuate the values embodied in law and thus help those who are powerful to stay in power. Further, those who have values, or interests, opposing those of the "winners" find themselves in the position of being the most likely targets of negative enforcement actions. In some areas, officials may attempt to sweep an area of prostitutes or adult bookstores or strip clubs if wealthy residents and constituents pressure them to do so.

On this issue, labeling theory dovetails with conflict theory to produce an explanation of the reaction process by which the less-powerful come to the attention of law enforcement agents. For example, the less-powerful (or the "losers") are stigmatized by the more-powerful because of their opposition. Laws are then created or modified to enhance official reaction to the less-powerful. A final point is implied in the relationship between the use of power and the creation of law. Because law embodies the values of those who create it, law is also more likely to criminalize the actions of those outside the power group. When power is essentially equal between two groups, a give-and-take relationship can develop. The abortion issue provides an excellent illustration of this phenomenon. As the groups involved have gained or lost power, laws have been passed to restrict the activities of the other side. Thus, we have seen laws that prohibit blocking the entrance of an abortion clinic, while a Florida law made it unlawful for a pregnant woman to take drugs and thereby "addict" an unborn child.

Social Control Theories

Social control theory, developed mainly in the 1960s, is probably the one theoretical approach most closely matching the public's conception of why people become criminals. Whether one believes a person becomes criminal because of associating with the wrong friends, an improper family upbringing, a lack of religion, or a lack of education, social control theory can be seen to reflect that belief. Social control theory takes a view of human nature that assumes deviance is natural (which makes this theory similar to labeling in this regard). Why people conform, then, is the real question worthy of explanation.

Social control theory argues that people are self-interested and have a strong motivation toward self-gratification. For that reason, from a very young age, everyone must be taught restraint and how to control impulses and urges. Individuals learn, particularly from their parents and close relatives, the rules and regulations for living in a society. Normally, when we behave according to these rules we receive acceptance, and when we do not, we are sanctioned or disciplined. When the institutions that teach and reinforce these conforming attitudes and values are weakened for whatever reason, social control theorists tell us, the bonds that tie individuals to the moral order are also weakened. These weakened bonds automatically permit a greater degree of deviance (self-interested behavior) to occur.

One of the most noted of social control theorists, Travis Hirschi, described the social bond as having four distinct components (1969, pp. 16-34): attachment, involvement, commitment, and belief. Hirschi appears to believe that attachment is the most important element; consequently, attachment is the most popular element for theory testing. Attachments are the ties one has to significant others (parents, friends, role models) or to institutions (schools, clubs) which inspire us to behave and avoid criticism. Attachments, then, help to reinforce conformity, as it is important to have the encouragement of those who mean the most to us. The second element, involvement, represents the degree of activity (the time and energy) that one spends in socially approved behavior, such as afternoon meetings or sports practice. When people are occupied by conventional activities, they will have less time to be involved in crime or delinquency. The hours we spend participating in civic organizations, athletics, and other extracurricular activities serve to increase levels of conformity.

The third element, commitment, is a measure of the investment one has already built up or dedicated to the norms and values of the surrounding community. This investment may take the form of paying one's own way through college, cultivating a good business reputation, or achieving sports or artistic awards through sacrifice and effort. Individuals with these forms of commitment to conventional society also have more to lose if they are caught engaging in deviant behavior. For example, career politician Maureen O'Connor was arrested on charges of stealing millions from her late husband's charitable foundation in order to cover debts from her compulsive gambling. The former Mayor of San Diego appeared to be so afraid to ruin her reputation with the truth about her addiction that she kept borrowing money she intended to repay under the mistaken belief that she would eventually win enough to settle everything evenly. It almost seems as if the threat of losing her status in society for gambling was worse than the risk of being exposed as a thief and an embezzler. In fact, as early as her first court appearance, she began to craft an image of herself as a victim of a brain tumor that altered her judgment and activities (Spagat, 2013).

The fourth and last element, belief, is the acknowledgment of society's laws and rules as being fair. The adherence to oaths, pledges or allegiance, and professional codes means that one has a respect for those rules and norms and feels a moral obligation to obey them. The key to this element is a respect for the common value system. And, the more one believes in "behaving properly," the more likely one is to be conforming.

Each of the four elements of the bond described by Hirschi shape an individual's relationship with society. Because all individuals exhibit some degree of bonding to society, a better question might be how much these bonds need to be weakened before deviance results. If any of the four bonds are weak, one may be more disengaged from existing constraints and feel free to deviate from social norms. Past research has found evidence that girls and women are more likely to be taught or conditioned to seek social approval and are more likely to view their stakes in conformity as a deterrent to deviance. Girls appear to have stronger ties to their parents and are more likely to avoid behaviors that would threaten their relationships at home.

It should be pointed out that social control theories all rely on a specialized methodology of discovering crime and criminality — self-report studies — for their evidence. Assuming that one's willingness to reveal information in a survey might result in "estimates" of higher rates of deviance, evidence gathered about the frequency of deviance and delinquency might be a direct product of one's own restraint in answering questions. Thus, if women indeed internalize greater social control, responses to these surveys could be gender biased with women reporting artificially lower rates of deviance. It would be possible to argue, if they were generally more honest in interviews and more revealing in surveys, women might report higher rates of deviance than they do. In other words, the very social controls the theory assumes will affect deviant behavior may also have the effect of suppressing female responses to questions about deviant behavior. Other methodologies, such as the use of official crime report statistics or victimization data, do not particularly lend themselves to providing good evidence for the social control approach.

Social Learning

The essence of social learning theory is that girls learn, through a standardized system of rewards and reinforcement, that certain behaviors are acceptable, while others, like criminal conduct, are not. The resources and support available within our culture for following the path of "good girls" are a powerful motivator. The messages transmitted through a woman's formative years emphasize the benefits of virtuous behavior. Privileges and constraints imposed by society encourage conformity with images of women as not only law-abiding family matriarchs but as individuals who should be cautiously and self-protectively aware of their vulnerabilities.

Social learning theories would argue that family, peers, and significant others modify the way we develop perceptions of crime risk and that the learning process associated with these perspectives is influenced to a great degree by gender. That is, parents not only instill definitions of proper gendered responses to potential victimization but also reward and encourage adoption of approved ways of dealing with gender-related fears. Theorists often refer to the "gender-fear paradox" as the survey phenomenon that women consistently score higher on indices of fear of crime even though their actual chances of victimization are lower (Rader & Haynes, 2011). Learning the values and benefits of responding appropriately to fear of crime takes place in a socialization process. Researchers allow that admitting to such fears is a gender-approved trait that becomes internalized as it is imitated and reinforced in a manner consistent with both Ron Akers's social learning theory and Edwin Sutherland's differential association theory (Rader & Haynes).

Biological Theories

It would be safest to say that biological approaches to female criminality are most often combined with sociological or psychological perspectives. That is, neurological and chemical differences in genetic makeup function within adaptive processes influenced by the social and psychological experiences of gender. Of particular interest is how physical differences between the sexes affect aggression and how aggressive responses might be mediated by socialization, conditioning, and learning. For instance, theorists have examined the way in which endocrine systems regulate certain hormones. Imbalances in those hormones may result in overly passive or aggressive behavior. Sex hormones in particular, may be related to stress-triggered disturbances in personality that might result in fighting, depression, anxiety, and even eating disorders (Fishbein, 1992).

Low Self-Control Theory

The writing of Gottfredson and Hirschi (1990) on the concept of low self-control presents an example of how a theory might integrate the concepts of socialization and temperament into biological explanations of gender differences in crime. Arguing that children from an early age are disciplined and parented in ways that mold the parameters for self-control, this theory assumes impulsive behavior is related to favorable attitudes toward risk taking in events such as crime and deviance. From Gottfredson and Hirschi's viewpoint, the goal of human behavior is the promotion of self-interest. Without the ability to self-regulate these propensities and traits toward impulsivity, one would be less prone to restraint and other mechanisms of coping with stress.

Attempting to operationalize the concept of low self-control, Grasmick et al. (1993) settled on components such as temper associated with a low tolerance for frustration, a preference for simple tasks over complex tasks, and a preference for physical activity over mental activity. A number of studies, primarily using youth populations, have found support for the idea that girls have higher levels of self-control than boys — which some are further able to attribute to parenting styles in support of the theory. In other cases, researchers like Shekarkhar and Gibson (2011) found evidence that Latino males had lower levels of self-control and self-reported involvement in violent and property crime but did not find any direct links between those findings and specific parenting methods. Thus, the effect of parenting styles on delinquency is not yet firmly established.

Feminist Perspectives and Female Crime

The most important point for virtually all feminist perspectives is that males fail to understand the importance of gender and sex roles in society. Thus, critique of traditional male-based theoretical positions is an essential part of feminist criminology. Central to a feminist perspective is the idea that one must acknowledge the complex history of social, economic, and cultural forces defining women's roles and supporting their oppression. They argue that the traditional method of studying crime is *androcentric*, that is, male-centered. Traditional theories and theorists are limited by a tendency to view gender as a dichotomous construct (either fully male or fully female), which would limit their ability to inform both theory and policy.

Another goal of work in this area is to create a distinctly feminist perspective on society. Some feminist scholars (see Daly & Chesney-Lind, 1988) assert that existing criminological knowledge is a product of "men's experiences"; therefore, criminology is a biased and power-centered view of the world. By analyzing and evaluating through female perspectives, these scholars assume that a different view will emerge of personal conflict, crime, and crime prevention. Many feminist criminologists focus on the intersection of social class, race, ethnicity, and gender in an attempt to understand and highlight the complexities of gender differences in crime.

Early Feminist Crime Theories: Liberation and Opportunity

Since the late 1970s (and early 1980s) feminist social scientists (Belknap, 2001) have examined gender differences in crime and victimization and, in particular, whether changes in gender roles and the impact of women's liberation would really alter female behavior in terms of increased criminality and propensity toward victimization (Simon, 1975) and incarceration (Pollock-Byrne, 1990). This puzzle has been studied across different types of offenses, from violent crime (Lauritsen, Heimer, & Lynch, 2009) to property crime (Mullins & Cherbonneau, 2011). However, as we will see, the question of whether female involvement in crime has really increased and thus represents a genuine shift in gender distribution has largely been unanswered.

Freda Adler's 1975 book *Sisters in Crime* is a good example of the argument that as a result of the women's liberation movement, the roles and behavior of women will become more masculine, more assertive, and thus, more crime prone. She expects that future rates of female offending, for not only violent crimes but also white-collar crimes, will increase. Despite some inherent logic in the "liberation hypothesis" that was particularly persuasive during that period of sweeping social and legal reforms, crime data never reflected the anticipated shift. There was instead some evidence that indicated young girls who were more "liberated" were less delinquent, and female prisoners identified with more traditional, stereotypical gender roles.

Another early liberation theorist, Rita Simon (1975) also postulated that rates of female offending would change but not as a result of any factors related to the nature of women's demeanor or behavior. Simon argued that as women obtained greater access to higher-level occupations and made inroads into jobs and positions that would open up opportunities for deviance (such as white-collar crime), their rates of these types of offenses and arrest would increase. Often referred to as "opportunity thesis," this perspective supposes that, whereas a female bank teller has strict monitoring, auditing, and accountability checks, the availability of new positions such as a loan officer or securities regulator will yield greater opportunities to surreptitiously engage in bribes, kickbacks, and fraudulent schemes.

The debate over the evolution of female criminality continued as research investigated the effects of liberation and opportunity in our changing society. Additional concepts also became part of the feminist dialogue that drew on the issues of the women's rights movement, sexism, paternalism, and chivalry.

Concepts Central to the Feminist Perspective

Sexism, Paternalism, and Chivalry

You will find the terms *sexism, paternalism,* and *chivalry* used throughout the literature of feminist criminology. Because these terms are essential to understanding feminist theories, they will be explained in detail here.

Sexism is the broadest of the concepts and is identified with the continued use of sex-role stereotypes that have little to do with the realities of modern work and family relations. Sexism generally refers to any official or personal policies or practices with the effect of introducing bias or discrimination against someone based on his or her gender. For example, a young male might argue that a college-town bar's refusal to hire him and instead employ only scantily-clad, attractive, young women is sexist. Women might likewise argue that having only three toilet stalls at a sports arena is a sexist design. Today, many of these complaints and challenges are answered by the courts. Feminists argue that the perpetuation of these actions and attitudes and the defense of these practices present evidence that sexism is alive and well in our society. And, for the purposes of our discussion here, both paternalism and chivalry will be discussed as more specific forms of sexism.

Paternalism is a term used to describe patriarchal (male-based) power relations and is contingent upon the female being viewed as weaker, childlike, and in need of the protective benevolence of a father-like figure. Throughout the juvenile justice literature, paternalism could refer to both boys and girls being taken under the control of the system and benefiting from what is deemed to be the "nurturing care of the state." Although the treatment of delinquents under a paternalistic system was somewhat gender neutral, feminists use the image to refer to a tendency to protect and shelter females from the harsh realities of life even after passage into adulthood. As long as women are presented as "childlike" (Embry & Lyons, 2012) in their needs and aspirations, the state can continue to manipulate and control their destiny, suppressing their progress and integration into the full range of citizenship benefits.

Chivalry for many is similar to paternalism without the "fatherlike" imagery. In chivalry, there is the connotation of a man functioning as a knight in shining armor, moved by the belief that the female has a distinctly different role in society as a person who must be taken care of, thus complementing and fulfilling the needs of the dominant figure of the male. Feminists argue that to truly benefit from the effects of chivalry, a woman must meet the image criteria of femininity, virtuousness, and embodiment of traditional subservient homemaking ideals. Those who do not are cast in a deviant and even "evil woman" context (Embry & Lyons, 2012). In the justice system, these women would suffer harsher sanctions, particularly incarceration, not only for their crimes but for their refusal to conform to passive and helpless stereotypes. As Brennan (2002) explains, the "evil woman hypothesis" argues that criminal women will be handed more punitive sentences because of the court's drive to enforce sexual standards of behavior. This chivalry "backlash," which Brennan (2002) calls the "antithesis of chivalry," has been particularly evident in not only the sentences given to mothers who kill their children as opposed to fathers who kill their children but also in the public condemnation of their deeds.

In 2009, the media reported heavily on a young woman hiker, Sarah Shourd, who was captured with two male companions after allegedly straying across the Iraqi border into Iran. After more than a year of isolation in captivity, it appeared that the woman might have some medical issues. This apparently triggered her release but not that of her male companions, as they were designated to serve out the rest of her sentence. To some perhaps, this gesture reflects the essence of chivalry. Although Sarah later denied there was ever a health risk, she did believe she was freed because she had been in solitary confinement which was perceived to be harsh treatment. Iran's governing political and clerical leaders, possibly pressured by calls for more humanitarian treatment of the woman, agreed to issue her a $500,000 bond and to have the male captives absorb her term, which they would seemingly agree to out of compassion and chivalry (Karimi, 2011).

U.S. Supreme Court Justice Thurgood Marshall made the following remarks in a landmark death penalty case, *Furman v. Georgia*, that seem to reflect the essential idea of chivalry:

> There is also overwhelming evidence that the death penalty is employed against men and not women. Only 32 women have been executed since 1930, while 3,827 men have met a similar fate. It is difficult to understand why women have received such favored treatment since the purposes allegedly served by capital punishment seemingly are equally applicable to both sexes (1972, p. 365).

Though there seems to be ample evidence that chivalry does indeed exist within the criminal justice system, the practice of chivalry appears to be complex. For example, in current death penalty cases, jurors in Texas must find in their deliberations during the sentencing phase that the defendant represents a continued threat to society. This may be something that many jurors observing a slightly built or timid-appearing female defendant are unlikely to find.

Research on Sexism, Chivalry, and Paternalism

In one of perhaps the classic studies on the effect of chivalry, Koons-Witt (2002) found that gender effects in sentencing were mitigated by whether the woman was perceived of as having family responsibilities, such as the primary care of her children. However, when attempting to replicate Koons-Witt's Minnesota study in Ohio, Griffin and Wooldridge (2006) did not find any evidence of differences between mothers and non-mothers in sentencing outcomes. Other studies have indicated that chivalry seems to be reserved more for middle- and upper-class female defendants. Lower-class women, particularly economically disadvantaged women of color, may be sentenced more harshly when controlling for type of crime (Brennan, 2002). There even seems to be a punitive aspect for failing to meet the expected criteria of chivalry. Women who recidivate and build more extensive criminal histories may be sentenced more harshly than even their male counterparts because they represent greater outliers in terms of expected gender behavior (Brennan, 2002).

Embry and Lyons (2012), in research examining the sentencing outcomes for male and female sex offenders, found support for the effect of chivalry. They suggest that because women are more likely to have histories of sexual abuse themselves, or because they may be viewed as more passive participants in a crime scheme directed by a male, or had victims from within the immediate family, they receive disproportionately milder sentences than men convicted of the same crimes. It appears, the researchers conclude, that women "continue to be viewed as individuals who should be protected by the justice system" even for what amounts to "atypical gendered behavior" (2012, p. 158).

Conflict and Economic Marginalization

Although there is no one feminist perspective on crime, there are similarities in their ideology and agreement on the sources of conflict in society that give rise to gender oppression and discrimination. Most build on the conflict orientation that is firmly established in criminology and make use of the unequal distribution of power and resources as well as the ability to control the context of law and law enforcement as explanations for disparate treatment in the criminal justice system. The concept of economic marginalization represents the view that the positive economic and political strides in power that women are making in society apply to only a few nonrepresentative women. The majority continue to struggle under the weight of poverty, unemployment, single parenthood, and discrimination. The fact that there are more women in today's workplace, feminists argue, does not mean that they are better off or enjoy equal status in the workplace. Most women are economically marginalized and live paycheck to paycheck, if in fact they can live without incomes that are subsidized either legitimately or illegitimately. Many writers refer to the feminization of poverty that disproportionately impacts minority women and is further exacerbated by divorce, and nonsupport for those with dependent children. For these women, neither liberation nor increased opportunities have altered their situations. Engaging in crime, or associating with those who benefit from crime, becomes a difficult choice as does the temptation of escape through drugs and alcohol.

Feminist theorists often use the term "pink-collar ghetto" to refer to the substandard living arrangements resulting from minimum- and even lower-wage jobs. Immigrant women in particular are more vulnerable to wage exploitation and the perpetual entrapment in menial jobs without benefits. As a result, pink-collar crime — the nonviolent and petty property offenses that provide some level of maintenance for a family — seems to be an inevitable consequence of their lack of options.

A Variety of Feminist Approaches to the Study of Crime

Feminist criminologists tend to identify themselves by the set of beliefs they hold about the root causes of sexism in society and their outlook on the likelihood that circumstances will improve for women more specifically in the criminal justice system and how that might occur (Williams & McShane, 2014). For example, early liberal feminists felt that equal opportunity would bring about positive changes that would overcome gender discrimination. With consistent challenges to the status quo, such as with litigation on prison conditions and the hiring of female law enforcement agents, women would be able to prevail against restrictive stereotypes and achieve more access to the full range of rights and protections available under the law.

Williams and McShane (2014) describe radical feminists, on the other hand, as believing that historical traditions of gender oppression are so ingrained in the fabric of societies that masculine control can only be overcome with the redefining of roles, the restructuring of social relationships, and the aggressive enforcement of laws giving women control over their own bodies. That control includes the ability to protect oneself from sexual domination and rape through measures such as recognition of marital rape and the ability to regulate one's reproductive destiny. Radical feminists are less optimistic about the ability to neutralize masculine privilege that they often view as the weapon-like use of biological determinism.

Recent reports from Juarez, Mexico, illustrate these principles. There, women hold 80% of the industrial jobs that sprung up when foreign countries settled in that area to save production costs (Althaus, 2010). The employment status of women, even for these extremely low-paying jobs, causes conflict in the home and between families. Men with more traditional mind-sets are frustrated and struggling to retain power and control. "As women and their advocates become more aware of their rights and more willing to demand them, complaints of discrimination and abuse have surged across Mexico" (Althaus, 2010). Under these conditions, rape and murder are viewed as means to revert to "discriminatory norms."

The conflict nature of feminist perspectives also implies the integration of a number of principles from Marxist ideology. In particular, theories in this area often address the nature of capitalist social structures and their maintenance of exploitive work environments. For Marxist feminists, gender is another form of the division of labor which allows women to be relegated into low-paying jobs that serve the interests of industries. Sexism legitimizes the sexual division of labor by emphasizing women's limitations as a capital resource because of their duties to the home and to their children (Radosh, 1990). In fact, it is profit, and not some type of biological imperative, that motivates men to dominate and control women.

As perhaps the most contemporary of the feminist perspectives on criminology, socialist feminism is an attempt to integrate gender with economic class to better view patterns of crime and perceptions of crime seriousness. This orientation believes that women are socialized into the various structures of our society that serve to create criminal opportunities and, in particular, opportunities for property crime. As Williams and McShane explain, this approach combines aspects of both Marxist and radical feminist criminology. "The social distribution of crime is derived from both the relationship to the production domain and the reproductive or family, domain. . . . Females are exploited by the capitalist patriarchal system both for their labor and for their sexuality" (2014, p. 154).

Power-Control Theory

Examining changes in family structures over time, John Hagan (1989, 1991) argues that parenting styles have been influenced by the way adults react to their position in the workforce. As couples experience different levels of power and responsibility, any stresses or strains generated from their employment status translate into different tolerance levels for delinquency when it comes to sons and daughters. For example, Hagan argues that the more traditional family structure is a patriarchal one where the father, by virtue of his income earnings, maintains more control over the children's discipline. In this context, he has more tolerance for a boy's delinquency than a girl's, and mothers are more likely to recognize and abide by the father's authority. The daughter is held to more traditional standards, is more tightly controlled, and is allowed less freedom or risk taking. On the other hand, in a more contemporary familial arrangement where the mother may have equal or even higher job status and earning potential, both sons and daughters are allowed similar rules and behavioral standards. Where parents maintain these egalitarian arrangements, as Hagan refers to them, it is difficult to set up differential rules for sons and daughters. Parents are at risk of being hypocritical if they were to say that they have different gender-role expectations for a girl than for a boy.

The effect of being parented in mostly the same fashion means that the two children should have similar outlooks and attitudes about taking risks. This would not necessarily mean that daughters are more delinquent, but it does indicate that either child is at risk for rule- and law-breaking behavior. Obviously the implication of Hagan's Power Control Theory is that the gender gap in delinquency will begin to narrow if more children are raised in egalitarian than in patriarchal family structures.

The Gender Gap: Theory and Research

As noted throughout this chapter, crime data for a number of offenses consistently show the existence of gender differences in the commission of certain types and levels of crime. For example, arrests for prostitution are predominantly female, while arrests for violent crimes are disproportionately male. In another example, Garase (2006) explains, most studies indicate that road rage is more likely to be exhibited by males than females.

Is the Gender Gap Narrowing?

Despite the body of research supporting these differences, a growing number of contemporary studies, using newer and more sophisticated forms of statistical analyses, provide evidence that in some areas the gender gap is narrowing. Results indicate that either there are fewer distinctions in the behavior of men and women or the justice system's reaction to the behavior of men and women is equalizing. One study argued that the type of neighborhood in which men and women live will determine the nature of the gender gap. That is, in poorer, disadvantaged areas, there will be less of a gender gap between residents, particularly when it comes to violent crime (Zimmerman & Messner, 2010). The authors of this study posit that close relationships with others who offend and exposure to the violence of those with whom we associate are influential in narrowing the differences between the likelihood of a person of either sex offending. This finding is significant and in accord with our discussions in the previous chapter about the complex effects of social disorganization in the lives of disadvantaged women. Limited housing options mean more exposure to drug-infested areas with few legitimate opportunities for employment, education, and health services.

Another variable related to the risks of becoming involved in crime appears to be the gender-specific nature of close relationships with others who offend. These relationships are mostly with men offenders, and research shows that women tend to participate in crimes whose plans and activities are dominated by men (Becker & McCorkel, 2011). These findings are particularly true of the research on delinquent girls and the influence of co-offenders. Girls are more likely to commit crimes in groups, and the risks go up if those groups include boys (Warr, 1996). The effect of girls following the lead of boys has also been found in gang research where exclusively female gangs have the lowest levels of crime and the rate of offending increases with the amount and importance of male associates (Peterson, Miller, & Esbensen, 2001). With co-offending the most common scenario for delinquency, we may see future rates of offending, arrest, and incarceration begin to equalize between the sexes.

Within this argument are two different views on the cause of a narrowing in the gender gap. Intrinsic or personal changes are the basis of one side, that the nature of women (i.e., their psychosocial drives and sentiments) is predisposing them toward more crime than ever before. The second perspective argues that other external forces are changing, that victims are pressing more charges against women, and that the system is changing to attribute more blame and accountability to women, all of which will result in a narrowing of the gap in rates of reported crime, arrests, and entry into supervision. This second view maintains that the perception of changes in the gender gap is, in reality, more superficial. Changed social control mechanisms targeting the female population (e.g., net-widening policy) (Steffensmeier & Streifel, 1991) might be responsible for the increased number of female arrests, which does not significantly affect the gender gap in terms of women's self-perceptions and identity (Schwartz, 2008).

Violence Datasets and the Gender Gap: Contemporary Analyses

The question of whether women now represent a greater proportion of all violent offenders has been controversial and seems to be influenced by the type of data analyzed. Lauritsen, Heimer, and Lynch (2009) relied primarily on victimization data from National Crime Survey/National Crime Victims' Survey (NCS/NCVS) interviews and postulated that the gender gap is narrowing relative to the commission of violent offenses. This would mean that differences in the rates of violent crime committed by men and women are shrinking. In contrast, studies by Schwartz et al. (2009a, 2009b) found that UCR data are less susceptible to personal bias and are a more accurate indicator of the true amount of violent crime committed by women. Using UCR data, the researchers did not find any meaningful or major shifts in rates of female violent offending over time. Schwartz et al. (2009a, 2009b) explain that the stability (and longevity) of the gender gap may be due not only to the overwhelming tendency for crimes like rape to be predominantly perpetrated by males, but also to the fact that female homicide and assault rates have been consistent over time, as have been rates of female incarceration for violent offenses. In addition, the researchers argue, mandatory arrest policies for domestic violence, zero-tolerance policies for certain crimes on campus, and a broadening of definitions of violence have artificially inflated the increase in the number of women who commit the more "traditional" violent crimes (Schwartz et al., 2009a).

What These Theories Tell Us

One of the themes underlying theory related to female criminality, particularly feminist theory, is that women proceed through different pathways or trajectories on the way to becoming involved in crime (Becker & McCorkel, 2011). Longitudinal research analyzing the life course of offending and factors related to desistence from crime sees differences in the careers of male and female offenders. These differences are evident in the risk factors for committing various types of crime as well as in the offenders' amenability to treatment and rates of recidivism.

For women offenders in the criminal justice system, the introduction of sentencing guidelines and mandatory sentences has done much to reduce the influences of gender-related bias that might produce differential sentencing outcomes. Nonetheless, feminists have argued that mandatory arrests at domestic violence incidents are not adequate solutions to the disproportionate effects of domestic violence.

To many feminists, the failure to address historical disparities in the status of women results in continued marginalization within society and the perpetuation of traits more generally associated with crime-proneness. Work in sexually segregated occupations that create low-wage clusters reflect the low value placed on women's contributions to the economy. Changes must result in increases both in the pay gap and in the authority gap.

Critical Thinking Questions

1. Can the same theories be used to explain male as well as female crime and delinquency? Why or why not?

2. What theories do you think best explain female criminality? Do the "best" theoretical explanations change over time?

3. Do you think parents raise boys and girls differently today? Does this influence a child's willingness to take risks?

Books, Websites, and Media Resources

Gaines, P. (1994). *Laughing in the dark.* New York: Anchor Books.
Lombroso, C. (1920). *The female offender* (translation). New York: Appleton. Originally published in 1903.

Popular Films

Helter Skelter (1976), Steve Railsback, Steve DiCenzo, and Nancy Wolfe.
Monster (2003), Charlize Theron.
The Quick and the Dead (1995), Sharon Stone.

References

Adler, F. (1975). *Sisters in crime: The rise of the new female criminal.* New York: McGraw-Hill.
Althaus, D. (2010, April 18). Juarez's women in power struggle. *Houston Chronicle,* p. A23.
Becker, S., & McCorkel, J. (2011). The gender of criminal opportunity: The impact of male co-offenders on women's crime. *Feminist Criminology, 6*(2), 79-110.
Belknap, J. (2001). *The invisible woman: Gender, crime, and justice* (2nd ed.). Belmont, CA: Wadsworth/Thomson.
Brennan, P. K. (2002). *Women sentenced to jail in New York City.* New York: LFB Scholarly Publishing.
Daly, K., & Chesney-Lind, M. (1988). Feminism and criminology. *Justice Quarterly, 5,* 497-538.
Embry, R., & Lyons, P. M. (2012). Sex-based sentencing: Sentencing discrepancies between male and female sex offenders. *Feminist Criminology, 7,* 146-162.
Fishbein, D. (1992). The psychology of female aggression. *Criminal Justice and Behavior, 19*(2), 99-126.
Furman v. Georgia 408 U.S. 238, 1972.
Garase, M. (2006). *Road rage.* El Paso, TX: LFB Scholarly Publishing.
Gottfredson, M. R., & Hirschi, T. (1990). *A general theory of crime.* Stanford, CA: Stanford University Press.
Grasmick, H. G., Tittle, C., Bursik, Jr., R. J., & Arneklev, B. (1993). Testing the core empirical implications of Gottfredson and Hirschi's general theory of crime. *Journal of Research in Crime & Delinquency, 30,* 5-29.
Griffin, T., & Wooldridge, J. (2006). Sex-based disparities in felony dispositions before versus after sentencing reform in Ohio. *Criminology, 44,* 893-923.
Hagan, J. (1989). *Structural criminology.* New Brunswick, NJ: Rutgers University Press.
Hagan, J. (1991). A power-control theory of gender and delinquency. In R. Silverman, J. Teevan, & V. Sacco (Eds.), *Crime in Canadian society* (4th ed., pp. 130-136). Toronto, Ontario, Canada: Butterworths.
Hirschi, T. (1969). *Causes of delinquency.* Berkeley: University of California Press.
Justice for all? Judge Kent's case. (2007, November 18). *Houston Chronicle,* p. 2E.
Karimi, N. (2011). Iran opens trial of 3 Americans on spy charges. *Houston Chronicle,* p. A9.
Koons-Witt, B. A. (2002). The effect of gender on the decision to incarcerate before and after the introduction of sentencing guidelines. *Criminology, 40,* 297-327.
Lauritsen, J. L., Heimer, K., & Lynch, J. (2009). Trends in the gender gap in violent offending: New evidence from the National Crime victimization Survey. *Criminology, 47,* 361-400.
McShane, M., & Krause, W. (1992). Examining the non-serious juvenile offender in out-of-home placement. *The Presley Institute Bulletin, 1*(1), 5-8.
Mullins, C. W., & Cherbonneau, M. G. (2011). Establishing connections: Gender, motor vehicle theft, and disposal networks. *Justice Quarterly, 28,* 278-301.

Peterson, D., Miller, J., & Esbensen, F. A. (2001). The impact of sex composition on gangs and gang delinquency. *Criminology*, 39, 411-439.

Pollock-Byrne, J. M. (1990). *Women, prison, and crime*. Belmont, CA: Wadsworth/Thomson Learning.

Rader, N. E., & Haynes, S. H. (2011). Gendered fear of crime socialization: An extension of Aker's social learning theory. *Feminist Criminology*, 6, 291-307.

Radosh, P. (1990). Women and crime in the United States: A Marxian explanation. *Sociological Spectrum*, 10, 105-131.

Schwartz, J. (2008). Gender differences in drunk driving prevalence rates and trends: A 20-year assessment using multiple sources of evidence. *Addictive Behaviors*, 33, 1217-1222.

Schwartz, J., Steffensmeier, D. J., & Feldmeyer, B. (2009a). Assessing trends in women's violence via data triangulation: Arrests, convictions, incarcerations, and victim reports. *Social Problems*, 56, 494-525.

Schwartz, J., Steffensmeier, D., Zhong, H., & Ackerman, J. (2009b). Trends in the gender gap in violence: Re-evaluating NCVS and other evidence. *Criminology*, 47, 401-425.

Shekarkhar, Z., & Gibson, C. (2011). Gender, self-control and offending behaviors among Latino Youth. *Journal of Contemporary Criminal Justice*, 27(1), 63-80.

Simon, R. J. (1975). *Women and crime*. Lexington, MA: Lexington Books.

Spagat, E. (2013, February 14). Ex-San Diego mayor's gambling wagers top $1B. Associated Press. Retrieved from www.denverpost.com

Steffensmeier, D., & Streifel, C. (1991). Age, gender, and crime across three historical periods: 1935, 1960, and 1985. *Social Forces*, 69, 869-894.

Tracy, P. E., Kempf-Leonard, K., & Abramoske-James, S. (2009). Gender differences in delinquency and juvenile justice processing: Evidence from national data. *Crime & Delinquency*, 55, 171-215.

Warr, M. (1996). Organization and instigation in delinquent groups. *Criminology*, 36, 11-37.

Williams, F. P., & McShane, M. (2014). *Criminological theory* (6th ed.). Englewood Cliffs, NJ: Prentice Hall.

Williams, F. P., & McShane, M. (2010). Walter Benson Miller. In K. Hayward, S. Maruna, & J. Mooney (Eds.), *50 key thinkers in criminology* (pp. 120-126). London: Routledge.

Wilson, D., & Barstow, D. (2007, April 12). All charges dropped in Duke Case. *New York Times*, p. A1.

Zimmerman, G. M., & Messner, S. (2010). Neighborhood context and the gender gap in adolescent violent crime. *American Sociological Review*, 75, 958-980.

The Female Victim and the Criminal Justice System

Introduction

Both Candace Lightner and Cindi Lamb lost young daughters in alcohol-related traffic accidents. In both cases, the offenders had four previous drunk-driving charges. When Lightner and Lamb joined forces to change the criminal justice system's approach to driving under the influence (DUI)/driving while intoxicated (DWI), they were mad. Today, more than 30 years later, the organization that they began, Mothers Against Drunk Drivers (now Mothers Against Drunk Driving) has evolved into a complex network of education programs, lobbying, and social awareness strategies aimed at reducing underage drinking as well as increasing penalties for drunk driving. MADD has a record of successfully backing tough laws. Today they have nearly 2 million members and supporters, over 600 chapters throughout the United States, a national hotline for victims, and a 97% name recognition rating. To get a clearer picture of the road from average citizen to crusading advocate that many family members of victims travel, read the background briefs on a number of women whose lives have been impacted by drunk drivers. In many of these cases, the women were inspired to become not only activists but also leaders in the campaign for zero-tolerance drunk-driving legislation.

The victims' rights movement has been propelled almost exclusively by victims and their families, often referred to as "survivors." Organizations like MADD, Parents of Murdered Children (POMC), Adult Survivors of Child

Abuse, and Survivors' Network of those Abused by Priests (SNAP) are all directed at changing aspects of the criminal justice system that would address the problem or crime by which they have suffered. And, a number of these founding activists are women.

Assessing Crime Victims' Risks

As larger data sets have been compiled and made available for sophisticated computer analysis, theories of victimization have become more popular and easier to test and revise. The National Crime Victim's Survey (NCVS), the National Incident Based Reporting System (NIBRS), the UCR Supplementary Homicide Report, Campus Crime Reports, Sexual Victimization in Prison Reports, and a national database on domestic violence are all examples of the types of information that contribute to theorizing about criminal events and the risks women face from certain types of crime. These databases tell us that in the United States, femicide (a term for the killing of women) is one of the leading causes of premature death (Messing et al., 2011). They also indicate that up to half of these murders are committed by men in current or former intimate relationships with the victims. Women are four times more likely to be the victims of intimate partner violence than are males (Truman, 2011).

In a broader look across all types of offenses, we could theorize that the victimization risks of males and females are equal for some crimes, for other crimes the risks are higher for males than females, and for yet others the risks are higher for females than males. There are also those offenses for which one might perceive the risks to be equal, according to some type of logical assessment of the scenarios, but in fact, they are not. For example, if more teachers are women, then increases in classroom violence and attacks on teachers will have a disparate impact on women. One might argue that both males and females would be at equal risk for identity theft and that they would perceive their risks in similar ways. However, according to a recent study (Choi, 2010), women are more afraid of being victimized by identity theft and online stalking than are men. Men were more likely to identify hacking as the computer-related crime they were most afraid of. Gender also seemed to be related to the types of online risks that individuals faced. For example, Choi explains, "males are more likely to engage in online risky leisure activities such as visiting unknown Web sites, downloading free games, free music, and free movies," while women were more likely to "open any attachment in the e-mail, click on any web-links in the e-mails, open any file through the instant messenger, and click on a pop-up message that interested them" (2010, p. 107).

For many of these differences we described above, gender is an apparent, direct factor in the unequal rates of victimization, such as rape. For others, the relationship between gender and risk may be more indirect, such as gender influences on other behavior and treatment differences that may lead to great or lesser risks of exposure to crime. For instance, data indicate that 60% of women who reported being victimized in the past decade identified their perpetrator as a nonstranger. For men, only 39% of those victimized indicated that the offender was not a stranger (Truman, 2011). Thus, the role of women in the workplace and more likely presence in the house, coupled with gender-oriented perceptions of intimacy, may help explain these differences in stranger/non-stranger victimization.

Differences in victimization risk for men and women as well as differences in the way they perceive their risks, if substantiated, give us clues as to how to go about addressing crime prevention. The quest for a more gender-sensitive response to victims was fostered by the National Organization for Women (NOW), which was founded in 1966. Some of the projects that NOW sponsored included rape crisis centers, domestic violence hotlines, and research on the causes and prevention of violence against women. As contemporary criminological theories based on victimization data tell us, lifestyle and expectations for behavior are intricately linked to crime risks.

Women and Fear of Crime

Throughout the research on fear of crime, gender has consistently been linked to more concern about personal safety, whether it is directly related to actual risk or not. As Sacco explains, "women are much more likely than men to state that they feel unsafe in their neighborhoods . . . and more likely to restrict their behavior because of crime" (1990, p. 487). Some studies indicate that exposure to media, television news, and reality shows has an effect on reported fear of crime. Other researchers have found that area crime rates and levels of social disorganization are also factors that mediate the fear of crime. Prior victimization does not appear to be as significant as one might think in producing fear of crime even across gender. In addition, a number of studies have pointed out that the way "fear" is operationalized in the questioning process of most surveys is likely to produce a distorted image, because "concern about crime" or "awareness of crime" may also be misinterpreted as fear. For example, a woman may report that she does not feel safe walking in her neighborhood at night, but that feeling may be related to being bitten by a loose dog or hit by a car because of poor lighting.

Others have looked at the problems of interpreting fear of crime that may affect measures in special population groups. Disadvantaged women may answer questions about concern for crime that reflect the problems associated with certain consequences of victimization. For example, if your car is your only access to work, you cannot afford theft insurance, and you must leave it parked at a curb without security at night, then there would be more serious ramifications for you than for someone with a secure garage and full insurance coverage. In another scenario, women in public housing may have a very realistic fear of their children being accidently shot or mistakenly being taken into custody or abused by police. As Alvi, Schwartz, Dekeseredy, and Maume (2001) explain, the graffiti, vandalism, decay, and a reputation for drug dealing in a public housing area might heighten perceptions of incivilities and the probability of victimization. Here, fear of crime is not an irrational misconception, but a daily reality and perhaps even a healthy assessment.

Theorists often argue that women may be socialized into adopting more fearful reactions to crime. Learning or conditioning based on being rewarded for being overly cautious is at the heart of this process. Fear may also be perpetuated by initiatives that extol the benefits of women being more trained and prepared to ward off attackers with self-defense courses and weapons (Gilchrist, Banniser, Ditton, & Farrall, 1998). These programs seem to claim that if the woman will take certain proactive measures, she will reduce her risks of victimization. A by-product of that would be perhaps a false sense of security in those who do attempt, however, ineffectively, to face down attackers, while those who realize they are untrained and unprepared may suffer higher levels of fear. Even the National Rifle Association (NRA) uses campaigns like "Refuse to be a Victim" in attempting to sell more firearms to more women (Thompson, 1996).

Theories About Female Victims

In some of the earliest writings on victimology, women were simply grouped together under the generic assumption that, as weaker and more vulnerable members of society, they represented a separate victim typology (von Hentig, 1948). Historically, the problem with not gathering detailed information about crimes and victims meant that stereotypes and unsupported assumptions could continue under the guise of "theory." However, as more crime data were gathered, criminologists began to see complex relationships between socioeconomic and cultural factors in cities that translated into areas, not people, being more prone to crime. The presence of social disorganization in areas, particularly in urban neighborhoods, often trapped women in cycles of poverty, illiteracy, and poor health. Sociologists of the Chicago School examined these areas and found that unemployment, delinquency, and substance abuse seemed disproportionally high. They then developed theories to explain the effect of socially disorganized areas on crime.

Culture Conflict

Culture conflict theory was developed during the early 1900s during a time of growth of American cities and waves of immigration that provided a way of studying how people adapt and conform to new societal rules. Sociologists noticed how recent immigrants moving into the poorer areas of cities were prone to conflict with authorities, particularly when they insisted on maintaining behaviors and customs from their "old countries." Primary culture conflict, according to Thorsten Sellin (1938), occurred when the individual's norms and values resulted in actions that put them in opposition to expected conduct in this country. Borrowing from the work of cultural anthropologists, he noted the following:

> [A]mong the Khabyles of Algeria, the killing of adulterous wives is ritual murder committed by the father or brother of the wife and not by her husband, as

elsewhere. The woman having been sold by her family to her husband's family, the honor of her relatives is soiled by her infidelity. Her father or brother has the right and the duty to kill her in order to cleanse by her blood the honor of her relatives (Sellin, 1938, p. 65).

A similar circumstance would arise today if, for example, an African father insisted on having a genital mutilation performed on his daughter. Though such a practice may be acceptable within his former culture, it would be considered child abuse here, as it was in Paris. In 1993, two African women from Mali were prosecuted for mutilating their 3-year-old daughters when they paid a woman $30 to cut out the children's clitorises and labia minora. As Tempest explains:

> On the stand, with the help of a Malian translator, they said they were only conforming to the ancient tradition of their homeland; that the act of "female circumcision" was something they had undergone, as had their mothers and grandmothers before them. . . . In two separate cases here in Paris recently, the father of one girl and the mother of another were ordered jailed by a French jury for allowing their daughters to be excised. Leaders in French organizations opposed to the practice of female genital excision hoped for more jail terms in the case. . . . However, after the two-day proceeding charged with emotional debate about cultural and ethnic relativism in a modern European state, the jury chose to be lenient, giving each of the women a five-year suspended sentence (Tempest, 1993, p. A10).

Other cases coming to the attention of authorities have involved forced marriages and the selling of daughters into marriages. Again, Tempest explains:

> In a 1988 Fresno (California) criminal case against Hmong immigrant Kong Moua, the defendant said he was only conforming to his Hmong tribal tradition of *zij poj niam* — marriage by capture — when he abducted a young Hmong immigrant woman from the Fresno City College Campus and forced her to become his bride.
>
> The woman called police and accused Kong Moua of kidnapping and rape. However, after hearing the cultural defense mounted by the man's attorneys, Fresno Superior Court Judge Gene M. Gomes accepted Kong Moua's plea on the lesser charge of "false imprisonment" and sentenced him to a relatively short 120-day jail term (Tempest, 1993, p. A10).

In what Sellin would refer to as secondary culture conflict, younger members of immigrant households found themselves struggling against the dictates of their parents and grandparents. Children may rebel against strict discipline and adopt dress and language customs of their new peer group much to the dismay of their more traditional elders. These youth may be more prone to what would be described as deviance within both cultures, or what he referred to as a subculture identity, one that eschews their parents' values and attitudes and even engages in law-breaking behavior in an attempt to assimilate with new-found delinquent friends. This will not only bring immigrant youth to the attention of teachers and law enforcement authorities but also promote extended conflict within their families.

In a more recent Arizona case, one Muslim immigrant ran down his daughter, Noor, with a Jeep Cherokee and killed her for not only rejecting the Iraqi suitor selected by her parents, but also for moving in with her boyfriend in direct defiance of her father's orders. According to Pitts:

> [T]he father "felt his Facebook-using, husband-rejecting daughter had become too 'Westernized.' His son, Peter-Ali, told a local TV news station that tensions ran high between father and daughter. Noor, he said, went 'out of her way' to disrespect their conservative Muslim father" (Pitts, 2009, p. B9).

Pitts (2009) further explains that "The U.N. Population Fund estimates that more than 5,000 women a year die in honor killings for such crimes as speaking to unrelated men or being raped." Although culture conflict theories would naturally focus more on immigrant populations and the process of assimilation into varying social environments, another commonly used perspective called rational theories are not tied so directly to culture.

Rational Theories

Rational theories argue that behavior is a predictable set of responses geared to maximize one's own benefit and self-interest and to avoid punishment or pain. Rational theorists see people as calculating and able to read cues in the environment that would indicate whether certain actions and activities might expose one to great risk of victimization — or for an offender, result in better chances of getting away with a crime. Victims, theorists tell us, are a critical part of the formula that offenders weigh before committing a crime. As a result, criminals might target those who seem more vulnerable or who seem more likely to provide greater rewards, such as the weak and the wealthy. Women may be disproportionally represented in these groups, not only for general disadvantages in height, weight, and strength, but also by dual vulnerabilities such as being elderly, pregnant, or handicapped.

Choosing a victim, theorists tell us, is a rational process involving a number of assessments and evaluations about the risk and the likelihood of a profitable outcome. The way a victim appears in specific environmental contexts would be critical, and crime prevention, under rational models, involves providing protection for the victim in the forms of escape, surveillance, and the presence of others who would deter potential criminals. The rational theories we will look at here are routine activities theory, rational choice theory, and lifestyle theory.

Routine Activities

After studying how patterns of everyday life in America had changed over the years, criminologists Lawrence Cohen and Marcus Felson (1979) attempted to show how types of victimization and risk of victimization would also evolve in similar patterns. At about the time World War II ended, they noticed, more couples moved away from their rural hometowns and more women began full-time work, thus entire families would leave home for the entire day. This change in the flow of people away from high-density neighborhoods and into business areas meant that some victimizations were less likely to take place at home and were more likely to occur in urban areas, parking lots, schools, and even at fast-food establishments on the way to and from residences.

For Cohen and Felson, the likelihood of someone becoming a victim at any given time is dependent upon three things: (1) the suitability or attractiveness of that victim as a target, (2) the willingness or motivation of the offender at that time, and (3) the perception that the potential victim will not draw the attention or assistance of any capable guardian. Guardians could be anything from neighbors looking out the windows, to security lights and surveillance cameras, to watch dogs. Routine activities theory further explains that if any one of the above three elements is lacking, then that would be "sufficient to prevent the successful completion of a direct-contact predatory crime, and that the convergence in time and space of suitable targets and the absence of capable guardians may even lead to large increases in crime rates without necessarily requiring any increase in the structural conditions that motivate individuals to engage in crime" (Cohen & Felson, 1979, p. 589).

Simply put, the patterns of everyday life determine the possible interactions of the three crime elements, which may explain variations in crime rates across different areas and different times. Cohen and Felson believe that even if the number of suitable targets and motivated offenders is stable over time, changes in the way the rest of society interacts and moves about our environment are enough to alter the crime rate through these variations in perceived opportunities. For example, we might see an increase in women being killed at their place of work by a former spouse, rather than in their home. This shift is most apparent when we consider the number of women who now work compared to the number of working women during our grandmother's and great-grandmother's time. Also, the relatively recent phenomenon of couples separating, and the ability to obtain restraining orders and home security, often means that angry exes will hunt down their former partners at neutral locations. Personal victimizations shift to adapt to where people are located. Burglaries and thefts may also shift to times when family members are not home, or not near their vehicles. The development of malls, parking garages, and even cyberspace alters the dynamics of interactions between offenders and victims.

Recently, one large city instituted a self-defense skills training session for homeless women after it was reported that three had been murdered in separate incidences in the past year (Gallegos, 2011). Twenty residents of a downtown shelter participated in the seminar because of the high-risk situations they found themselves facing every day. "Trainers from the Main Boxing Gym taught the women where to hit attackers and how to use their hair against them. More importantly, they wanted women to flee to public places and make themselves known. They were given flashlights and whistles to help" (Gallegos, 2011, p. B4).

Rational Choice Theory

Like routine activities theory, a rational choice perspective is grounded in the notion that a decision process, regardless of how good or bad, is the impetus in any criminal action. According to Cornish and Clarke (1986, 1987), a potential offender uses a two-step evaluation process that is characterized by varying degrees of rationality. If a particular course of action appears likely to succeed, or net a large profit, then he or she is likely to follow through with the crime. If on the other hand, it seems as if one is likely to be caught or not gain enough benefit from the adventure, then the potential offender may withdraw from that particular crime event. As the idea of a crime unfolds, the first step is an involvement decision that is then followed by an event decision. As Williams and McShane explain:

> Involvement decisions are those in which the choice is made to become involved in an offense, continue with an offense, or withdraw from an offense. These types of decisions are instrumental in weighing the costs and benefits. . . . The other form of decision making, event decisions, is that in which the tactics of carrying out an offense (the demands placed on the offender) are determined. If the tactics are easy, the involvement decision gains potential benefits. If the tactics are difficult, the involvement decision loses potential benefits (2014, p. 196).

As an example, Barrow (2008) concludes in her dissertation that the deaf may be more vulnerable targets because they may not hear the offender approaching or be able to call out for assistance. It is also possible that the deaf may have adopted more insular and socially isolated patterns of activity, and they may be less likely to even contact the police because of the difficulties they anticipate in attempting to interact with the hearing-based justice system.

For rational choice theorists, the goal then would be to reduce the chances that weaker or more vulnerable members of society would be selected or targeted for victimization. Any time there are concentrations of children, the disabled, and the elderly, strategies should be in place to strengthen crime prevention aspects of the environment such as surveillance. Support systems should be in place that would encourage greater interaction with the general population and discourage those who might attempt crimes that exploit those less able to protect and defend themselves.

In a sense, we have done this in many jurisdictions simply by enacting statutes imposing more serious sanctions for those who commit crimes against children, the elderly, those who are pregnant, or persons with disabilities. Thus, any benefit from having a more suitable target is offset by the enhanced penalties.

Lifestyle Theory

One of the dominating themes of victimization statistics is that males, young people, minorities, and the poor appear to be at much higher risk for victimization than the rest of the population. Those in multiple categories, such as young, Black females in high-crime areas, exponentially increase the probability of victimization (McShane & Emeka, 2011). The way personal characteristics or demographics influence one's risk of becoming a victim is explained through lifestyle theory (Hindelang, Gottfredson, & Garofalo, 1978). If we use these traits as qualifiers or simply the starting point, it would still be necessary to attempt to clarify why not all poor, Black females are at equal risk. As with other contemporary crime theories, researchers need to construct predictive models that might be powerful enough to distinguish between those at risk, even within specific population subsets.

Lifestyle theory argues that the choices women make when they adapt to the constraints of their demographic limitations will set the stage for the type of jobs, recreation, and lifestyle activities she may become involved in. That is, if a young woman's parents insist that she live at home, it may mean that they expect her to be home before midnight and to have not been drinking. If a young woman rents the only apartment she can afford in perhaps a higher-crime area, she may be exposed to greater risk of victimization. Having made these lifestyle choices, one then accepts specific routines that increase contact with certain types of people at certain times and in specific places (exposures). The more one comes in contact with potential offenders, exhibits behavior with high-risk traits, and makes oneself available at high-risk times, the more likely it is that one will experience victimization (McShane & Emeka, 2011). If girls associate with delinquents or are in an area with a high concentration of delinquents, then lifestyle theory would predict that they are more likely to be preyed upon by those willing to offend. This means that the more your lifestyle exposes you to disproportionate levels of high-risk people, places, and times, the more likely it is that you will be victimized.

According to the theory, a lifestyle is a product of forces shaped throughout one's formative years. The opinions and pressures of others, as well as the choices one makes, evolve to place one at greater or lesser risk of victimization because of the times, places, and other people that one is likely to come into contact with. One's demographic traits, such as age, race, and gender, are influential in setting up the role expectations as well as the structural constraints one will be faced with every day. Even though our family and friends may have certain goals or expectations for us, those must be in line with the legal, economic, and educational barriers or limitations in our lives. As we adapt, we make personal choices that come to represent our lifestyle. That lifestyle, including our jobs and leisure activities, determines our associations and thus the various risks we are exposed to, in particular, the likelihood of coming into contact with dangerous people and places perhaps late at night or in high-crime areas. It could even be that a higher-risk job, like being a clerk in a pawn shop or a waitress at an after-hours club, is sufficient to set one up to become a victim.

In an account that demonstrates lifestyle theory, Catherine Woods, daughter of the famous Ohio State University Marching Band leader, Jon Woods, came to New York City from Ohio with "dreams of making it big on Broadway. Instead, she wound up working as a topless dancer" (McShane, 2005, p. A9). Her family was shocked to find out, upon her death, that she had such a secret life.

Pretending to have gained a part in an off-Broadway show, she worked as a stripper on Manhattan's Upper East Side until she was stabbed to death in 2005. In the trial convicting Paul Cortez of the murder, "prosecutors claimed she rejected him and his self-appointed role as a white knight who would stop her from working as a stripper" (McShane, 2005, p. A9).

Although individual cases and anecdotes highlight the elements of this theory, the theory is really designed to explain changes in rates of risk across different demographic groups. One of the best examples would be the increase of murders among young women working in the factories along the border of Mexico near Juarez. The lack of alternative jobs or shifts as well as protective transportation through the area expose young women to potential predators at high rates almost always late at night. Thus, an entire demographic group suffers the disproportionately high risk of murder and sexual assault according to the lifestyle theory model.

Alternating Roles as Victims and Offenders

One of the important contributions of victimization research has been the ability to see that the roles of victim and offender often are neither clear cut nor absolute. Motivating forces such as anger or revenge imply that the subject was first wronged, or harmed (a victim), and then went on the offensive to seek retribution (perpetrator). This more complex crime scenario is offered by theorists who believe that lifestyle choices give us exposures to opportunities for both victimization and offending. In some cases, the victimization predates the offending, such as the scenario in the movie *The Brave One* starring Jodie Foster. After Erica (Foster's role) and her fiancé are attacked and brutally beaten (her fiancé dies), Erica slowly recovers, buys a gun, and begins to prowl the streets committing revenge murders in vigilante fashion. In reality, however, most victims transition much less slowly and in less dramatic ways as they react or even adjust to the effects of victimization. For social learning theorists, the victimization experience seems to provide a context where the behaviors that become important are those that provide rewards and reinforcements. As one delinquent girl explains:

> I was with this foster lady who was very cruel. She was abusive, and I was no more than a maid as a child. That was my purpose. She received welfare for foster kids; that was her purpose. I stayed there until I was 13, then I ran away. I was tired of the physical abuse. I ran to my mother's. The man who she lived with sexually abused me and I ran away again. I was in the street. I got arrested for shoplifting. I was picked up for vagrancy (Chesney-Lind & Shelden, 1992, p. 170).

In other cases, women can routinely drift from being the victim to being the offender. Although far from the typical offender, serial murderer Aileen Wuornos clearly characterized these circumstances. Wuornos was abandoned by her mother as an infant, and her father, a convicted child molester, committed suicide in prison. While still very young, she lived in the woods and on the streets, and by 13 years of age, she was pregnant. Wuornos went on to a life of prostitution where she stole from and murdered men with whom she engaged in sex. Most often, she claimed, her victims were those who were abusive or violent toward her. From the criminal histories we compile on those who come into the criminal justice system, we often see how the roles of victim and offender overlap and alternate.

High-Profile Cases and Victims

Another model, used by social problems and labeling theorists, tells us that certain crimes are more likely to become high priority for law enforcement and receive a disproportionate amount of resources from the criminal justice system. These celebrated cases are like the top tier of a wedding cake. This model has been used in describing the justice system's treatment of offenses for many years. One of the major assumptions in this model is that these high-profile cases are statistically rare compared to the large bottom layers of everyday crime. Still, because they receive more publicity and may dominate the news for months, they often skew public understanding of the realities of crime and justice. Some of these cases may become media events because of who the victim is, such as a celebrity, politician, or wealthy businessperson, like actress Sharon Tate or singer Selina. Others occur to regular people who suddenly become the center of a media storm because of the unusual nature of the crime, such as the child beauty queen Jon Benet Ramsey or the pregnant wife Lacy Peterson or the Central Park jogger Trisha Meili.

High-Profile Victims

High-profile victims have status and name recognition prior to the events that seem to change their image and reputation in our society. Because of their notoriety, their victimization becomes more "newsworthy" than perhaps other similarly situated victims. Even though they may suffer a crime similar to that suffered by many other Americans, such as a mugging or theft of their savings from a corrupt investment banker, their cases draw more publicity. The ways their cases evolve stand out in our minds as news pundits, and our colleagues around the water cooler dissect all the elements of the victimization. As an example, after Nicole Brown Simpson was murdered, the media replayed tapes of her calls to police in earlier domestic violence incidents. As Lauber (n.d.) wrote:

> "It was that tape," said Kim Scott, a spokesperson for Heartly House, a shelter for domestic violence victims in Frederick, MD, referring to the much-broadcast 911 message of Nicole Simpson pleading for help. "The sounds in the tape hit close for a lot of women," . . . following the week that the tapes were

broadcast in the summer of 1994, calls to abuse hotlines went up 80 percent . . . the Simpson drama, gave a face to the statistics and awoke a nation to what the U.S. Surgeon General had 10 years earlier called "this nation's number one health problem" (http://www.villagelife.org/news/archives/ DV_coverstory/DV_nolongersecret.html).

And, as Burgess et al. explain, "Pervasive media attention that tends to focus on high-profile crime cases sometimes serves to confuse the general public on who the most likely victims of crime are. For example, Ronald Goldman and Nicole Brown Simpson were certainly victims of a violent crime, but their case is in no way typical or representative" (2010, p. 68).

From the time Nicole was discovered murdered through the trial of her former husband, the case seemed to fuel myths about domestic violence. When O. J. Simpson was acquitted on the murder charges in criminal court, people felt it was not uncommon for spousal murderers to be set free, which is far from the truth. The Bureau of Justice Statistics analyzed data on 318 husbands accused of murdering their wives, and as Walker (2011) explains, the criminal justice system was tough on these offenders at every stage of the process. Only 2% of those on trial were acquitted. Forty-six percent pleaded guilty, 41% were convicted at trial, and 81% served prison terms averaging 16.5 years. Still, one high-profile case is often all it takes to give people the impression that offenders "get away with murder," particularly the murder of their wives.

High-Profile Cases

Before she was murdered, Katie Sepich was a typical low-profile, 22-year-old graduate student at New Mexico State University. Her rape and murder in 2003 were the beginning of a legislative movement within the state to mandate the collection of DNA from every felony offender. Prosecutor and later New Mexico Governor Susanna Martinez tried that case but regretted that it took three years to locate Katie's killer because, even though they had his DNA from the crime scene, he had only been arrested and not convicted in the years following the crime. In signing the popular but perhaps expensive legislation, Governor Martinez argued that waiting for someone charged with a violent crime to be convicted before DNA could be legally processed would be too late and lead to more victimizations. Passing the recent *Katie Sepich Act* made New Mexico one of 13 states to mandate DNA collection upon arrest for all violent and nonviolent offenses. Similar legislation at the federal level in 2011, entitled *The Katie Sepich Enhanced DNA Collection Act* of 2012, was finally passed by the U.S. House and Senate in December 2012 and signed by President Obama in January 2013. The Katie Sepich Act, as it is popularly known, offers financial incentives for states that participate in DNA collection efforts.

As in the case of Katie Sepich, parents and loved ones, legislators, media, and social networking systems all unite to make some criminal events and victims more high profile than others. Katie was a very attractive young woman who projected a girl-next-door image, and she was the random victim in a senseless killing — suggesting that this is something that might happen to any of our daughters, anywhere. Her cause is now the focus of a website *DNA Saves* that is committed to more extensive passage of laws collecting DNA on felony offenders. Each of the stories included on that website, as you will see, concerns a woman. Another of the victims on that website also has started her own victim-based support network (http://www.h-e-a-r-t.info/debbieact.php). Of note is that Debbie Smith, the wife of a former police officer, has a law named for her, the 2004 *Debbie Smith Act* (reauthorized 2008), which was part of a larger victims' crime bill package.

Capital murder cases, like the one involving victim Katie Sepich, often remain high profile up until the execution of the offender. As Williams et al. (2007) note, data across the years have been fairly consistent in demonstrating that cases with female victims of capital murder and, in particular, with White females are more likely to result in death sentences than those in which the victim is male.

> Defendants who murder women may be perceived as more dangerous and morally blameworthy than defendants who kill men and, hence, more deserving of punishment. . . . Defendants may also be viewed as creating additional hardship for families, the community, and the state. For example, killing a female victim might disrupt childcare or social support networks more than killing a male. . . . Furthermore, female homicide victims may be perceived as engaging in less disreputable or contributing conduct associated with their own victimization compared with male victims. . . . Similarly, sexual assault is an aggravating factor . . . in most jurisdictions . . . juries are more likely to impose death sentences in homicides involving rape (Williams et al., 2007, p. 870).

In researching the feelings expressed in the execution process, Scott Vollum (2008) explained that the co-victims, or survivors, in his study were more likely to adopt a restorative approach to the offender and sought closure when the victim was a female. This may be because female victims are often killed by someone known to the family, and there may still be children or relatives connecting the families. This makes some type of conciliatory resolution, some type of spiritual approach to dealing with the situation, more practical. For example, when Bart Whitaker, a Sugarland, Texas, youth, arranged for the contract killing of his family, his surviving father, Kent Whitaker, was caught between his love for his murdered wife and son, and retribution from the offender, also his son.

Restorative justice may offer options for co-victims or survivors, and these stories seem to attract considerable media attention, perhaps because mediation and forgiveness seem so difficult in cases of violent crime. We have talked about mothers becoming activists in the wake of losing a child to a crime, and there are those who have engaged in peacemaking opportunities that are an essential component of restorative justice. Vollum (2008) argues that such efforts have been "transformative processes" for both surviving families and offenders within the context of capital punishment.

College Coeds as Crime Victims

A college campus is often an environment where individuals spend a significant amount of time during what might be considered the higher-risk years of a young adult's life. Daily routines for most undergraduates involve not only attending classes, but also working in financial-aid jobs on campus and engaging in leisure activities and student organizations. Tracking crime and victimization risks on college campuses is a relatively new responsibility for institutions of higher learning, and the collection of these data gives us insight into a number of offenses and their relative risks for female students.

Early research on campus crime seemed to indicate that only about 60% of victims reported offenses to campus police. Victims as well as authorities seemed to be confused about jurisdiction, and many students indicated that they did not report crimes because they did not have confidence in campus police or believed that the officers would not be able to do anything. Those who were younger and more economically disadvantaged were also less likely to report. Still, studies reflected that women were more worried about crime on campus regardless of the time of day or the location (parking lots, gyms, auditoriums, library, etc.). Ironically, the crimes most likely to be experienced, larceny/theft, harassment, vandalism, and threats, were not even those that would be tracked by the early reporting systems (Fisher, 1995).

Given that much victimization occurs away from the campus, at events such as spring break, off-campus fraternity houses, and local bars and nightclubs, it has taken a long time for the concept of liability to become attached to the university itself. After 19-year-old Jeanne Clery was raped and murdered in hr Lehigh University dorm room in 1986, her parents pressed for changes in Pennsylvania law that would require reporting campus crime. They, like many other parents, were unaware that their daughter's school had recorded 38 violent campus crimes in the three years prior to Jeanne's murder.

The passage of the *Campus Security Act of 1990* began a long and slow process of developing a culture of accountability in colleges and universities. Campus crime data are now part of the Uniform Crime Report (UCR), and each school must publish an annual crime report that provides data on homicide, sex offenses, robbery, aggravated assault, burglary, motor vehicle theft, and arson. The data are also submitted to the U.S. Department of Education that conducts analysis and research on issues related to campus crime. Schools must also make available to all current and prospective students, as well as staff, policies on reporting crime and basic victims' rights (in a variety of formats). The 2000 *Jeanne Clery Disclosure of Campus Security Policy and Campus Crime Statistics Act* added crimes committed in areas bordering campuses, as well as the reporting of hate crimes and manslaughter. To provide some incentive for compliance, sanctions have been put in place for not meeting reporting mandates. The circulation of crime statistics and emergency alert notifications when offenders are suspected on campus are all mandated under the *Clery Act* and its amendments.

To date, a number of sexual harassment issues have been litigated, all of which seem to clearly spell out the types of measures that officials should take to not only deal with allegations but also prevent it from occurring. For women in college, the most practical approach to sexual harassment litigation may be through *Title IX of the Education Amendments of 1972*. Under that law a person may not be "excluded from participation in, be denied the benefits of, or be subjected to discrimination under any educational program" that receives federal funds, which is essentially most any college campus. Title IX offers protection from both student-student harassment or teacher-student harassment, and damages may be awarded if intentional conduct results in harms covered by this statute. Obviously, courts would be looking for a determination that the school knew of the harm and was "deliberately indifferent" to that harm before assessing liability.

In several cases, the high court has clarified that officials will be evaluated on both post-harassment conduct as well as pre-harassment conduct if it is obvious that they knew or should have known that a substantial risk for harassment existed (Davis & Smith, 2009). In the first case, a student reported being raped in her dorm room by one of the university football players, but her claim was initially dismissed by a lower court. Although the University of Washington might not be able to prevent a rape from occurring, the higher court would reason in their reversal, fault was found with administrators' subsequent actions. In finding sufficient grounds for "deliberate indifference," the court submitted an extensive list of what officials did wrong:

> A lack of appropriate discipline of [the plaintiff's] rapist, minimizing the effects of her rape, treating the victim equally with the rapist in the mediation process, allowing her rapist's denial of wrong-doing to be accepted at face value at the mediation, keeping the matter out of the public eye to avoid negative publicity, offering only a repeated mediation as an alternative remedial measure, discouraging [the plaintiff] from filing a police report, top administrators not notifying the UW's own police force of the report of a violent sex crime, repeatedly suggesting that [the plaintiff] leave her job with the football program while her rapist would remain, wearing [the plaintiff] down until she believed that further complaints would be futile, a decision not to investigate — or cause to be investigated — her rape report, and — in the absence of a proper investigation — questioning her truthfulness when she expressed dissatisfaction with the results of the mediation [*S. S. v. Roc Alexander (defendant)*, 2008 Wash. App. LEXIS 333, (Ct App. Wash., Feb. 11, 2008)].

The second case involved a coed, Tiffany Williams, who was gang raped by three basketball players in a dorm room. The court noted what they referred to as "pre-harassment evidence," namely, that one of the athletes accused of raping a student at the University of Georgia had a history of disciplinary proceedings and criminal conduct, all of which were known to officials when he was recruited and admitted (Davis & Smith, 2009). The ruling indicated that the university's "knowledge of an alleged harasser's past sexual misconduct and its failure to properly supervise the athlete with these known proclivities 'substantially increased the risk faced by female students'" (*Williams v. Bd of Regents University System of Georgia*, 477 F.3d. 1282 [11th Cir. 2007]).

Assisting Victims in the Criminal Justice System

By most state statues, women must not only file official crime reports in order to be eligible for assistance and compensation, but they must also participate in the prosecution of alleged offenders. Fear of retaliation may discourage many victims from seeking help, as will concerns about having to make arrangements for family and work responsibilities in order to pursue a case in court.

Under the terms of most programs, in order to be eligible for victims' compensation/assistance, victims must report the crime to law enforcement within three days of the offense and file the claim within a fixed period of time. All private sources of health care or insurance must be exhausted before one is eligible to receive victims' compensation from these funds. States usually distribute their monies through public and nonprofit organizations that provide victim-related services at the local level. The seemingly bureaucratic red tape encountered in navigating many of these agencies may discourage all but the most committed. In addition, victims with health, immigration, or language difficulties are less likely to avail themselves of whatever resources might be in their area. The availability of specific victims' advocates, outreach networks, and support (such as self-help and survivors) organizations serves to alleviate some of the problems in this process.

Victim compensation usually includes medical costs, funeral and burial costs, psychological services, lost wages or support, and repair of eyeglasses, prostheses, or dental work. Money may also be available for crime scene cleanup but does not cover property damage or loss. Victim assistance, on the other hand, may include a variety of services such as crisis intervention, emergency shelter or transportation, and the provision of advocacy representation in the criminal justice system. In many cases this means making sure that victims can get to treatment, appear as witnesses, or obtain restraining orders in court. Even with assistance, though, the strict criteria for admission to many programs, such as battered women's shelters and a lack of available beds, make this option difficult for many victims.

Finding Solutions to the Epidemic

According to a 2005 report by Amnesty International, the current level of violence against girls and women worldwide represents an epidemic, a major human rights scandal, and a public health crisis. In the report, gender-based violence is defined as follows:

[P]hysical, sexual and psychological violence occurring in the family, including battering, sexual abuse of female children in the household, dowry-related violence, marital rape, female genital mutilation and other traditional practices harmful to women, non-spousal violence and violence related to exploitation; physical, sexual and psychological violence occurring within the general community, including rape, sexual abuse, sexual harassment and intimidation at work, in educational institutions and elsewhere; trafficking in women and forced prostitution; and physical, sexual and psychological violence perpetrated or condoned by the state, wherever it occurs (Amnesty International, 2005, p.2).

In the chapters to come, we will look more closely at some of these specific forms of violence. We will also examine ways the criminal justice system in this country has responded to challenges raised by these issues. Over the last few decades, victims have made monumental strides toward incorporating a full range of rights in the criminal justice system. From the domestic violence legislation of the 1990s, to the Victim Rights Act of 1996, to the federal Crime Victims Rights Act of 2004 and subsequent laws that provided assistance to victims of trafficking, stalking, and sexual harassment, prosecutors have additional resources and tools to combat the victimization of women.

Critical Thinking Questions

1. After reading through the following cases, think about any factors that may make mothers more receptive to the processes of restorative justice than perhaps fathers. Do father's relationships with their daughters involve more "protective" features that make forgiveness less likely? What is it about mother-daughter relationships that would encourage such an undertaking? (You might want to look at two websites: http://www.abpnews.com/content/view/4777/9/ and http://newsweek.washingtonpost.com/onfaith/guestvoices/2010/06/forgiving_my_daughters_killer.html)

2. What should be a college campus' responsibility regarding safety and crime prevention? How should the liability of a university be assessed following any particular crime?

3. Discuss some high-impact cases or high-profile victims from recent crimes in your region. What factors relative to these incidents seem to influence public opinion the most?

4. Do we as a society seem to blame victims for their role in a crime as some of the theories in this section appear to suggest? What can women do, according to these theories, to reduce their risk of victimization?

Books, Websites, and Media Resources

Amnesty International: www.anmesty.org/en/womens-rights
DNA Saves: http://www.dnasaves.org
Meili, T. (2003). *I am the Central Park jogger: A story of hope and possibility*. New York: Scribner.
Mothers Against Drunk Driving: http://www.madd.org/about-us/history/madd-presidents.pdf
National Center for Victims of Crime: http://www.victimsofcrime.org/
The U.S. Department of Justice, Office for Victims of Crime — Training and Technical Assistance
    Center: https://www.ovcttac.gov/
Van Derbur, M. (2003). *Miss America by day*. Denver: Oak Hills Ridge Press.

Popular Films

Panic Room (2002), Jodie Foster.
Thelma & Louise (1991), Susan Sarandon and Geena Davis.

References

Alvi, S., Schwartz, M., Dekeseredy, W., & Maume, M. (2001). Women's fear of crime in Canadian public housing. *Violence Against Women, 7*, 638-662.

Amnesty International. (2005). Women, violence and health. Retrieved from http://www.amnesty.org/en/library/info/ACT77/001/2005/en

Barrow, L. M. (2008). *Criminal victimization of the deaf*. New York: LFB Scholarly Publishing.

Chesney-Lind, M., & Shelden, R. (1992). *Girls: Delinquency and juvenile justice*. Pacific Grove, CA: Brooks Cole.

Choi, K. (2010). *Risk factors in computer-crime victimization*. New York: LFB Scholarly Publishing.

Cohen, L., & Felson, M. (1979). Social change and crime rate trends: A routine activities approach. *American Sociological Review, 44*, 588-607.

Cornish, D. B., & Clarke, R. V. (Eds.). (1986). *The reasoning criminal: Rational choice perspectives on offending*. New York: Springer-Verlag.

Cornish, D. B., & Clarke, R. V. (1987). Understanding crime displacement: An application of rational choice theory. *Criminology, 25*, 933-947.

Davis, T., & Smith, K. (2009). Eradicating student-athlete sexual assault of women: Section 1983 and personal liability following Fitzgerald v. Barnstable. *Michigan State Law Review, 2009*, 629-667.

Fisher, B. S. (1995). Crime and fear on campus. *Annals of the American Academy of Political Science, 539*, 85-101.

Gallegos, A. (2011, October 23). Homeless women learn to be their own best defense. *Houston Chronicle*, pp. B1, B4.

Gilchrist, E., Bannister, J., Ditton, J., & Farrall, S. (1998). Women and the "fear of crime": Challenging the accepted stereotype. *British Journal of Criminology, 38*(2), 283-298.

Hindelang, M., Gottfredson, M., & Garofalo, J. (1978). *Victims of personal crime: An empirical foundation for a theory of personal victimization*. Cambridge, MA: Ballinger.

Lauber, M. (n.d.). Domestic violence: No longer a quiet secret. *Village Life*. Retrieved from www.villagelife.org

McShane, L. (2005, December 1). Slaying reveals aspiring dancer's secret life in New York's topless bars. *Houston Chronicle*, p. A9.

McShane, M. D., & Emeka, T. (2011). *American victimology*. El Paso, TX: LFB Scholarly.

Messing, J. T., Campbell, J. C., Cimino, A., Patchell, B., & Wilson, J. S. (2011). Collaborating with police departments: Recruitment in the Oklahoma Lethality Assessment (OK-LA) Study. *Violence Against Women, 17*(2), 163-176.

Pitts, L., Jr. (2009, November 9). Honor killing was act of cowardice. *Houston Chronicle*. Retrieved from http://www.chron.com/disp/story.mpl/editorial/outlook/6712167.html

Sacco, V. (1990). Gender, fear and victimization: A preliminary application of power-control theory. *Sociological Spectrum, 10*, 485-506.

Sellin, T. (1938). Culture conflict and crime. *The Social Science Research Bulletin, 41*, 63-70.

Tempest, R. (1993, February 18). Ancient traditions v. the law. *Los Angeles Times*, pp. A1, A10.

Thompson, C. (1996). Women's crime concerns and gun ownership: Evaluating media images. *Journal of Contemporary Criminal Justice, 12*,151-172.

Truman, J. L. (2011). Criminal victimization, 2010 (NCJ 235508). Washington, DC: Bureau of Justice Statistics.

Vollum, S. (2008). *Last words and the death penalty*. El Paso: LFB Scholarly.

von Hentig, H. (1948). *The criminal and his victim: Studies in the sociobiology of crime*. New Haven, CT: Yale University Press.

Walker, S. (2011). *Sense and nonsense about crime, drugs and communities*. Belmont, CA: Wadsworth.

Williams, F. P., & McShane, M. (2014). *Criminological theory* (6th ed.). Upper Saddle River, NJ: Prentice Hall.

Williams, M. R., Demuth, S., & Holcomb, J. E. (2007). Understanding the influence of victim gender in death penalty cases: The importance of victim race, sex-related victimization, and jury decision making. *Criminology, 45*, 865-892.

Prostitution and Sex Crimes

Introduction

As labeling theory tells us, societal reaction to a crime depends in large part on who the victim is, who the offender is, and the current cultural values and attitudes of the time. A stigma or master status may be conferred upon someone whose image is altered by the way people view his or her deviant behavior. Ironically, for example, more people recognize Mike Tyson as the championship heavyweight boxer who bit off an opponent's ear than the boxer who was convicted and imprisoned for rape. It seems almost as if the rape was not deviant enough or unusual enough to cause a lasting impression.

In two books, *Out of Bounds: Inside the NBA's Culture of Rape, Violence, and Crime* (2005), and *Pros and Cons: The Criminals Who Play in the NFL* (1998), Jeff Benedict argues that high-profile, professional athletes like members of the NFL and the NBA can often commit very serious crimes, including sexual assaults and domestic violence, with very few repercussions. In his research, journalist Benedict found that of the 509 NFL players tracked, 21% had formal charges for serious crimes of which most of the victims were women. In examining the careers of 177 NBA players from 2001 to 2002, Benedict determined that 40% had arrests for serious criminal charges including rape and domestic violence. Interviewing over 400 prominent criminal justice system figures, Benedict found that charges were often "negotiated." Individual sports franchises and their parent organizations like the NBA and NFL held firmly to a legal rather than a moral benchmark—if someone is not convicted, than charges don't mean a thing.

59

To many, the cover of celebrity and wealth means protection from the types of penalties that most citizens would face under similar charges. It also means access to a lifestyle of privilege and opportunities to have whatever one wants. Regardless of what happened between Kobi Bryant and his young accuser, Benedict argues, the L.A. Laker superstar checked into a resort at 10:00 PM and by 11:00 PM had already had what the future Hall of Famer agreed was sexual intercourse with someone he hardly knew.

In this chapter we will look not only at a wide range of sexual offenses, but at the values and norms with which society interprets and reacts to sexual behaviors in general. Feminist theory often focuses on the way identities are shaped by sexual roles. It is also important to examine how the law has evolved around changes in our interpretation of acceptable sexual behavior. Perhaps of even more concern in our society today is the protection of special populations such as children and victims of human trafficking from inappropriate sexual contacts or exploitation and sexual abuse.

Prostitution

Prostitution has always been a controversial occupation. Even though it may not actually be "the oldest profession," as the saying goes, it continues to reflect cultural values, varying levels of social tolerance, and ties to the political and economic well-being of any area. One hundred years ago, Cesare Lombroso (1911, p. 186) reasoned that if prostitution were calculated in crime statistics, men and women might be on par for criminality.

Early American sexual mores were tied to puritanical values that may have made prostitutes seem exotic and tempting. As Evans explains:

> In the prudish Victorian era women did not go barefooted or bare-armed. Ankles were not to be seen. The average middle-class housewife left the front steps wearing twenty-two pounds of clothing. Sexual inhibitions abounded and rarely did husbands and wives see each other naked (2002, p. x).

In addition, painful childbirths and fears about high-risk pregnancies often meant that women eschewed marital relations, and families would never consider divorce. The services of prostitutes were readily available across the United States and up and down the East Coast and in the nation's capital. In Washington, DC, by the time of the Civil War (1860), there were at least 500 brothels and over 5,000 prostitutes (Evans, 2002). However, by the start of World War I (1914), most of the active establishments were more discreetly hidden as a result of religious and moral crusaders.

As urban growth, industrialization, and immigration changed the shape of U.S. cities, prostitution was relegated to certain areas associated with illegal drinking and gambling during Prohibition and, in general, high-crime areas. Perhaps as a result of significantly different social forces, prostitution in the West had a much more open and colorful history. Parlor houses, as author

Max Evans (2002) refers to them, remained centrally located and legal through the mid-twentieth century. As Anne Seagraves (1994) explains, adventurous women who were willing to sacrifice their virtue to move out into the daunting Western Territories were, for the most part, some of the first females to settle in rough mining areas. As towns developed, most of the brothels

> were situated in what was called the red light district or tenderloin. This was the designated area for the "houses of sin," saloons, and gambling establishments. The term "red light" is said to have originated in Dodge City, Kansas. Dodge City was a major stop for the railroad, and a convenient place for the train crews to visit the ladies of negotiable virtue. When these men entered the brothels . . . they would leave their red lanterns outside so they could be located in case of an emergency. The madams soon realized that a red light was an excellent way to advertise, and the custom spread. The red light in front of a place of prostitution eventually became a law . . . cities also insisted that a red shade or curtain be hung in the windows of these establishments during the day (Seagraves, 1994, p. 28).

Alliances between the working men and prostitutes hinged on mutually beneficial arrangements. Often the women cared for the sick, donated to charities, and sewed and cooked as needed. As Seagraves explains:

> The soiled doves were good for the western economy and helped support the community. They spent their money locally, buying fancy clothing, expensive wines and ornamental jewelry. These women paid for business licenses, when required, and fines when they were arrested for breaking the law. The lawmen and ladies usually lived in harmony. There were seldom any special accommodations for women in the jails, so they learned to co-exist — it was easier on the taxpayer (1994, p. xviii).

Within the world of prostitution, there are classes or castes differentiating members into levels of status just like any other sociological typology. In her book, Soiled Doves, Seagraves describes the most successful call girls as having their own parlor house, cottage, or saloon. They would have wealthier patrons, and this allowed them to entertain less frequently and with only a few select clients. On the next rung down were the less-prosperous majority of women working in larger brothels and in the more run-down saloons and dance halls, with some of the more transient prostitutes taking up in tents outside of mining camps. Below that, and at the lowest level, are the street workers. As one autobiography read, "the social gulf between the first-class courtesan and those who have become dregs of prostitution is as great as the gulf between the sheltered woman in her home and the streetwalker" (Rosen, 1982, p. 107). Some of the less fortunate prostitutes were sick, alcoholic, and forced into exploitation by pimps.

As time went on, however, politicians on the East Coast realized that a tamer and more conservative image of the frontier West would encourage families to move there. Shootouts and land fights, the vast wealth that changed hands daily, the proliferation of bars and brothels, as well as the absence of churches and schools, emphasized the dangerous lawlessness that was the Wild West. Officials were afraid that reports of outlaws and vigilante justice would discourage the migration of decent, God-fearing families who were needed to make their area a model of successful democracy. Governments were focused on having peaceful, law-abiding areas that appealed to young, healthy families who would help build the fledgling country by securing its resources and strengthening the national economy. More ranches, farming, and mining would contribute to a more powerful world position for the United States. Oversight and regulation of the West was then a priority for policy makers, and efforts were made to reduce the perceptions of scandal in the territories. Weak or ineffective law enforcers were quickly replaced, competent judges were routed through court circuits, and territorial jails and prisons were funded and built (McShane, 2008, p. 27).

Prostitution Today

Today the law clearly differentiates between street-level and indoor prostitution. There are certain rural areas in Nevada where prostitution is legal, and in Rhode Island, codes make prostitution within closed establishments legal though it is still illegal to street-walk or advertise or solicit outside. In regard to the decriminalization of prostitution indoors in Rhode Island, the move appears to be both a compromise and a possible social experiment. As Shapiro explains, during the late 1970s, a number of factors came together to prompt this change. For example:

> [C]itizens demanded police action against street prostitution in their neighborhoods. The existing prostitution laws made criminal procedures slow, and since prostitutes remained on the streets awaiting jury trials, it was ineffective to reduce prostitution. In addition, a prostitutes' rights group filed a federal sex discrimination against the state of Rhode Island because more women than men were being arrested for soliciting sex even though the statute was gender neutral (Shapiro, 2009, p. 6).

Obviously, levels of enforcement of prostitution laws vary from place to place and over time. In one General Social Survey, about 2% of American women admitted to ever engaging in acts of prostitution, or the more common sociological phrase "sex work" (Smith, 2006). Concern about sexually transmitted diseases and efforts to track and expose patrons of prostitutes may have also decreased the extent and visibility of the sex trade in many cities. Data on arrests show that over the years, arrests for prostitution have appeared to decline. Again, this could reflect changes in enforcement priorities rather than any significant change in the actual commission of the crime. As Cunningham and Kendall (2009) explain:

> During the late 1970s and early 1980s, the prostitution arrest rate grew substantially, reaching a peak of 70 arrests per 100,000 women in

1983 . . . prostitution arrest rates began declining after 1983, while arrests for other crimes continued to rise until the early 1990s . . . prostitution arrest rates declined in most years during the peak years of the crack epidemic, 1984–1991; however, this may be due to the hierarchical structure of UCR data, in which those arrested for multiple crimes (e.g., prostitution and drug possession) are recorded in the data only by the most serious crime (drug possession, in this example). To the extent drugs and prostitution became more closely linked after 1983, UCR data may be limited in accurately describing trends in prostitution activity. Nevertheless, by 2007, prostitution arrest rates were lower than their 1970 value, at 26 per 100,000 women.

One could also argue that for a sex worker, the risks of a regulated brothel are far less than those of street-walking. As Quinet (2009) notes, prostitutes have been victimized in disproportionate numbers, particularly at the hands of serial killers. Looking at cases with only female victims, prostitutes make up 32% of the victims of serial murderers in this country. The data also indicate that those who kill prostitutes tend to murder more victims and offend over a longer period of time than perpetrators who kill nonprostitutes.

From Baby Pros to Trafficked Victims

In the 1970s one of the early female pioneers in criminal justice, Dr. Dorothy Bracey, was finishing her field research on juvenile prostitutes. With an Ivy League education in social anthropology, Bracey became one of the founding members of the criminal justice department at John Jay College of Criminal Justice in New York. Her monograph, *Baby-Pros: Preliminary profiles of juvenile prostitutes* (1979), quickly became a classic and was one of the few pieces to have been written about the subject in the discipline. Schulz (2002) explains that Bracey's work continues to be

> . . . the conventional wisdom of feminist criminology. She voiced concern about the background of neglect and abuse from which juvenile prostitutes came. She also pointed out their further abuse not only by pimps, customers, and muggers, but by the juvenile justice system itself. She documented the tendency of the juvenile courts to deal severely with girls accused of sexual activity and she criticized the system for treating the girls not as victims, but as "criminals in need of punishment" (Schulz, 2002, p. 38).

In her writing, Bracey linked the issues of runaways and prostitution and questioned the tendency to consider such offenses as "victimless crimes." She wrote:

> The twin frustrations of a paucity of effective treatment alternatives and a rising rate of violent juvenile crime have supported [treating juvenile offenders as criminals rather than as victims]. There is, in addition, the well documented fascination of juvenile justice officials in the sexuality and sexual activities of female juvenile offenders. It is the combination of these factors that dictates

that when presented with the young prostitute in the dual role of offender and victim, the odds are very high that the latter will be subsumed in the former (Bracey, 1984, 151).

One of the more interesting changes in law since Bracey wrote, and what certainly reflects the mind-set of Americans today, has been a decline in the use of the term "juvenile prostitution." As that phrase seems to emphasize the youth's criminal activity, the shift has been to adopt the term "sexual trafficking in minors" that reflects the victimization or exploitation of the underage youth.

Recent research has found that when cases are classified as child sexual abuse with payment, the juvenile was more likely to be treated as a victim (Mitchell, Finkelhor, & Wolak, 2010). In Halter's (2010) research, only 60% of youth involved in prostitution were viewed as victims by police. Those who were identified as being local residents, cooperated with the police, were able to identify their exploiters, and did not have a prior criminal record were more likely to be considered as victims. In addition, more of the current research tends to link together a complex system of associated factors that evolve over time prior to juvenile prostitution. These include involvement in behaviors with escalating risk that appear to begin with caregiver strain and child maltreatment. From there, a youth may be more disposed toward running away, early onset of substance abuse, and sexual denigration of one's self and others (Reid, 2011).

Barriers to Exiting Prostitution

According to the literature there are a number of barriers to women successfully exiting careers in prostitution. These include drug addiction, mental illness, physical injury or health problems, exhaustion, strained family relations, a criminal record, and the lack of housing, job alternatives, or education. Often, years of estrangement from support groups like family and friends mean that the prostitute is socially isolated. Prior sexual abuse within a family may also make assistance or reunification unlikely (Cimino, 2012; Baker, Dalla, & Williamson, 2010). A study by Martin, Hearst, and Widome (2010) found that young girls who entered into prostitution were less likely to be using drugs when they begin what researchers refer to as "survival sex," and they had more negative outcomes than women who began selling sex later in life. Adult females were more likely to have children and to be using drugs when they enter prostitution.

In a study of participants in a residential program specifically designed to facilitate the process of exiting prostitution, Roe-Sepowitz (2012) found that challenges for the women included homelessness, a history of attempted suicide, and involvement with friends who engaged in prostitution. For many, exiting the prostitution lifestyle requires a series of steps that Baker, Dalla, and Williamson (2010) outline as first having doubts, then exploring alternative roles, followed by experiencing either a gradual or sudden turning point from which they may eventually be able to develop the ex-role and a new identity.

Rape

In 1925, famed blues singer Billie Holiday was only 10 years old when she became a victim of rape. Immediately after the rape happened, she was brought, still bleeding, to the police station:

> Instead of treating me like somebody who called the cops for help, they treated me like I had killed somebody . . . they threw me into a cell and gave me filthy looks and snickers. After a couple of days in a cell, they dragged me into a court. Mr. Dick got sentenced to five years. They sentenced me to a Catholic institution (Holiday, 1976, pp. 32-33).

Fortunately, victims of rape today receive far more support from the public and from the criminal justice system than they did in Billie Holiday's era. Reforms in rape law have also made it less intimidating for a woman to report rape and to follow through in the criminal justice system with an offender's prosecution. As Samaha (2002) explains, statutes have been revised so that a victim's testimony does not have to be independently corroborated, the victim's past sexual behavior cannot be introduced into evidence (rape shield laws), and victims do not have to demonstrate significant levels of resistance, particularly when a reasonable woman would believe that to do so would lead to further injury and harm.

Research available today indicates that women are more likely to report rapes when threats and weapons are used and when the offender is not someone with whom they have a close, intimate relationship. Research also shows that older women are more likely to report a sexual assault, yet, conversely, women overall are less likely to report having been raped if they were intoxicated at the time of the offense (Menard, 2005).

From the development of sex-crime response units within police departments and specialized prosecution units within the courts, progress has been made in sensitizing our society to the seriousness of the crime and the need for both legal and social service interventions. The Sexual Assault Response Team (SART) is a recent government-supported initiative to put more effective coordinated resources in place, thus benefitting from uniform strategies. The SARTs include primary and secondary team members who work together to respond to criminal events and strengthen community prevention efforts. Primary members include victim advocates, law enforcement officers, forensic medical examiners (including sexual-assault nurse examiners, SANEs), forensic laboratory personnel, and prosecutors. Secondary or supplementary members have been identified as dispatchers, emergency medical technicians, correctional staff, culturally specific organization representatives, sex-offender management professionals, policy makers, federal grant administrators, faith-based providers, and civil and victims' rights attorneys.

Mandatory treatment programs for sex offenders can also be seen as both recognition of the serial nature of many sex offenses and a commitment to preventing recidivism. The registration requirements and community monitoring imposed on sex offenders also reflect the prevailing view that these crimes are serious enough to warrant restrictions on offenders' civil liberties. Reducing the stigma of being a rape victim and increasing the likelihood that sex offenses will be taken seriously if reported have helped to build confidence in the contemporary criminal justice system.

The collection of more sophisticated data on sex offenses has stimulated academic interest in studying rape and led to improvements in the way these crimes are defined and classified. As social norms more broadly recognize the appropriateness of reporting rape, available data will not only grow but more accurately reflect the true nature of rape. And, rather than viewing rape as one generic category of crime, we have been able to distinguish a number of different types — acquaintance rape, date rape, marital rape, stranger rape, rape of a child, statutory rape — which helps us to develop laws and policies that best fit the circumstances. Critics charge, however, that more recent sex-offender registration practices may actually result in having taken backward steps by lumping too many disparate types of sex offenses into one generic group. They suggest that more specific and offense-appropriate sanctions are necessary.

Rape: The Challenges of Measuring Risk

Although many websites purport to contain information on the occurrence of rape, few contain up-to-date or carefully explained data. (See data published on RAINN | Rape, Abuse and Incest National Network.) Some use "crime clocks" showing that a rape occurs every so many minutes, but these simplistic portrayals do not accurately convey the nature of risk and the differential risks for certain groups within the general population. In fact, crime clocks make it look as if everyone has the same degree of risk, which is simply not true. Others, including a 2006 Report on the National Violence Against Women Survey, use information collected a decade earlier in 1995/1996 (Tjaden & Thoennes, 2006). Even some of the more recent postings from the SART website include data that were collected before the year 2000 (see note in italics added after each posting):

- American Indian women suffer rape at twice the rate of any other race [this figure comes from data 1993-1998].
- The risks of being sexually assaulted are at least one and a half times greater for individuals with disabilities than for people without disabilities of similar age and gender [published in 1994].
- Among college students nationwide, between 20 and 25% of women reported experiencing completed or attempted rape [based on data collected in 1997].
- Nearly half of all women who served in the military encountered physical or sexual violence while enlisted [from a 2000 publication based on even older data with events that may have occurred as many as 10 years before the data were collected].
- Between one-third and one-half of battered women are raped by their partners [from a chapter in a book published in 1996].

- While living on the streets, 32.3% of homeless women, 27.1% of homeless men, and 38.1% of homeless transgendered persons were sexually or physically assaulted [*data gathered in interviews in 1996*].

You could argue that it is somewhat misleading to read facts on a website in 2013 that was constructed of data drawn in the 1990s, but few studies have been funded beyond that time for the collection and analysis of sexual assault against women. In a 2011 article by Cook, Gidycz, Koss, and Murphy, the following data were noted in the literature review:

> Fisher et al. (2000) found that 10.1% of their national sample of college women had experienced a rape prior to their assessment. Similarly, Kilpatrick, Resnick, Rugiero, Consoscenti, and McCauley (2007) reported lifetime prevalence rates of rape of 18% for the general population and 11.5% for college student samples. In contrast, the prevalence of rape among at-risk samples of women is often much higher. For example, sexual assault prevalence rates among inmates in correctional facilities approach 100% (see Blackburn, Mullings, & Marquart, 2008; Cook, Smith, Tusher, & Raiford, 2005) (Cook et al., 2011, p. 204).

The key is to check the dates and, if the data are older, to see if any more recent figures are really out there. Remember that with the time lags generally associated with the publication process, data collected in 2005 may not appear in a published source until 2008 or 2009 (or even later if the data are being used in a secondary analysis).

Time is not the only threat to the ability to develop accurate measures of the frequency or risk of rape. As Cook, Gidycz, Koss, and Murphy (2011) explain, health services definitions might differ from those used by various researchers or by social service workers or by police. In the field of criminal justice, legal definitions used in charging defendants are those given highest priority. The ability to gain convictions and to prevent recidivism is predicated on the legal elements of the crime, regardless of how appropriate other descriptions might appear.

The Prevalence of Rape

The risk of any victimization occurring is referred to as "prevalence." Because we are concerned with rape victims, our prevalence rate incorporates the number of victims rather than the total number of crimes in an area. It is calculated by dividing the total number of victims by the total population. This provides an estimate of proportion or percent of the population who have been victimized. Of course, we frequently don't know the number of actual victims and as a result cannot calculate a prevalence rate directly. Another version of a prevalence rate can be expressed as a percentage of those who report having been victims of a specific crime out of the total population at risk. Let's call this one an "at-risk" prevalence rate. For instance, let us say that there are 12,000 reported rape victims within a population of 100,000, or 12 per 100 people. Changing this into an individual's "risk level," we could estimate a risk of rape equivalent to 12% for each individual. This is still not satisfactory, because even though both males and females are victims of rape, females are more at risk for rape than males. In our hypothetical example, if females represent about 90% of rape victims and 50% of the population, then the "at-risk" prevalence of females raped over the course of a year would be about 21.6%, with males having a risk rate of 2.4%.

Unfortunately, for our attempt to construct a reasonable risk rate, there are even more issues involved. Think of it this way — if we can predict victimization to any degree, then the likelihood of victimization is not the same for all. Not only can victimization be predicted for certain groups of people, but as discussed earlier, lifestyle and routine activities theories are based on and explain differences in victimization. Each argues that the daily choices made by members of the population affect the likelihood of their victimization. For example, a young person who goes to nightclubs on the weekend has a greater chance of being victimized than an elderly person who is at home at night. In fact, as Kavanaugh points out, "nightlife spaces such as bars and clubs are intensely sexualized social spaces where victimization outcomes such as rape, attempted rape, stalking, harassment, and other instances of unwanted sexual contact occur with regularity" (2013, p. 21).

Geographical criminologists have also shown that there are areas much more disposed to crime than others. All of this tells us that a simple number or rate based on the incidence of crime or some general population figure will be misleading. We need an approach that will tell us the risk of victimization, rather than the rate of crime events for a given population. Geographical criminologists try to take this into account by using concentration rates, which are based on the average number of incidents per victim in a given area. Even this, though, does not account for the different chances of victimization among various types of people engaged in various lifestyle practices.

As should be obvious by now, one of the major dilemmas confronting researchers in calculating the rate of any specific crime or victimization is precisely what goes into both the numerator and denominator of the constructed fraction. Disagreement occurs on who the actual victims of any offense are, as well as on who the potential victims might be. Altering either of these could result in greatly overestimating or underestimating the actual risk of any individual, or group of individuals, being a victim of any offense. In our rape example above, where should the data on the actual number of rape victims come from? Moreover, should all claims of rape be included? Should rape be inferred if the small child, Alzheimer's patient, or otherwise mentally or psychologically impaired person cannot confirm what actually took place? Who should be included in the list of potential victims? By placing everyone of any age in the potential victim category, have we watered down the picture of the true risk of rape?

Acquaintance Rape and Recurrent Sexual Victimization

You have probably heard people talk about "date rape." Researchers have indicated a preference for the term "acquaintance rape" because it is more

Table 1	**Calculation of Rape Risk**

Which approach below would you argue most accurately represents the risk of rape?

$$\frac{\text{\# of Reported Rape Victimizations}}{\text{Population of U.S.}}$$

$$\frac{\text{\# of Police-Reported Rapes}}{\text{Population of U.S.}}$$

$$\frac{\text{\# of Women Ages 10 to 75 Reporting Rape Victimization}}{\text{Total of Women in U.S. Ages 10 to 75}}$$

What other calculation might you use for demonstrating the rate of rape in the United States?

---

meaningful to focus on the relationship rather than the context of a "date," as that is more contextually ambiguous. According to a report issued by the Community Oriented Policing Services (COPS) office, young women in the 16- to 24-years age bracket are raped four times as often as other women. It was even determined that women attending college are more at risk for sexual assault and rape than their peers not in school. The rates are estimated at about 35 per 1,000 female students over a 7-month school period. It is thought that access to alcohol, privacy in housing areas, and lack of supervision may create environments not only conducive to rape, but also to not reporting rape. Sampson's (2003) report disclosed that

> [A]lmost 25 percent of college women have been victims of rape or attempted rape since the age of 14. Ninety percent of college women who are victims of rape or attempted rape know their assailant. The attacker is usually a classmate, friend, boyfriend, ex-boyfriend, or other acquaintance (in that order). Most acquaintance rapes do not occur on dates; rather they occur when two people are otherwise in the same place (e.g., at a party, studying together in a dorm room). Fewer than 5 percent of college women who are victims of rape or attempted rape report it to police. However, about two-thirds of the victims tell *someone*, often a friend (but usually not a family member or college official). In one study, over 40 percent of those raped who did not report the incident said they did not do so because they feared reprisal by the assailant or others (Sampson, 2003, pp. 3-4).

In the 1990s, a disturbing trend of date-rape drugs being used, particularly Rohypnol (flunitrazepam), to render women unconscious and to disrupt any potential memory of the rape event, prompted legislation in the form of the *Drug Induced Rape Prevention Act*. The bill enhanced penalties for crimes associated with the use of such drugs and dictated punishments for importing or trafficking in such substances. Funds were also appropriated for college education programs on ways to avoid being victimized by date-rape drugs.

Research by Fisher, Daigle, and Cullen (2010) tried to determine if any of the factors suggested by lifestyle theory or routine activities theory could predict which women would face a single versus multiple sexual victimizations. This includes being close to potentially motivated offenders, the presence of other family or household members (guardians), and engaging in risky behaviors such as alcohol use. None of those factors were significant, but the researchers did find that "women who used self-protective action during the first incident reduced their likelihood of being a recurrent victim" (p. 103). McFarlane et al. (2005) worked with 148 physically abused women and found that reporting the first rape to police reduced the likelihood of a subsequent rape by more than half. On the other hand, Daigle, Fisher, and Cullen (2008) determined that a one-time rape victim was no more likely to report that incident to police than a victim who suffered multiple rapes. According to Fisher, Daigle, and Cullen:

> The National College Women Sexual Victimization (NCWSV) study reported that 47% of the respondents experienced recurrent sexual victimization during an academic year with 23% of the rape victims reporting having been raped two or more times during this time (Daigle, Fisher, & Cullen, 2008). Two recent single-campus studies support the notion that recurrent sexual victimization is an all-too-common occurrence among college women. Gidycz, Hanson, and Layman (1995) showed that among the women who were sexually assaulted during their first quarter, 38% experienced a subsequent sexual victimization during their second quarter. . . . Gross and his associates (2006) reported that 37% of women reported experiencing more than one forced sexual incident since enrolling in college (2010, p. 103).

Theories About Rape

A number of assumptions about rape are subsumed within general theorizing about violent crime. Some of these theories focus specifically on the rapist, and describe profiles or typologies of rapists motivated by anger, power and control, or degrees of pathological sadism (Grana, 2002). General theories about victimization often examine the environment or the context in which a crime occurs. Many of these theories use an individual's lifestyle and routine activities to predict that certain areas, times, and associations are more high risk, particularly within certain demographic groups such as young college students who are drinking heavily on spring break.

Along with theories about rape, writers explore the myths that seem to persist in our society regarding sexual victimization. Many of these myths seem to be behind popular "theories" explaining why women are raped. These myths include (Grana, 2002):

- Women provoke men to rape by the way they dress.
- Women may say no, but they really mean yes.
- Women often lie about rape when they regret decisions to have sex.

When examples of these myths are exposed in the media, particularly when they are repeated or espoused by noted figures, they tend to bring attention to the damage that such assertions may cause. For instance, during the 2012 political season, one politician claimed that a woman's body biologically reacts to "legitimate" rape by preventing pregnancy (perhaps he thought that fallopian tubes are able to identify something different about a rapist's sperm), but the ensuing uproar cost him the election. Another politician espoused that any pregnancy following a rape is legitimate because it was obviously God's will. He failed to get elected as well. In regard to the damage such assertions may cause women, these politicians tend to sponsor legislation expessing their beliefs which sometimes get enacted into law. Thus, one might argue that past and existing laws concerning rape contain expressions of various rape myths, and various components of the criminal justice system act to perpetuate these "truths."

Overcoming the Effects of Rape

Studies have consistently indicated that rape survivors have to overcome significant hurdles to physical and mental health following victimization. In one study it was found that women with a history of sexual assault had lower levels of self-efficacy and were less able to deal with risk situations (Bryant, 2001). According to Campbell and Raja (2005), most of the African American female veterans they interviewed who reported being victims of sexual assault also indicated they had experienced secondary victimization or victim-blaming in the legal, military, and medical systems. Those who sought help reported that interactions with officials in these systems made them feel "guilty, depressed, anxious, distrustful of others, and reluctant to seek further help" (Campbell & Raja, 2005, p. 98). Victims of date rape also cited fear of contracting AIDS, guilt, and sexual dysfunction. College acquaintance-rape victims often drop out of school because they dread facing their attacker in classes, in the dorms or dining areas, or at various campus activities (Sampson, 2003).

Charlotte Pierce-Baker was raped by two men who had broken into her home. Sharing the journey of recovery with millions of readers, she reached out to other survivors and told their stories, too. In her book *Surviving the Silence: Black Women's Stories of Rape*, she explains that her relationships with these women compelled her to testify against her attacker:

> While I was nervously awaiting my turn on the stand at my own preliminary hearing . . . I learned implicitly that a woman's word is not enough, that we, the women harmed by rape, serve merely as witnesses. The rendering of our specific brutalities, as in any other case in court, becomes "The Commonwealth vs. the Defendant." Our names do not appear. . . . I also didn't realize that going to trial meant I would be dragged through harsh details time after time after time, until I persuaded a jury that my rape had actually occurred and that the "alleged perpetrator" was, in fact, the man who raped me. There were many women, on that day and others, who were not given a trial date due to "insufficient evidence" (Pierce-Baker, 2000, p. 17).

Control of Pornography and Sexually Explicit Media

Rapid advances in technology have created greater access to sexually explicit and pornographic materials. The distinction between these two terms is important, because even though media may be required to provide warnings and means to regulate access to sexually explicit material, pornography is more strictly regulated by the law, and the failure to control access to pornography subjects one to legal prosecution and sanctions. This access, as well as ways to control it, has opened debate about social control and reinterpretation of basic rights and freedoms vis-à-vis the dangerousness of pornography and unfettered sexual conduct that ostensibly leads to criminal behavior. Controversial associated issues range from free speech and expression to commerce between consenting adults and the possibility of civil rights violations in the promotion of practices that subjugate, discriminate, and oppress groups protected by age, race, gender, and religion (Williams & McShane, 1995).

In this section readers may find themselves polarized in their views about how much freedom should be associated with the production, sale, and use of pornographic materials. Perhaps we need to see some type of evidence that there are direct harms caused by exposure to sexually explicit and pornographic materials before we support increased efforts to control this material. To justify more strict controls, what would that evidence need to be? When we finish this section, you must decide for yourself if that evidence is worth additional regulation and enforcement and how we might go about such interventions.

The U.S. Congress Permanent Subcommittee on Investigations on Child Pornography and Pedophilia issued a report in 1986 that, among other things, contained the following statements:

> No single characteristic of pedophilia is more pervasive than the obsession with child pornography. The fascination of pedophiles with child pornography and child abuse has been documented in many studies and has been established by hundreds of sexually explicit materials involving children.
>
> Detective William Dworin of the Los Angeles Police Department estimates that of the 700 child molesters in whose arrest he has participated during the last ten years, more than half had child pornography in their possession. About 80 percent owned either child or adult pornography.
>
> Child pornography plays a central role in child molestations by pedophiles, serving to justify their conduct, assist them in seducing their victims, and provide a means to blackmail the children they have molested in order to prevent exposure.

It is worth noting, however, that these statements are derived primarily from anecdotal testimony of victims and those who investigate and prosecute child molesters. Very little actual research information was present in the congressional report.

In a Canadian report, Rettinger states that there appears to be a link, although far from an empirically strong one, between pornographic material and other sex offenses such as pedophilia:

Anecdotal information from police officers provides compelling evidence of the collection of child pornography by pedophiles. . . . According to Lanning, an FBI agent, preferential child molesters "almost always" collect child pornography and/or child erotica (1992). Lanning (1985) and Hames (1993) provided several evocative examples where child pornography was found in the possession of individuals suspected or convicted of sexual offences against children. . . . Abel, Mittelman, and Becker (1985) found frequent use of pornographic materials in their sample of sex offenders who were outpatient volunteers at a sexual behaviour treatment clinic. This study is notable because the sample was not under a court order to attend the clinic and there was an elaborate system to protect the confidentiality of participants. It was found that 88 percent of males who had sexually abused children under the age of 14 years used pornography (Rettinger, 2000, p. 2).

The literature on television and movie violence supports the notion that exposure to material of a violent nature leads to more aggressive behavior displays, reported acceptance of violence, and desensitization to violence, particularly in younger children (Donnerstein, Linz, & Penrod, 1987; National Institute of Mental Health, 1982). Studies of sexual violence seem to find similar results (Donnerstein & Linz, 1986; U.S. Department of Justice, 1986). However, there is some debate over whether exposure to sexually explicit materials, in general, affects established attitudes or sentiments regarding sexual morality (Scott & Cuvelier, 1993).

Early Studies on the Nature of Pornography

Past studies have examined and categorized the content of sexually oriented books, magazines, films, and videos. The themes presented and the typical profiles that emerge give us insight into the nature of the material and perhaps its social meaning. For example, Winick (1985) examined the content of all (430) magazines available in a New York City Times Square adult bookstore. He found that practically all of the magazines were intended for men, and more of the descriptive material was about women than about men. Where bondage-discipline practices were used, 85% represented unequal distributions of power. In almost three-quarters of those cases, the men were dominant.

Palys (1986) conducted a content analysis of 150 adult or XXX videos in Vancouver, Canada. Some were particularly selected because of violent sexual content or because the titles had been listed as violating obscenity codes. Overall, females were more frequently portrayed and more often in solitary sexual depictions. Women remained the most commonly dominated figures, and the most common theme of aggression was verbal anger and humiliation in the context of sexual activity. Although the adult movies had more aggression (murder, weapons, beating, and torture) and more general sexual aggression, the XXX versions had more of some selected types of sexual violence. Men were clearly perpetrators and women the victims. The coders agreed that, in general, the videos reaffirmed or encouraged traditional rape myths.

Cowan et al. (1988) conducted a content analysis of 45 adult (X-rated) movies. As a percentage of the total of sexually explicit scenes, more than half used dominance and exploitation. Twenty-three percent of the scenes involved physical aggression, 20% verbal aggression, 39% status inequalities (males were professional and women had clerical positions, were students, or were housewives), and 29% voyeurism (predominantly male). Of the genitalia full-screen exposures, 69% were female. Fifty-one percent of the movies included a rape scene. All of the rape victims were female, and 90% of the perpetrators were male.

In Prince's (1990) analysis of 32 "classic" pornographic feature films produced between 1972 and 1985, the one area that supported the traditional charges leveled against pornography was in the portrayal of violence. In sexually violent scenes, men were more likely to be abusers and women the victims. Also, he explained, the violence tended to encourage the rape myth that pain is sexually stimulating.

Yang and Linz (1990) selected 90 video rentals, 30 each from the categories of R-rated, X-rated, and XXX-rated. Twenty-six percent of the videos had exploitative/coercive sex, 19% had sadomasochism and 33% had individual or group rape. Violence or sexual violence was more likely to occur in the R-rated (60%) than in either the X- (47%) or XXX-rated (37%) films.

These themes and profiles found in earlier research also led researchers Malamuth and Donnerstein to conclude that "after repeated exposure to pornography, viewers became desensitized to women's pain and degradation and callous toward rape and other violent acts" (Grana, 2002). Feminists have long argued that the way images of women are conveyed reflects the values and attitudes that transcend into law, politics, and everyday interactions in our society. Overall, women are presented as eagerly available for casual sex, as property, and as generally subservient to males. Arguably, a message is often presented that some degree of sexual violence is acceptable for men, and that it may be necessary to treat women roughly and aggressively because "they really want it that way."

Law and the Regulation of Pornography

As the result of a number of court cases challenging restrictions on the First Amendment, the Supreme Court has attempted to more clearly carve out a distinct definitions of trafficking in child pornography. Terminology in most laws today includes the commercial use of visual depictions that involve sexually explicit conduct and that conduct involves what appears to be a minor (Sternberg, 2001). However, jurists have had much more difficulty regulating the parameters of these concepts in cyberspace. Frequently, materials are available free and are not being sold or are simply available to all who subscribe to a much larger generic information service. In 1991 a federal judge ruled that CompuServe was like a bookstore owner and could not be held accountable for the contents of books on the shelves (Harmon, 1993). Recent raids and arrests, however, are bringing that ruling into question, and more recent court cases have held independent providers liable for content on their bulletin boards. To this mix, one must add the effect of Germany, Malaysia, and a number of other countries with their recent attempts to regulate the sexual content of the Internet.

The *Child Pornography Prevention Act* passed in 1996 made it unlawful to create, own, manufacture, or distribute child pornography to include enhanced video imaging that could be sold or advertised as such. In this legislation, "images," such as computer-generated or "morphed" depictions, were also included in the definition of pornography. It is the intent of the law that even if the subject of the film or pictures is not a child, it is illegal to attempt to sell the material as if the person were underage.

Human Sex Trafficking

One of the largest sting operations and rescues of sex-slave workers occurred in Houston, Texas, in 2005. Girls and young women from El Salvador, Nicaragua, and Honduras were deceived as they were smuggled into Texas and placed in cantinas dominated by Salvadoran Maximino Mondragon. Believing that they were going to get legitimate work, the girls were instead beaten and forced into prostitution (Olsen, 2008). Similar cases have occurred in many other cities across the globe, according to a report by Amnesty International (2005):

> Trafficked women and girls are deprived of fundamental human rights and face considerable risks. During transit to their destination country they may face rape by those transporting them or by others; at the point of arrival they risk rape by their new "owners," who use rape as a means of control and coercion. Violence is part of the process of coercion. Trafficked women are repeatedly subjected to psychological abuse. This can include intimidation and threats, lies and deception, emotional manipulation and blackmail, in particular threatening to tell their family about the nature of their work or making threats regarding the safety of their family. Traffickers keep women insecure by making their lives unpredictable and their environment unsafe. Once in their destination country they are forced into exploitative work.
> (Retrieved from http://www.amnesty.org/en/library/asset/ACT77/001/2005/en/fa8b3814-d53a-11dd-8a23-d58a49c0d652/act770012005en.html)

The figures on trafficking appear to be startling. Texas accounts for more calls to the National Human Trafficking Hotline than any other state, and Houston is the city posting the most calls. As disappointing as that may seem to residents there, it is also important to know that forces at work to address this problem may be responsible for the increased number of calls. According to Rick Casey, "Texas was one of the first states to outlaw human trafficking making it a second-degree felony in 2003 and requiring that a national hotline number be posted in certain businesses" (2011, p. B4). The mandate to prominently display that number may be an explanation for the disproportionate number of calls.

As Casey (2011) explains, only 1 in 200 victims of sex slavery is ever identified, and Harris County's (Houston) record for following through on prosecutions is poor. Although one task force addressing sex and forced labor trafficking has been able to charge 29 defendants based on 169 foreign victims rescued, the number of cases that have been assigned and activated by the District Attorney's office in the last few years can be counted on one hand. Conversely, of the 45 U.S. citizen minors being exploited as sex workers, all 22 of the perpetrators charged were convicted (Casey, 2011).

From the almost 100 young women swept up in the 2005 raids, a few have been deported. A small number have been reunited with the children they left behind in their native countries. Sixty-seven have been issued T-visas and work permits that will last four years. The T-visa is a mechanism that will allow victims to stay in this country long enough to testify against their captor-exploiters. The *Trafficking Victims Protection Act of 2000* developed the T-visa, and Congress has approved up to 5,000 being issued each year, though relatively few are actually awarded. Nineteen of the Houston victims were left waiting for the visas, and more than a dozen others were stuck in limbo three years later, still frightened and still ashamed (Olsen, 2008).

Critical Thinking Questions

1. How have views about prostitution and rape changed over the years? What factors do you think account for those changes?

2. How should we as a society evaluate adult entertainment media from a cost-and-benefit perspective? Do women (and men) have a right to make a living in this industry, and if they are satisfied with their portrayals in this format, is it a private choice? Is it too difficult to distinguish between adult and underage participants? Do we simply say that if you don't like this material, do not buy or subscribe to it?

3. How could we address sex trafficking on local, national, and then international levels? What efforts do you think are most and least effective?

Books and Media Resources

RAINN | Rape, Abuse and Incest National Network: http://www.rainn.org

SART Toolkit: http://ovc.ncjrs.gov/sartkit/about/about-sa-fsa.html

Smart, E., Smart, L., & Morton, L. (2003). *Bringing Elizabeth home: A journey of faith and hope.* New York: Doubleday.

Warshaw, R. (1994). *I never called it rape: The MS report on recognizing, fighting, and surviving date and acquaintance rape.* New York: Harper.

Popular Films

Extremities (1986), Farrah Fawcett.
Taken (2008), Liam Neeson.
Taxi Driver (1976), Jodie Foster.
The Accused (1988), Jodie Foster.
The Day My God Died (2003), Anuradha Koirala, Tim Robbins, Winona Ryder, and others.

References

Amnesty International. (2005). *Women, violence and health.* Retrieved from http://www.amnesty. org/en/library/info/ACT77/001/2005/en

Baker, L., Dalla, R., & Williamson, C. (2010). Exiting prostitution: An integrated model. *Violence Against Women, 16,* 579-600.

Benedict, J. (1998). *Pros and cons: The criminals who play in the NFL.* Boston: Grand Central Publishing.

Benedict, J. (2005). *Out of bounds: Inside the NBA's culture of rape, violence, and crime.* New York: It Books (Harper Collins).

Bracey, D. (1979). *Baby-Pros: Preliminary profiles of juvenile prostitutes.* New York: John Jay Press.

Bracey, D. (1984). The juvenile prostitute: Victim or offender. *Victimology: An International Journal,* 8(3-4), 151-160.

Bryant, N. L. (2001). Child sexual abuse and its relationship to perceived vulnerability, powerlessness, self-efficacy, and sexual assault. Doctoral dissertation, Ohio University. *Dissertation Abstracts International,* 61, 4973.

Campbell, R., & Raja, S. (2005) The sexual assault and secondary victimization of female veterans: Help-seeking experiences with military and civilian social systems, *Psychology of Women Quarterly,* 29, 97-106.

Casey, R. (2011, February 13). The ladies saw hell's slavery pit. *Houston Chronicle,* pp. B1, B4.

Cimino, A. (2012). A predictive theory of intentions to exit street level prostitution. *Violence Against Women,* 18, 1235-1252.

Cook, S., Gidycz, C., Koss, M., & Murphy, M. (2011). Emerging issues in the measurement of rape victimization. *Violence Against Women,* 17, 201-218.

Cowan, G., Lee, C., Levy, D., & Snyder, D. (1988). Dominance and inequality in x-rated videocassettes. *Psychology of Women Quarterly,* 12, 299-311.

Cunningham, S., & Kendall, T. (2011, July). Prostitution, technology and the law: New data and directions. Chapter 10 in L. Cohen and J. Wright (Eds.), *Research handbook on the economics of family law.* Northampton, MA: Edward Elgar Publishing.

Daigle, L., Fisher, B., & Cullen, F. (2008). The violent and sexual victimization of college women: Is repeat victimization a problem? *Journal of Interpersonal Violence,* 23, 1296-1313.

Donnerstein, E., & Linz, D. (1986). Mass media sexual violence and male viewers: Current theory and research. *American Behavioral Scientist,* 29(5), 601-618.

Donnerstein, E., Linz, D., &Penrod, S. (1987). *The question of pornography.* New York: Free Press.

Evans, M. (2002). *Madam Millie: Bordellos from Silver City to Ketchikan.* Albuquerque: University of New Mexico Press.

Fisher, B., Daigle, L., & Cullen, F. (2010). What distinguishes single from recurrent sexual victims? The role of lifestyle-routine activities and first-incident characteristics. *Justice Quarterly,* 27, 102-129.

Gidycz, C. A., Hanson, K., & Layman, M. (1995). A prospective analysis of the relationships among sexual assault experiences. *Psychology of Women Quarterly,* 19, 5-29.

Grana, S. J. (2002). *Women and (in)justice.* Boston: Allyn & Bacon.

Halter, S. (2010). Factors that influence police conceptualizations of girls involved in prostitution in six U.S. cities: Child sexual exploitation victims or delinquents? *Child Maltreatment,* 15, 152-160.

Harmon, A. (19 March 1993). New legal frontier: Cyberspace millions of Americans swap information. *Los Angeles Times*, p. A1.

Holiday, B. (1976). *Lady sings the blues*. New York: Avon.

Kavanaugh, P. (2013). The continuum of sexual violence: Women's accounts of victimization in urban nightlife. *Feminist Criminology*, 8(1), 20-39.

Lombroso, C. (1911). *Crime: Its causes and remedies*. (H. P. Horton, Trans.). London: Heinemann.

Martin, L., Hearst, M., & Widome, R. (2010). Meaningful differences: Comparison of adult women who first traded sex as a juvenile versus as an adult. *Violence Against Women*, 16(2), 1252-1269.

McFarlane, J., Malecha, A., Watson, K., Gist, J., Batten, E., Hall, I., & Smith, S. (2005). Intimate partner sexual assault against women: Frequency, health consequences, and treatment outcomes. *Obstetrics & Gynecology*, 105, 99-108.

McShane, M. (2008). *Prisons in America*. New York: LFB Scholarly Publishing.

Menard, K. (2005). *Reporting sexual assault*. New York: LFB Scholarly Publishing.

Mitchell, K. J., Finkelhor, D., & Wolak, J. (2010). Conceptualizing juvenile prostitution as child maltreatment: Findings from the National Juvenile Prostitution Study. *Child Maltreatment*, 15, 18-36.

National Institute of Mental Health (1982). *Television and behavior: ten years of scientific progress and implications for the eighties* (DHHS Publication No. ADM 82-1196), Washington, DC: U.S. Government Printing Office.

Olsen, L. (2008, November 24). Trafficking victims' lives in visa limbo. *Houston Chronicle*, p. A1.

Palys, T. S. (1986). Testing the common wisdom: The social content of video pornography. *Canadian Psychology*, 27, 22-35.

Pierce-Baker, C. (2000, reprint edition). *Surviving the silence: Black women's stories of rape*. New York: W. W. Norton.

Prince, S. (1990). Power and pain: Content analysis and the ideology of pornography. *Journal of Film and Video*, 42(2), 31-41.

Quinet, K. (2009). Prostitutes as victims of serial homicide: Trends and case characteristics, 1970–2009. *Homicide Studies*, 15, 74-100.

Reid, J. A. (2011). An exploratory model of girl's vulnerability to commercial sexual exploitation in prostitution. *Child Maltreatment*, 16, 146-157.

Rettinger, L. J. (2000). *The relationship between child pornography and the commission of sexual offences against children: A review of the literature*. Ottawa, Ontario, Canada: Department of Justice Canada.

Roe-Sepowitz, D. (2012). Juvenile entry into prostitution: The role of emotional abuse. *Violence Against Women*, 18, 562-579.

Rosen, R. (1982). *The lost sisterhood: Prostitution in America, 1900–1918*. Baltimore: Johns Hopkins University Press.

Samaha, J. (2002). *Criminal law* (7th ed.). Belmont, CA: Wadsworth Learning.

Sampson, R. (2003). *Acquaintance rape of college students*. COPS Office, Washington, DC: U.S. Department of Justice.

Schulz, D. M. (2002). Many interests, many talents: Dorothy Bracey's career has crossed intellectual and national boundaries. *Women & Criminal Justice*, 13(2/3), 29–50.

Scott, J., & Cuvelier, S. (1993). Violence and sexual violence in pornography: Is it really increasing? *Archives of Sexual Behavior*, 22(4), 357-371.

Seagraves, A. (1994). *Soiled doves: Prostitution in the early west*. Hayden, ID: Wesanne Publications.

Shapiro, M. (2009, April). Sex trafficking and decriminalized prostitution in Rhode Island. Senior Honors Thesis, University of Rhode Island. Retrieved from http://digitalcommons. ri.edu/cgi/viewcontent.cgi?article=1137&context=srhonorsprog&sei-redir=1#search=%22 PUMA+prostitutes+union+of+massachusetts%22

Smith, T. W. (2006). *American sexual behavior: Trends, socio-demographic differences, and risk behavior*. GSS Topical Report No. 25. Chicago: National Opinion Research Center.

Sternberg, S. (2001). The Child Pornography Prevention Act of 1996 and the First Amendment: Virtual antitheses. *Fordham Law Review*, 69(6), 2783-2823.

Tjaden, P., & Thoennes, N. (2006). Extent, nature, and consequences of rape victimization: Findings from the National Violence Against Women Survey. Washington, DC: National Institute of Justice.

U.S. Department of Justice (1986). Attorney General's Commission on Pornography Final Report. Washington, DC: U.S. Department of Justice.

Williams, F. P., & McShane, M. (1995). Getting your kicks on cyberspace's Route 66: Erotica, the information highway and freedom of access. Paper presented at the annual meeting of the American Society of Criminology, Boston.

Winick, C. (1985). A content analysis of sexually explicit magazines sold in an adult bookstore. The Journal of Sex Research, 21(2), 206-210.

Yang, N., & Linz, D. (1990). Moving ratings and the content of adult videos: The sex-violence ratio. Journal of Communication, 40, 28-42.

Women and Domestic Violence

Introduction

Our popular media, literature, movies, and music tell us much about how we view domestic violence. You may have heard the song by Meat Loaf on his *Dead Ringer* album where an angry lover tells his girl, "*In every way I want you out of my life but I'll kill you if you don't come back.*" There is even a website devoted to music that is domestic violence oriented (http://creativefolk.com/abusesongs.html). Some songs tell the story of relationships that become violent, but the ones that seem to get the most negative public reaction are those that appear to "glorify" or promote abuse in gender relations. Country music, like rap, seems to have a controversial amount of material. Carrie Underwood's best-selling *Before He Cheats* describes a vengeful and criminal attack on a car by a woman who believes that her boyfriend is or would be cheating on her. Even the Dixie Chicks, *Goodbye Earl*, startled audiences with its frank portrayal of revenge and retaliation, a shift in the balance of traditional gender relations. After years of perhaps exploiting couple violence, Eminem has done a piece with Rihanna (no stranger to couple violence herself) that seems to be more of a comment on the futility of domestic conflict than a macho anthem for it. Some critics feel that Eminem's arrival at a place where domestic violence seems more like a vicious cycle represents a major turning point in his career.

Domestic violence has been a popular theme in movies as well. *Enough* starring Jennifer Lopez is typical, like Julia Roberts in *Sleeping with the Enemy*, in that it highlights the female victim as wronged, scared, running, and hiding, although ultimately prevailing in the end. The late Farrah Fawcett's dramatic portrayal of a victim of domestic violence who murders her sleeping abuser in *The Burning Bed* won both Emmy and Golden Globe nominations. This true story of events that occurred in 1977 surrounding Francine Hughes's acquittal on murder charges also inspired Martina McBride's hit song *Independence Day*. Still, people from the small town in Michigan say events were not as simple as the film suggests.[1] Others wonder if the movie would have had the same impact if it had not been the gorgeous *Charlie's Angel* star transformed into a battered and bruised character, but instead was someone perhaps plain and pudgy like actress Kathy Bates, who in reality looked more like Hughes. The fact that the gritty work was a made-for-television movie also allowed for a wider general audience, one that was accustomed to seeing the actress as a glamorous Hollywood icon. Still, most agree that the film represented a major rallying point in society's transition to a more active agenda on domestic violence, as it seemed to bring the problem right into people's living rooms.

Books, movies, and music give us access not only to the stories of domestic violence but also to their social interpretation. Some of the recent narratives by women who were allegedly trapped in sexually exploitative plural marriages as young minors have been so popular that they have been developed into various prime-time television shows. Our fascination with the more high-profile domestic violence cases has resulted in their distorting the realities of less dramatic but more common forms of domestic violence.

Research Issues

Being an intelligent consumer of information about domestic violence requires us to ask important questions about how the data were gathered, where and when they were collected, and by what methods they were garnered. Carefully reading through studies on domestic violence, we will see that findings are ultimately tied to the ways questions were asked and the ways behaviors or answers were measured. Some of the features that will impact these studies are as follows:

- Where the sample of respondents/participants was drawn from
- The method used for gathering the data
- The survey or study response/completion rate
- The various definitions of abuse and domestic violence used

First, the origin of the sample will undoubtedly have implications for the generalizability of the study. That is, the ability to say that your research findings could be replicated or reproduced in other geographic areas might be undermined if there were specific features of your sample that are not commonly

---

[1] For one explanation of the importance of the film for the fight against domestic violence, see http://www.lansingstatejournal.com/article/99999999/NEWS01/909270304/-Burning-Bed-turning-point-fight-against-domestic-violence

found across other, more general, populations. Even though it is important to study underrepresented groups such as Native Americans, ex-offenders, and teens, it is also necessary to indicate the special traits of the group under study. This is so researchers and, ultimately, readers can determine if the characteristics of that group might somehow have influenced the outcome of the study and whether the findings might differ across other demographic groups. In the past, studies have indicated that the domestic violence experiences of female offenders, immigrants, and women in battered women's shelters are significantly different from the general population of women in America. Although it is often easy to access high-risk groups for research purposes, it is also a trade-off in that you might have a group that is substantially different from the population at large. The rule is simply to acknowledge the possible limitations of using any particular sample and continue to provide detailed research information so that we all might learn more about domestic violence. Thus, when you are reading any literature on domestic violence, particularly information containing facts and figures, you need to take the time to understand where that information was drawn from and assess how representative it might be.

Second, the method of gathering the data has implications for the accuracy and reliability of the data. In particular, when researching sensitive issues that people may be reluctant to discuss, it is important that they feel protected, that the information is gathered anonymously, and that their identities will not be revealed. There are many ways we do this from some high-tech solutions to simply not recording names or not storing information on participation in the same location as the results or data. Depending on the type of study being done, participants may feel more comfortable if it is an officially designated endeavor complete with letterhead, contact information, or websites. Others types of studies may do better distancing themselves from authorities, while focusing on assuring participants that their privacy will be protected and information will not be shared with authorities.

The third feature of research for us to consider is the response or completion rate. This is conveyed as the participants representing some percentage of those eligible to respond. If response or completion rates are low, then it is equivalent to saying that the average or even majority of respondents did not respond. With that being true, your question should be, "what is different about these people that made them choose to respond or participate?" Actually, there is even a statistical problem using low-response-rate samples to discuss the likelihood of important characteristics. A related issue here is the overall sample size. Studies where the sample sizes are small will have difficulty using many forms of statistical analysis, and their results are prone to error (the smaller the sample, the larger is the error). By not meeting the minimum size for some types of statistical tests, the results would be viewed as less meaningful or interpretable. Also, in these situations the characteristics of the sample may skew the results, as it takes a substantial number of subjects in any research "pool" before they begin to resemble the general population.

Finally, how terms are defined in a study is critical for determining the way they will be addressed and measured. This is particularly important in domestic violence research where the terms "domestic," "abuse," and "violence" may mean many different things. In trying to compare the results of one study with another, any differences in how terms were defined or "operationalized" during the research will be a problem. For example, one study of incest may include mothers and another may not; even whether "mothers" includes step-mothers can be important. As you can predict, a study that includes a broader range of offenders and victims will have higher rates of incidence, which could then affect the way we view the problem. Differences you will commonly see in domestic violence research are which family members are considered "domestic," how age groups are delineated, which types of abuse are included, and how far into the past abuse might be tracked.

Relying on victims and abusers to accurately remember events in the past subjects any study to "recall error," or the various mistakes people make in accurately recalling and describing past events. This problem is particularly prevalent in cases where adults are asked to describe events from their childhood. This may seem like an approach that is risky in terms of reliability, but it is often used because it is too difficult for researchers to get consent to interview children and teens about these issues, particularly when the young subjects are not in some type of treatment program.[2]

Although there are many aspects to domestic violence that have been studied and addressed in interventions and treatment programming, we will concentrate here on those most common to the study of women in the criminal justice system, namely infanticide, matricide, and spousal abuse. In a later chapter, we will discuss child abuse and child sexual abuse as they are related to female delinquency.

Battered Women

There are a variety of reasons offered for the increased reporting of domestic violence that takes place today. These include the changes in values and attitudes that people have toward reporting, the fact that there is less social stigma for reporting family violence, and the presence of more support organizations and services for victims of domestic abuse. With mandatory reporting in hospitals and schools, and mandatory arrest policies in law enforcement agencies, there are mechanisms in place to bring cases that were once hidden behind the doors of private homes to the attention of authorities. Changes in terms and definitions have also expanded the cases eligible to be reported and recorded in domestic violence databases. What was earlier restricted to "wife battering" has been expanded over the years to include a much wider range of circumstances under the umbrella of spousal assault, including wives battering

---

[2] Consider here the possible psychological harm caused when a child is asked to remember a potentially painful episode in his or her past. Research review boards will generally not allow such research to take place.

husbands. The use of the term *domestic violence* now includes same-sex partners and unmarried couples living together. Often, caseworkers investigating child-abuse allegations will find a complex web of domestic violence in the home which makes developing treatment strategies for the children that much more difficult.

Theories of Intimate Partner Violence

According to Resko (2010), there are various theoretical arguments that can be used to predict levels of domestic violence at any given time in society. Stress theories, she explains, link higher levels of intimate partner violence to worsening economic conditions or a decline in the couple's income status. Periods of unemployment, underemployment, bankruptcy, poverty, and a cycle of low-status jobs place women at greater risk of being abused and beaten. Batterers often talk about frustration and loss of role identification as providers and authority figures in the home. Bargaining theories, on the other hand, suggest that as women earn more, are able to obtain better jobs, and provide increasing support for the family, they also gain power and leverage. This shift into a position of workforce value allows women to avoid being victimized, and rates of intimate partner violence would decline. Access to resources either permits women to be self-supporting if they must leave a violent partner, or acts as a control factor whereby the husband cannot risk the loss of income from the woman's job or being detected and arrested as a batterer as she would be more likely to call the police. Finally, the backlash theory argues that any advance or economic achievement a woman might make would be interpreted as a threat to the male partner and would increase her risk of domestic violence victimization. This means that employment success for the woman becomes a catalyst that increases violent outbursts from an abusive partner (Resko, 2010).

Correlates of Domestic Violence

Research has found considerable support for the premise that times of economic hardship, unemployment, and stress also seem to correlate with higher levels of reported domestic violence. Just recently, officials in New Zealand indicated that a prolonged period of earthquakes and aftershocks there triggered widespread reporting, even epidemic levels, of domestic violence:

> Professor Doug Sellman of the National Addiction Centre in Christchurch says people have hit the booze, smokes and junk food since the quakes. "We've noticed a relapse after each major earthquake" he says. Tony Milne of the Problem Gambling Foundation says the stress and anxiety caused by the ongoing aftershocks has caused the people of Christchurch to pump around $4 million extra into poker machines during the past quarter. Nicola Woodward, who heads the Christchurch Women's Refuge, says there has been a "significant" increase in family violence since the quakes. After the June earthquake, she

says the city's five women's refuges were full within hours and have stayed that way. "The whole of the city is living with significant uncertainty and anxiety" she says. (Stewart, 2011, p. 40)

A previous study in New Zealand (Houghton, 2010) had evidently already attributed increases in domestic abuse to natural disasters. Houghton found evidence that floods and snowstorms could increase domestic abuse by as much as three times. She attributed that increase to anger created by feelings of instability and insecurity, with no good outlet for its release.

Although women of all socioeconomic groups are represented in domestic violence statistics, the data are clear that poorer women are at far greater risk than those with more financial resources. As Buzawa explains:

> Women with less income have higher rates of victimization. For example the NCVS data reported that women in households with incomes less than $7,500 reported a rate of nonlethal violence at a rate 10 times higher than those women who have an income of $75,000 or more. Women who are supported by welfare experience higher rates of abuse than women in a similarly low socioeconomic bracket. One estimate reports that approximately one-third of women on welfare are current victims of abuse, while slightly more than half had been victims of abuse during their lifetime (2007, p. 68).

Gender Roles and Values

According to Wright (2011), sexism, patriarchy, and more traditional perceptions of the roles of women are frequently correlated with tolerance for domestic violence or intimate partner violence (IPV). Explanations based on imbalances of power and control are also tied to theories about economic hardship as unemployment or underemployment may escalate those conflicts as a point of contention in the relationship. She explains that:

> Males and females who believe in traditional gender roles, such that women's primary roles in life revolve around domestic activities while males' primary roles include providing for and protecting the family, are more likely to engage in IPV. . . . The relationship between gender roles and IPV has often been explained in terms of dominance and control within the partnership; when gender roles are not adhered to, or where power imbalances in the relationship exist, males (in particular) may feel threatened . . . and may attempt to re-establish their dominance within the relationship by using violent means (Wright, 2011, p. 20).

Women holding more traditional values may also be less likely to leave dysfunctional partnerships and believe that they have fewer options to do so. Neil Websdale's (1998) in-depth look at rural woman-battering explains that residents of isolated small towns may have lower tolerance for diversity, more preindustrial traditions, and subcultural values steeped in fundamentalist religious dogma.

In his research, he found that not only murder, but also murder-suicide were almost exclusively male-perpetrated events. He notes that the cumulative losses of tobacco and coal as resources in the regions of Kentucky that he studied have stressed areas that are not only economically depressed but also maintain stereotypical family roles.

Some of the difficulties in confronting rural domestic violence are related to the ways women often justify the abuse as acceptable. This is similar to ideas common in certain immigrant populations. For ethnic minorities, these values may represent traditional cultural expectations that become a source of culture conflict when acted out in this country.

Social Learning as an Explanation of Battering

Criminologists have long argued that domestic violence can be explained by social learning theories. Domestic violence appears to be intertwined with the popular concept of a "cycle of violence" or the generational passing down of attitudes associated with abuse in families. According to social learning theories, the acceptance or status that is gained by modeling certain behaviors, particularly those of close relatives and friends we emulate and seek approval from is the key. Feedback, whether overt or subtle, that validates violence lays the foundation for continuing to engage in abuse. Although much of the content of definitions favoring abuse may be learned early in life through families, social learning theorists also believe that peers play an important role in encouraging certain definitions of appropriate conduct. Hypermasculinized roles such as those adopted by gangs may reward rape and sexual abuse of female "property," so that relationships are distorted by these commonly held values.

Social learning theory would also explain the adjustment that victims make in dysfunctional dyads. Learning to accommodate the abusive spouse so that punishments are minimized and rewards are optimized is part of the conditioning process central to this theoretical approach. It is even possible to view social learning as the foundation for cultural or subcultural values supportive of abuse, as the passing down of abuse-supportive definitions from one generation to another becomes institutionalized as culture.

Marital Rape

Although domestic violence seems to be a general category for unwanted force in a home, nothing muddies the waters like unwanted and forced sex within a marriage. Historically, one of the basic tenets in common law is the principle that there can be no prosecution of a husband as the sole actor in the rape of his wife. This is known as the spousal rape exemption as it indicates that the husband is exempt from being prosecuted for rape. Historically, marriage meant that a wife became the property of the husband; therefore, it was deemed unreasonable that a man could be accused of harming his own property.

Legal Issues

In the mid-seventeenth century, the concept of wife as property was modified with a new legal precedent. By viewing marriage as a contract, the concept changed to a consideration that the wife irrevocably entered into a consent status that would be incompatible with a legal definition of rape, which implies "without consent" (Hale, 1680). Other legal arguments examine the restrictiveness of rape definitions in that an element might be "unlawful" sexual intercourse, which would be difficult to establish given the "lawful" union of marriage in most jurisdictions. Patriarchal courts also viewed the privacy of families as sacred and were reluctant to invade marital relations.

It wasn't until the late 1970s that courts began to critique the historical tradition as an artifact that was out of touch with modern times. In *State v. Smith*, the first case to attack the spousal rape exemption, it was held that the antiquated doctrine resulted in a kind of bondage for the wife which "leads to insidious deprivation of sexual privacy to a victimized married woman" (1977, p. 391). The court urged that as in other areas of contemporary law, the concept of equal protection should be used to give married women the same protection as women in general. Cases like *Smith* led the way for the erosion of the spousal rape exemption. Courts initially provided relief to women who were legally separated and had filed for divorce, recognizing that they had withdrawn that implied consent and then later provided relief to those who were physically (but not legally) separated.

As Ferro, Cermele, and Saltzman explain:

> It was not until July 5, 1993, that marital rape became a crime in all 50 states. However, by May 2005, only 20 states had completely eliminated the marital rape exemptions from state laws; in the remaining 30 states, there were still some exemptions given to husbands from rape prosecution.... The Violence Against Women Act ..., 2006 led to changes in existing state rape laws, which treated spousal rape as a lesser crime than rape occurring with other victims (2008, p. 765).

In some states like Pennsylvania and Maine, lawmakers have simply removed the exemption, which means that they have adopted a "rape is a rape" approach, and prosecutors may charge as such. Other states have specified circumstances under which those who are married or cohabiting may face charges of sexual assault. Spousal rape may be considered a separate crime — "spousal sexual assault" — which may be a lesser offense than rape. For example, in California, the restriction that there can be no probation applies to nonspousal rape only. Still in other states, such as North Carolina and Washington, DC, the law is written to specifically convey that "marriage is not a defense to the crime" of rape.

Although the 2006 *Violence Against Women Act* has helped to further reduce disparity between the legal treatment of rape and marital rape cases, feminists will argue that legal barriers remain. The progress spousal-rape victims have made in the last 20 years has been hampered by inherent problems built into law. In many jurisdictions there are reporting requirements such as the victim has to report the offense within a specified number of days (30, 90, 365) which is usually a shorter period of time than that required for report of nonspousal rape. In some, force, bodily harm, or threats may be required. In Tennessee a weapon must be used, the couple must live apart, and they must have filed for divorce. Thus, marital rape remains less than a "normal" rape for women in many jurisdictions.

Incidence Rates of Marital Rape

Researchers looking at sexual assault in domestic violence have been aided by the development of the government database known as the National Incident Based Reporting System (NIBRS). This allows for the collection of much more detailed information about crime context as well as many variables relative to the victim and offender. Sociological studies on rape in marriage have primarily dealt with the frequency with which it occurs, or incidence rates across various demographic groups. Often data come from selected samples, such as women who have sought refuge in battered women's shelters. One study by Giles-Sims (1983) found that 36% of the women in her analysis had been sexually assaulted, and in a similar study Pagelow (1984) reported 37%. In a clinical sample (those who had sought treatment or therapy) of battered women (Walker, 1979), most felt that they had been raped at one time or another, a finding that is common in this particular group. Because of the special nature of these groups, though, it is hard to argue that they represent all women or even all women who have been raped. After all, these women sought either refuge or treatment for battering and represent a unique group. Recognition of the serious consequences of battering may drive more of these women to seek help and to openly discuss these issues, while the general population may have been more likely, especially 20 years ago, to avoid the perceived stigma of admitting sexual abuse in a committed relationship. Random sample surveys of the general population, like those conducted by Finkelhor and Yllo (10% in 1982) and Russell (12%, 1980), may be the most accurate indicator of the true marital rape rate. What should be noted here is that the evidence from these earliest estimates comes mainly from testimony, reports, and essays, all of which are less formal and reliable sources than research published in peer-reviewed outlets. Until more rigorous random sampling techniques were used in the research design, studies on this subject were unlikely to be published in academic journals.

Criminal Justice System Responses to Domestic Violence

The criminal justice system is not able to effectively address the problems of domestic violence without appropriate laws and resources as tools. In most cases, the federal government attempts to develop model legislation and programming, but it is up to states to adapt and implement those strategies in order to guarantee family safety at the local level.

The *Violence Against Women Act* of 1994 (VAWA) was one of the most sweeping pieces of legislation to address domestic violence in the United States. Since its passage, amendments and extensions have been added to adapt to changes in social perceptions of the most critical needs of family and the best ways to provide for them. Under this act, gender-motivated violence is treated as a form of discrimination that is protected like any other civil right. It makes it a federal crime to cross state lines to injure, harass, or intimidate a spouse or intimate partner. If any of these actions result in harm to a victim, an offender can be punished by up to 5 years in prison. There are additional enhancements to this provision for circumstances where an offender uses a weapon (10 years), causes life-threatening injuries (20 years), or kills the victim (life).

What has perhaps had the greatest effect on the ability of police departments to address domestic violence is the funding provided under VAWA for training and developing pro-arrest policies, for working with prosecutors and court personnel to bring cases into the courts, and for providing battered women's shelters and hotlines. In addition, the law allows immigrant women who might be staying with an abuser for immigration status to petition for reclassification without having to rely on the papers and documentation authority of a spouse. The VAWA also included longer sentences for repeat sex offenders and provided more rape-shield protection for women testifying as victims in rape cases.

Because federal law only applies to interstate crimes (or crimes on federal property), states have had to develop their own criminal codes relative to domestic violence, and most have done so by using guidelines from the VAWA. The model provided by the government set a precedent for states to extend "full faith and credit" to any protection order that a woman might bring in from another state. In the past, women fleeing from domestic violence were frustrated to find their valid protection orders were not recognized in their new state of residence. Although it was a federal crime for a suspect to cross state lines and violate a valid protection order, each state had to adopt the full faith and credit clause on this issue in order to ensure that local police departments would recognize and enforce such orders.

One of the perhaps more controversial trends has been for states to assume more power and decision-making ability over cases. In the past, battered women or men were able to drop charges or choose not to file charges, but now the states have the ability to proceed with charges under certain circumstances without the support or involvement of the victim. For feminists, this has been a win-lose situation. Although it is important for the ultimate protection of a woman who may be too frightened to file charges and who may otherwise be killed if her abuser is not taken into custody, it also usurps the power of a woman to make decisions for herself about the escalation of a domestic dispute and the initiation of formal criminal charges.

Mandatory Arrest

During the 1980s, the new idea of mandatory arrest for batterers in domestic violence incidents was controversial. Because police traditions rely so heavily on the discretion of the individual officer responding to a call, the proposal seemed to contradict the very nature of policing. There were concerns raised both by officers and administrators that departments' morale would suffer. Many felt that a mandatory arrest policy was a rejection of police competence and the benefits that discretion could potentially provide. Other issues were raised by skeptical women's groups, policy makers, and civil rights activists.

One concern was that the arrest would only escalate violence in the home and that angry arrestees would return home later to retaliate with more abuse. The fear of reprisals was based on the assumption that the arrest was not a deterrent and was too short of an intervention to change the long-term prospects of the relationship.

Another concern was that mandatory arrest would have a disproportionate effect on poor, minority populations who were less likely to be able to arrange bond or legal representation. In economically depressed areas like housing projects and apartment complexes, disputes are more likely to be overheard and authorities called, so that it appeared that arrests would disproportionately take place in certain residential areas.

Related to that issue, there was some fear that more women would be drawn into the criminal justice system under these policies if the women had defended themselves and there was any evidence of injury to their attackers. In the past, women who had engaged in domestic violence had been given tremendous latitude by investigating officers, particularly if the women had small children in the home and it did not appear that there were reasonable placements for them readily available. For example, one of my former students tells the story of growing up with ten brothers and sisters in a poor rural area. His mother found work cleaning up after receptions and had been given a large pot of stock broth to take home. The father came in intoxicated while she was preparing the broth to feed the family and criticized the effort, throwing the liquid to the floor. She stabbed him in the chest and then told the eldest child to call the sheriff. The responding sheriff's deputy took one look at the spilled food, the ten hungry children, and the frustrated mother, and hauled the victim off to the hospital urging him not to go back for a long time. The effect that pro-arrest policies would have on children was a concern for many jurisdictions. Without adequate resources to provide quality supervision, it was possible that more harm than benefit could come from the policy, particularly when the benefits were still unknown. To better address the issues of the unknown effects of mandatory arrest, the federal government sponsored a series of research tests that became known as the Minneapolis Experiment.

The Minneapolis Experiment

Distinguished researcher Lawrence Sherman and colleagues (Sherman & Berk, 1984; Schmidt & Sherman, 1993) designed a study during 1981 and 1982 that would compare three different police responses to domestic violence. In order to tell in any meaningful way what the effects of a certain response would be, it was necessary to distribute the treatments (or responses) randomly at each call. When participation was discussed with patrol officers in Minneapolis, some officers declined to participate, believing that they could not support the method that was essential for interpreting the outcome. As this was anticipated, officers were excused because Sherman needed treatment integrity (actually following the random pattern of responses) more than he needed everyone participating. The experiment was structured so that when officers went to a domestic violence call, the color of the top sheet of their report pad would dictate the response to use: arrest the suspect, order the suspect to leave the premises for eight hours, or try and mediate and restore order without doing either of the other two options. Of course any time an officer had reason to believe violence or injury was pending, or a felony had been committed, they were to resort to the safest options and report that incident outside the experiment.

The study concluded that arrest was the best way to reduce the likelihood of violence in the six months following an incident. Still, there were criticisms of the findings as many of the victims were not located for follow-up. This phenomenon, called "attrition," diminishes the strength of the results because you do not know the outcomes for the missing cases, the lost individuals may be somehow different from the ones remaining in the study, and you may not have a large-enough sample size remaining on which to base conclusions about treatment.

The study was replicated in several other cities, including Milwaukee, Wisconsin, over the next few years. There, the range of responses were revised as a normal arrest with 11 to 12 hours in custody, an expedited arrest that was about 3 hours in custody, and a warning that police would return if there was any further disturbance. In the nine months of follow-up, researchers did not find any significant differences between the treatment groups. They did reason, however, that the effects were strongest for those individuals who had the most to lose by an arrest. This means that batterers with a job, community status, and stakes in conformity were more likely to be deterred with the threat of an arrest. Specifically, people who had employment, regardless of how modest that position was, responded differently to the possibility of going to jail than those who had the least to lose.

Torrington and Liability

Research seemed to support the idea of mandatory arrest, but the evidence was neither overwhelming nor conclusive. Across the country, the issue appeared to hang in limbo. Perhaps departments would have hesitated even longer if it had not been for the landmark ruling in *Thurman v. City of Torrington, Connecticut* in 1984. The case of victim Tracey Thurman was an excellent test of just what the "duty to protect" meant, as she not only had a restraining order against her abusive estranged husband, Charles, but it was also a condition of his probation to stay away from her. Thus with two legal mechanisms in place, it was not hard for the court to determine that authorities did have an obligation to protect her and her son from further attacks. It is no wonder that the court took up this case to make a clear example of what type of police response was expected, as the details below will show:

> On June 10, 1983, Charles Thurman appeared at the Bentley-St. Hilaire residence in the early afternoon and demanded to speak to Tracey. Tracey, remaining indoors, called the defendant's police department asking that Charles be picked up for violation of his probation. After about 15 minutes, Tracey went outside to speak to her husband in an effort to persuade him not to take or hurt Charles Jr. Soon thereafter, Charles began to stab Tracey repeatedly in the chest, neck and throat. Approximately 25 minutes after Tracey's call to the Torrington Police Department and after her stabbing, a single police officer, the defendant Petrovits, arrived on the scene. Upon the arrival of Officer Petrovits at the scene of the stabbing, Charles Thurman was holding a bloody knife. Charles then dropped the knife and, in the presence of Petrovits, kicked the plaintiff Tracey Thurman in the head and ran into the Bentley-St. Hilaire residence. Charles returned from within the residence holding the plaintiff Charles Thurman, Jr. and dropped the child on his wounded mother. Charles then kicked Tracey in the head a second time. Soon thereafter, defendants DeAngelo, Nukirk, and Columbia arrived on the scene but still permitted Charles Thurman to wander about the crowd and to continue to threaten Tracey. Finally, upon approaching Tracey once again, this time while she was lying on a stretcher, Charles Thurman was arrested and taken into custody (Thurman v. City of Torrington, 1984).

Tracey Thurman's well-documented history of calls to police suggested that prior to that incident, she was virtually ignored by several City of Torrington police officers even though she had followed all of the legal procedures under the restraining order. In fact, some beatings were even witnessed by officers responding to her calls. Still, Charles Thurman, Sr., was allowed to live and work in the City of Torrington.

The district court in Connecticut found that police officers have the responsibility to provide equal protection under the law to all persons, including spouses and children. The court found that conduct of the police officers represented deliberate indifference to the safety of the plaintiff. Tracey's unprecedented award ($1.9 million reduced on appeal from $2.6 million) was instrumental in clarifying the nature of police responses to domestic violence and set the stage for implementing mandatory arrest policies. Because the city was fiscally unprepared to deal with such a judgment, the outcome alerted municipalities across America to buy liability insurance to protect against potential bankruptcy.

Variation in Mandatory Arrest Policies

Today most mandatory arrest policies focus on two key factors, the presence of the offender and the existence of probable cause. Some states require the victim to have some type of visible injury or to have been threatened with a deadly weapon. Other states may have regulations that consider the length of time that has elapsed between the incident, the call to authorities, and the officer's arrival upon the scene. In some jurisdictions the response may vary by the marital status of the subjects or whether it is a same-sex couple. Some may require officers to complete an official statement whenever an arrest is not made in response to a domestic violence incident. In many areas, the terms have been revised to what officials believe is a more practical position, that of "preferred" or "pro-arrest."

Other Tools in Combating Domestic Violence

In the years following the Minneapolis experiment, the research evidence is pretty consistent in its support for various forms of mandatory or preferred arrest. Methodologies for analyzing outcomes have improved, as have methods for tracking victims and giving those victims incentives for remaining in contact with the research study. The term "first responders" is now associated with the role of police, while training has been aimed at increasing options and resources at that level. Other changes have also taken place such as increasing support for confiscating weapons found at the scene, greater aid for dependent families with children, and increased prosecutorial sensitivity so that more cases come before the court once arrests have been made. In some areas, increasing the penalties and sentences handed down for domestic violence offenses has also been linked to decreases in repeat calls on domestic violence cases.

Restraining Orders and No-Contact Orders

Although logically, restraining orders (ROs) and temporary restraining orders (TROs) seem to be the best ways to officially restrict undesired conduct, they are not as easily obtained as they could be. In many instances, filing fees are in place that may make it difficult for low-income women to opt for such orders in lieu of other basic family needs such as food and diapers. One problem, noted in several jurisdictions, was that the formula for determining whether a woman needed to pay fees was based on the earned income of the person she was trying to flee from — her spouse. Most women approach the court *pro se*, that is without a lawyer. Research seems to indicate that those without an attorney are less likely to be issued an RO or to be given an award of temporary financial support. Some victim assistance programs or support groups have services to assist women in this process, but these programs are not spread evenly throughout the country. To make matters more daunting, the batterer may have the resources to hire representation, and the victim may be intimidated by cross-examination or simply the threat of undergoing a confrontational exchange.

Because the RO or TRO is a legally binding order, clerical persons need specific training in order to properly issue and maintain the paperwork on these orders. Mistakes caused by untrained personnel could jeopardize the well-being of women throughout the community. Another problem that has been documented is the discrepancy between when the court offices are open to apply for these orders and when they are actually needed. A system where emergency orders, even temporary orders, could be issued (particularly on holidays and weekends) would enhance the safety of some applicants. And finally, ROs must be served by designated authorities, a function that may be backlogged in some jurisdictions. Delays in serving orders are a serious risk as the person named has the right to be officially notified of any potentially prosecutable consequences of his or her behavior.

Overall, the proper monitoring and enforcement of ROs are critical to ensuring that they protect as they were designed to. In response to violations, the court may issue criminal or civil contempt charges.

No-Contact Orders (NCOs) may also be issued by a police department for several reasons. One is when they believe that person is a threat to a domestic partner but that partner has declined to act in his or her own best interests. This has been an effective option that gives police leverage over a suspect when the victim may have dropped charges that were supported by probable cause. They may also be issued when both parties appear to be at fault or it is too difficult to determine who the instigator might be. This is a more general notice that neither party is to contact the other, which is often referred to as a mutual order of protection. NCOs are state issued by way of enabling statutes and ordinances, and if either of the subjects violates them, there are then grounds for filing charges.

Full Faith and Credit Clause

In the past, efforts of victims who have moved their residences in order to remain safe have been hampered by the reluctance or refusal of authorities in the new state to honor or enforce the terms of a restraining order they may have obtained in another state. Federal legislation in the VAWA tells states that valid restraining orders are to fall under the parameters of the Full Faith and Credit Clause of the U.S. Constitution. This means that the document would be recognized just like a marriage or driver's license, and its terms are to be executed wherever one may live.[3] In a sense, it transfers the power of restraining orders to the receiving or enforcing state. The measure was created through legislation in recognition of the gaps and problems arising as victims move from state to state, often in fear of their safety. As mentioned earlier, the VAWA also made it a federal crime to cross state lines in order to pursue or threaten a victim. Legislators obviously felt that without the full faith and credit measure, there would be little to deter someone intent on tracking down and attacking a former partner.

---

[3] The International Association of Chiefs of Police provides a guide to enforcement of protection orders (http://www.theiacp.org/portals/0/pdfs/ProtectingVictimsOfDV.pdf). On page 3, as you will see, the guide outlines the criteria for accepting an order as valid and enforceable.

Domestic Violence Shelters

Many believe that going to a battered women's shelter is a good solution to domestic crises, but there are nowhere near enough beds available in those shelters to meet current demands. In some areas, the criteria for shelter admission may be too inclusive and result in overcrowded, noisy, and contentious surroundings. Victims may end up returning to high-risk environments just to avoid the chaos and confusion of an unstructured environment. But policies that are too exclusive mean that desperate victims with no other alternatives are turned away. Usually the criteria for admission include that a woman is able to live communally, is not on drugs or is not an alcoholic, is not avoiding the police, or is not suicidal. Shelters may not be able to admit clients after hours or on weekends or during holidays which are some of the periods of highest demand. In some cases, shelters do not accept women with older children or more than a couple of children. Screening often excludes those who are not truly "battered" and may require women to call multiple times to prove that they are truly committed to making changes in their lives. The process often requires women to quit their jobs, remove their children from schools, and have no contact with the batterer for any reason. Critics have also argued that few, if any, bilingual services are available, and women with disabilities are less likely to be served.

Domestic Violence Victims in the Courts

Battered Women's Syndrome

The use of battered women's syndrome (BWS) in court is frequently misunderstood, and many falsely assume that it is used more often and more easily than it actually is. In and of itself, BWS is not a defense and is not used alone. Rather it is an element used to support a defense and, most commonly, used in an argument of self-defense. This means that the use of expert testimony is important to establish if the defendant meets the criteria for BWS and, thus, contributes to a finding that self-defense was necessary or justified. This is the scenario that would fit when a battered woman kills her spouse, alleging it was self-defense. Under a claim of duress, a battered woman would establish BWS to demonstrate why she was compelled or coerced into committing a crime on her partner.

In order to meet the requirement for BWS, three circumstances must be clearly established. The first is that the defendant honestly believed that she was in danger. For this, remember, the fact of danger does not necessarily have to be true, it just has to be something that in the defendant's mind was true. Of course, this type of subjective judgment is often difficult for jurors as they cannot let what they personally believe get in the way of their determination of the defendant's mind-set. Jurors must be convinced that the accused really does believe that she was directly in harm's way.

Second, and this is where the juror gets to assess the validity of that belief, the defendant's belief must be reasonable. This is more objective, although courts are now requiring that jurors consider and evaluate this element in terms of what any other "reasonable woman" would believe, given the same circumstances. In the past, a simple reasonable person standard often meant that gender differences were magnified and men did not perceive danger or impending harm in the same way that a woman would. Thus, the court now asks all jurors to assess the risks the defendant believed to be true in terms of what another reasonable woman would have felt.

Third, the defendant using self-defense must be facing real, imminent danger. The use of self-defense is thought of as a last resort, and the defense must be able to clearly establish that no other recourse was viable. Thus, if someone kills a batterer while he is sleeping or follows him after he leaves the house to shoot him, then establishing this third element is more difficult. Jurors would want to be convinced that there was no opportunity to run, or to call someone for help. The question of imminent danger is something the jury must treat as a matter of fact in the case. Previous court decisions established that prior contacts with, and the prior conduct of, the deceased cannot be the sole basis of the imminent danger — which means that something specific this time, in this incident, must be used to trigger the perceived need to use self-defense.

The courts have dealt with and clarified the legal concept of imminent harm in a number of cases. Various precedents include a ruling that the use of obscene words, gestures, or threats does not justify an attack. However, BWS may even explain why a defendant would find it necessary to dismember a body, even after the attacker is dead. The courts have also ruled that a defendant's happiness over the death of her abuser or attacker is immaterial. And, in other cases, the use of drugs and alcohol may be viewed as having impaired the defendant's reasoning. This means that intoxication may increase the difficulty of convincing jurors that the battered woman's perception of imminent danger was, in fact, reasonable.

Because of difficulties inherent in the second and third elements used to establish BWS, its successful use may seem daunting. Fear is a very personal and uncontrollable reaction that hindsight hardly seems to treat fairly. As Supreme Court Justice Oliver Wendell Holmes once said, "detached reflection cannot be demanded in the presence of an uplifted knife," so jurors may need to be reminded of the situational nature of "reasonableness."

Conclusions

Over the years, society, and thus the criminal justice system, has shifted expectations for intervening in cases of domestic violence. Although preferred arrest policies, stalking laws, and noncontact orders have been implemented, some critics argue that such measures may also be responsible for increases in the number of women offenders who have been incarcerated because police have less discretion and flexibility in settling domestic disputes. A number of studies have indicated that a significant portion of workplace violence incidents may be related to domestic disputes, from harassing phone calls and e-mails while on the job to actual onsite attacks.

Although the use of mandatory treatments, such as anger management classes, and the collection of information in national databases have increased our ability to respond to and possibly prevent domestic violence, there is room for improvement. Educating the public about domestic violence and the resources available to address it are important efforts as the system is basically a responsive mechanism that depends on timely reporting in order to best help victims.

Critical Thinking Questions

1. Is domestic violence best reduced with strategies aimed at the victims or the offenders? Why do you think so?

2. Compare and contrast the advantages and disadvantages of preferred versus mandatory arrest for their impact on offenders, victims, and law enforcement officials.

3. What might be done to improve the effectiveness of restraining orders and the process of obtaining them?

Books, Websites, and Media Resources

Abuse, Rape and Domestic Violence Aid and Resource Collection (AARDVARC): http://www.aardvarc.org/

Abused Deaf Women's Advocacy Services (ADWAS): http://www.adwas.org/

Academy on Violence and Abuse: http://www.avahealth.org/

Bui, H. (2004). In the adopted land: Abused immigrant women and the criminal justice system. Westport, CT: Praeger.

Violence Against Women Office: http://www.ovw.usdoj.gov/

Popular Films

The Burning Bed (1984), Farrah Fawcett.
Enough (2002), Jennifer Lopez.
Sleeping with the Enemy (1991), Julia Roberts.

References

Buzawa, E. (2007). Victims of domestic violence. In R. Davis, A. Lurigio, & S. Herman (Eds). Victims of crime (3rd ed., Chap. 4, pp. 55-74). Thousand Oaks, CA: Sage.

Ferro, C., Cermele, J., & Saltzman, A. (2008). Current perceptions of marital rape: Some good and not-so-good news. *Journal of Interpersonal Violence, 23,* 764-779.

Finkelhor, D., & Yllo, K. (1982). Forced sex in marriage: A preliminary research report. *Crime & Delinquency, 28,* 459-478.

Giles-Sims, J. (1983). *Wife battering: A systems theory approach.* New York: Guilford

Hale, M. (1680/1847). *History of the pleas of the crown* (Vol. 1, published 1680) (Emlyn, Ed., published 1847).

Houghton, R. (2010, September). *Domestic violence and disasters: A fact sheet for agencies.* Palmerston North, NZ: Massey University, Joint Centre for Disaster Research.

Pagelow, M. (1984). *Family violence.* New York: Praeger.

Resko, S. M. (2010). *Intimate partner violence and women's economic insecurity.* El Paso, TX: LFB Scholarly Publishing.

Russell, D. (1990). *Rape in marriage.* New York: MacMillan.

Schmidt, J. D., & Sherman, L. W. (1993). Does arrest deter domestic violence? *American Behavioral Scientist, 36,* 601-610.

Sherman, L. W., & Berk, R. A. (1984). *The Minneapolis domestic violence experiment.* Washington, DC: Police Foundation.

State v. Smith 148 N.J. Super. 219, 372 A.2d 386 (1977).

Stewart, C. (2011, August 20). Six months after the earthquake that shattered Christchurch, people are still living on the edge. *The Australian Magazine,* p. 40.

Thurman v. City of Torrington 595 F. Supp. 1521 (1984).

Walker, L. E. (1979). *The battered woman.* New York: Harper and Row.

Websdale, N. (1998). *Rural woman battering and the justice system.* Thousand Oaks, CA: Sage.

Wright, E. (2011). *Neighborhoods and intimate partner violence.* El Paso, TX: LFB Scholarly Publishing.

Other Domestic Offenses

Introduction

Although domestic violence is most commonly associated with married or common-law husbands and wives, family violence is a more general term used to describe any of a number of offenses that may take the form of homicide, assault, sexual abuse, and threats. From prenatal to elderly victims, the types of harms that are perpetrated within the home range from minor to serious and may be associated with anything from ineffective parenting to psychosis. In this chapter, we will discuss a number of family-related offenses that are often overlooked when we focus too intently on the most common forms of spousal abuse or child abuse.

Many of the concepts we will cover have a variety of cultural interpretations as well as legal definitions that have changed over time. For example, at different times and in different places, it would be considered the parents' choice to withhold certain types of medical treatments from their children, even if a child eventually died. Religious and class preferences may have justified individual decisions irrespective of the outcomes. Prosecuting parents for such decisions is a feature of our contemporary American legal system, but one that remains controversial. It is important to remember that the more unanimity of public opinion there is about child welfare and parental misconduct, the more aggressive the criminalization and prosecution will be.

Mothers as Murderers

The act of a parent killing a baby or a young child is considered one of the most reprehensible in our modern society. Yet, early laws in the colonies (1600s) permitted a parent to put to death an unruly child. The concept of *patria potestas* in ancient law meant that one who gave life could ultimately take it away. Even though it is often medically difficult to determine exactly how many infants die of unnatural causes, estimates are that up to 200 may be killed by their mothers every year. Data also tell us that about 30% of children under the age of five who are murder victims are killed by their mothers and another 30% by their fathers. That means the majority of all children under the age of five who are murdered are killed by a parent.

Mothers who kill their children are usually classified into psychotic and nonpsychotic cases. The nonpsychotic will use less violence, usually smothering or drowning a child. Neither type is likely to use a gun. Psychosis is evident in most cases where a woman uses a knife to kill a child, and weapons are more frequently used in the murder of an older child (Shipley, 2007).

Further classifying the killing of children by a parent, Philip Resnick (1969) defined neonaticide as the murder of a child within the first 24 hours after birth, infanticide as the murder of a child up to one year of age, and filicide as the murder of a child older than one year. He argued that mothers who committed filicide usually were suffering from severe depression and believed that some greater good or protection would be served by killing a child. Deaths, often including their own, were viewed as a means to alleviate suffering or some greater impending harm. When 25-year-old LaShanda Armstrong drove her minivan into a lake with her four children inside, she had been raising children on her own since she was 15:

> Neighbors said Armstrong took community college classes while holding down a job and caring for her family. Christine Santos . . . described Armstrong as overwhelmed by having to raise four children alone, and fed up with her predicament. "She was depressed," Santos said. . . . The Associated Press reported that a supervisor at the day-care center where Armstrong's children spent time had described her as under immense stress when she arrived to pick them up Tuesday. "The only thing she'd say was that she was so alone," Shaniesha Strange said. "She's a single parent. She takes great care of her kids, goes to school and works. She really needed a helping hand" (Susman, 2011, p. AA1).

On the other hand, those who commit neonaticide are usually "young women who deny they're pregnant to themselves and others and fear, not psychotic illness, motivates the crime" (Oberman, 2003, p. 494). Shipley hypothesized that those who commit neonaticide do so:

> . . . because the child isn't wanted due to illegitimacy, rape or social stigma, rather than altruistic reasons. . . . These young women may feel unable or unwilling to pursue alternatives such as adoption or abortion . . . make no

plans for labor and often labor on the toilet and in silence . . . they may have a history of dissociative states related to a history of early abuse and chaotic family life and are frequently emotionally isolated from adults in their lives (2007, pp. 69-70).

In 1922, British law responded to the obvious link between women being ostracized and stigmatized for a pregnancy out of wedlock and high rates of infant mortality when they passed the *English Infanticide Act*. The focus was on allowing the mother a chance to give up the child quickly, within a time span that would reduce the likelihood of others finding out. In that legislation, no specific age was noted until an amendment added in 1938 set the baby's age at one year or less. Although no similar laws existed in the United States at that time, women who killed their infants were usually charged with manslaughter rather than murder (Donnelly, 2010). This may be because such deaths would be considered unusual circumstances, evoking a wide range of public sentiments that would have made more serious charges unpredictable for trial. Also, without sophisticated medical tests and equipment, it was often difficult to say for sure what circumstances led to the death of an infant.

Baby Moses Laws

In a movement that began in Texas in 1999, jurisdictions all across the country initiated laws allowing a desperate parent to drop off a newborn at a fire station or hospital emergency room, allegedly without repercussions. In Michigan, the law is called the *Safe Delivery of Newborns Act*, and in California it is called the *Safely Surrendered Baby Law*, while in many jurisdictions they are simply referred to as Baby Moses laws. Although in place for at least a decade now, there have been some legal challenges to these laws and their implementation.

There are several common elements in the Baby Moses laws of most states. First, they usually define a newborn as being 72-hours, one-week, ten-days, or one-month old. Most limit who can turn in a baby for adoption to only one of the parents, although some states say only the mother. Although most relinquishing parents are promised anonymity, some procedures may ask for identification in order to officiate the process and then give the parent the option of anonymity in conclusion.

One of the unexpected consequences resulting from the passage of these laws is that a significant number of overwhelmed parents abandoned much older children at hospitals and fire stations. This usually occurs when the child has special, serious needs that are not being met because of limited resources. When the laws do not specify an age limit for which the safe haven or amnesty is covered, as in the Nebraska statute, for example, this loophole creates a situation where parents faced with financial and personal crises use the law to relinquish their parental responsibilities.

Prosecuting Infanticide: Perceptions and Realities

Of interest to the study of crime is whether women who murder their children are judged more harshly than men and why. Religious views, culture, and ethnic backgrounds may influence one's perception of infanticide as motives, rituals, and punishments may vary on this issue around the world. In a multicultural society, it is often difficult to gauge how receptive a jury might be to medical, psychiatric, and legal distinctions in these cases. The behavior of defendants who may use body language that we do not understand, or have values and symptoms that are difficult to accept, can also be difficult for a jury to interpret. We look at four different Texas cases where a mother murdered her small child (children). The information presented to the juries about these women influenced the outcome because it altered the jurors' perceptions about the mental health of the mothers and their states of mind at the times of the offenses.

Andrea Yates drowned her five children, and her case is the only one presented here in which the mother was originally eligible for the death penalty. Deanna Laney used rocks to crush the skulls of her three children; one child survived. Lisa Ann Diaz drowned her two children. Dena Schlosser cut off the arms of her toddler.

Deanna Laney and Lisa Diaz were both found not guilty by reason of insanity in their original trials. In the case of Lisa Diaz, the jury deliberated for 12 hours. The prosecutor in that case had tried to use her calm, flat demeanor against her — as if she were cold and unfeeling. They also projected her subsequent shame and unhappiness as not only indicators that she felt guilty, but also that she had known better all along. What may have swayed the jury in Diaz's case, however, was the substantial documentation of her decomposition at the time of the murders. She had over 90 documented trips to doctors complaining of worms, mad cow disease, seizures, multiple sclerosis, germs, and evil spirits. She had even tried to commit suicide by stabbing herself more than 20 times. Diaz heard voices of doom; she drank her own urine. All of this psychiatric background likely contributed to the jurors' sense that Diaz believed that what she was doing was right, although it was legally wrong.

Dena Schlosser had a history of postpartum psychosis but had not been taking any of her prescribed medication nor had she been under a doctor's care. She had previously abandoned her children by running away, and her husband was aware of her mental health problems. Dena and her husband had been attending a charismatic church that did not recognize mental illness but instead used often violent approaches to demonic possession. Her pastor claimed to have cast out demons, including one 6-feet tall with a long tail, but had no formal religious training. He did, nonetheless, have his own cable television show in the Dallas area. This spiritual adviser, Doyle Davidson, had been arrested for attempting to strangle the evil spirits out of another female parishioner while intoxicated in her home just before the baby's murder in 2004 (Korosec, 2006). The influence of this church and this televangelist were the subject of a number of investigative news stories (Whitely, 2006).

Like Diaz, Schlosser had stabbed herself as an act of punishment, atonement, or attempted suicide. She was originally found incompetent to stand trial but was eventually tried with the result of a hung jury. In a bench trial in 2006, she was found not guilty by reason of insanity and was sent to Rusk State Hospital. Her husband was granted a divorce and custody of the remaining children with whom Dena has been ordered to have no contact. In 2008, she was released to community outpatient services but was recommitted in 2010 (Crawford, 2010).

For all of these cases, an understanding of postpartum depression was critical for the outcomes. Milder forms of postpartum blues involving mood swings, anxiety, and crying affect up to 80% of women, and the depression normally lasts only a limited number of days. Postpartum depression is a more serious illness that may affect about 15% of new mothers and can last several months. Even more rare, postpartum psychosis strikes only about 0.2% (two-tenths of a percent) of women and is so serious as to constitute a psychiatric emergency. In this state, hallucinations, thought disorders involving commands from spirits, and delusions are not uncommon.

The similarities between the two women, Yates and Laney, are somewhat striking. Both were loving moms who gave their children Biblical names, and both home-schooled their children. Both had called 911 directly after the offense and were extremely remorseful. Why Laney was found not guilty by reason of insanity (NGI) and Yates guilty of capital murder and sentenced to death in her original trial may have to do with what expert testimony the jurors heard. In the Laney trial, jurors were shown videos of Laney in the initial investigative stages of the case, where her mental illness was full blown and she was so disoriented that it undoubtedly had an impact on anyone watching. In contrast, by the time Yates went to trial, she had been medicated for a significant period of time, and her psychotic manifestations were no longer evident. In fact, Yates appeared so flat and unemotional that jurors were probably shocked by her apparent numbness. She also failed to cooperate effectively with her attorney, often making statements that directly served the interests of the prosecution. On appeal, errors in the testimony given by an expert witness in the Yates' trial, including false insinuations that she had copied the crime from a television drama, were considered so prejudicial that she received a new trial. In that subsequent trial, Yates was found not guilty by reason of insanity. It appears that in the time that elapsed between the trials, the public, media, and criminal justice system all seemed to have been educated as to the serious, debilitating mental illness that seems to underlie many of these crimes.

Legislation on Postpartum Psychosis

In the wake of these sensational trials, several Texas legislators introduced bills to address this problem. First, in 2003, House Bill 341 (The Provision of Information on Postpartum Depression to Pregnant Women Act) was passed. However, this legislation simply required prenatal health care providers to offer pregnant women information on agencies that provide counseling and assistance for postpartum depression. Medically, this may be important, but few women are likely to anticipate postpartum depression prior to the birth of their children. Further, it does not seem to recognize that only a small portion of women actually receive medical supervision after delivery which would do little to address social concerns about the prosecution of these cases in the criminal justice system (Cheng, Fowles, & Walker, 2006)

In 2009, Representative Jessica Farrar introduced a bill that would allow the court to consider a postpartum condition during the punishment phase of a woman's trial. In these cases, a finding of guilty in an infanticide case would have to initially occur. Then, at sentencing, a judge or juror would be able to determine whether the defendant did suffer from the disorder. As a result, the maximum punishment would have been two years in jail. Although such a law would have made Texas one of the first in the country to have such a provision, it has yet to pass (Tovino, 2010). Proponents argue that while the insanity defense can still be used, the Texas version of this legal approach is very strict and difficult to use effectively in court.

Similar cases continue to take the same confusing route through the District Attorney's Office. In 2010, Narjes Modarresi was booked on capital murder charges in the death of her two-month-old son. Having twice been treated for postpartum depression, the Muslim woman's family conceded that she had been walking around like a zombie for the past two months. Unfortunately, only the textbooks seem to remember that "walking around like a zombie" is a classic symptom of postpartum psychosis, a lesson that came a little too late.

Munchausen Syndrome by Proxy

Another way that children may be killed or seriously injured by a parent is through the complex set of psychiatric symptoms called Munchausen syndrome by proxy. Depending on which source you read, eighteenth-century German storyteller Baron von Munchausen was a cavalry officer, a mercenary, or simply an aristocrat who was noted for spinning wildly fanciful stories. Medical experts used his moniker to refer to the unbelievable accounts that patients would relate about their illnesses or injuries which later were determined to be self-induced. For example, a young woman in Washington stunned media audiences across the country when it was determined she sprayed acid into her own face and fabricated an account of a mystery assailant. The incident gained notoriety over the young woman's initial claim of an African American woman attacker. After being hospitalized for severe burns to her face, Bethany Storro has been ordered to live in a mental health facility until she faces trial on charges related to filing false police reports and misappropriating funds that were donated to offset her medical expenses. The motive for her actions is not entirely clear, although she has claimed she tried to kill herself or at least change her appearance (Duara, 2010).

Munchausen syndrome characterizes someone creating dubious tales of his or her own medical complaints and their etiology. Munchausen syndrome by proxy is a form of child abuse that occurs when a parent who might him- or herself be seeking attention and support intentionally infects, injures, or causes unnecessary medical procedures and medicines to be administered to a child. As people often bestow a great deal of sympathy or support on the mother of a sick child, this may be a way that the woman is able to create a helpful and caring environment for herself. Apnea and other respiratory ailments as well as difficult-to-diagnose immune deficiency disorders are common complaints that the mothers bring to the pediatrician.

Accomplished by lying, exaggerating, or deceiving, Munchausen syndrome by proxy is a phenomenon that is predominantly exhibited (98%) in females (mothers), although child victims are equally likely to be boys or girls (Kindschi Gosselin, 2003). According to the website kidshealth.org:

> In some cases, the parents or caregivers themselves were abused, both physically and sexually, as children. They may have come from families in which being sick was a way to get love. The parent's or caregiver's own personal needs overcome his or her ability to see the child as a person with feelings and rights, possibly because the parent or caregiver may have grown up being treated like he or she wasn't a person with rights or feelings (http://kidshealth.org/parent/general/sick/munchausen.html).

In one of the most high-profile cases to date, an episode of television's *Extreme Home Makeover* featured a couple with two young girls that the family, mostly the mother, claimed were seriously ill (Mayes, 2011). The mother claimed the 8- and 10-year-old girls suffered from combined immunodeficiency disease, and their current home, dilapidated and mold ridden, was toxic. In March 2009, the show tore down and rebuilt a high-end, air-quality-controlled home with an elevator, solar-heated swimming pool, and gourmet kitchen. Later, when the family couldn't afford the larger home, they sold it and moved to Oregon where doctors were less supportive of all the medical claims. In fact, the girls' tantrums and screaming convinced emergency room specialists that there were no respiratory ailments, and further testing confirmed their suspicions. With evidence of Munchhausen syndrome by proxy, child services placed the girls with a relative who found them to be fit, active, and healthy, only using medical complaints when it suited their interests (Mayes, 2011).

Experts also indicate that Munchausen syndrome by proxy may be interpreted as a cry for help similar to threats or attempts to commit suicide. In these cases, the abusing parent or caregiver may be suffering from depression or anxiety or insecurity, particularly related to their ability to care for the child. The mother may seek out confirmation from medical professionals on the adequacy of their parenting or may bask in the attention afforded in the treatment environment. It is also possible that "the suspected person may also have symptoms similar to the child's own medical problems or an illness history that's puzzling and unusual. He or she frequently has an emotionally distant relationship with a spouse, who often fails to visit the seriously-ill child or have contact with doctors" (http://kidshealth.org/parent/general/sick/munchausen .html).

Over the years, a number of cases of this unusual psychiatric illness have been documented at Texas Children's Hospital, as they have been caught on surveillance cameras in rooms. In June 1991, 23-year-old Cathy Knighton was videotaped trying to suffocate her 7-month-old daughter. Hers was the third case in six years with similar circumstances at the hospital and one that was investigated by Child Protective Services. The unmarried mother with two other children was observed on multiple occasions putting her hand over her daughter's face, allegedly in attempts to suffocate the child, officials said. According to the *Houston Chronicle*, in another case caught on tape, a woman pressed down on her 2-year-old's throat. She was subsequently sentenced to 20 years in prison.

In the next case, we see what might appear to be a classic example of Munchausen syndrome by proxy except that it also involves new technologies and media that might allow someone to not only reach out to a much larger audience for consolation in the great cyber system, but to make money as well. By using Facebook and other social networking media, a person could not only gain sympathy and support from around the world, but donations as well. We can see how the solicitation and use of funds gained through the misrepresentation of a child's illness would make it difficult for jurors to view events in the context of a mental illness. As Lezon (2008) explains:

> A Spring woman was sentenced to 15 years in state prison Wednesday in connection with two surgeries on her young son that prosecutors said were unnecessary. Laurie Williamson, 40, was convicted April 24 of two cases of injury to a child in connection to the implantation of a nerve-stimulation device and a gastric-feeding button in her son. . . . Harris County prosecutor Mike Trent said Williamson manipulated doctors and her son's condition to get the surgeries. . . . But defense attorney Allen Isbell said Williamson was listening to doctors who said her son needed the procedures. . . . State child welfare officials and prosecutors have said Williamson has Munchausen syndrome by proxy. . . . Yet, Trent said the syndrome is not considered a mental illness and does not fit the legal definition of insanity. He also said that she fabricated the children's medical conditions to solicit money from organizations and people. She raised about $150,000 between 2000 and 2005, he said. Prosecutors said Williamson took her three children to at least 500 appointments with doctors in a 10-year period and that she told the children they suffered from a rare illness and would not live past their teens. . . . Officials said the children were malnourished when Child Protective Services took custody of them in March 2006. Two had feeding tubes and were in wheelchairs. Williamson's son is 13 now. Her other two children are 11 and 8. Child welfare officials said the children are now physically well and are in the care of a relative. Their mother is not allowed contact with them (Lezon, 2008, p. B2).

The interesting feature of this case is that state welfare officials and the prosecutor introduced the Munchausen syndrome by proxy traits, and the defense denied them. The defense strategy appears to be that doctors made these diagnoses and engaged in these treatments as it is beyond the expertise and capability of the rest of us as laypersons to do so.

Although Munchausen syndrome by proxy may not be considered a mental illness or a qualifying condition under some state laws regarding insanity, its treatment varies between jurisdictions according to each penal code. For example in *People v. Phillips*, a California court ruled that evidence of Munchausen syndrome by proxy was admissible. In that case, however, the defense had not introduced a diminished capacity defense, which is what a finding of the syndrome would have been used to support. To be clear, these examples illustrate that Munchausen syndrome by proxy is not an excuse that defendants use to avoid prosecution or conviction. It is not a defendant-friendly finding and most often would result in lengthy treatment, psychiatric commitment, and permanent loss of child custody as well as incarceration. On the contrary, the syndrome would be useful to a prosecutor to establish motive and intent where jurors might otherwise wonder, "Why would a mother do this?" Evidence of the syndrome, with its documentation in medical and psychiatric journals, is a way that the prosecution can use the data and literature on this behavior to convince the jurors that the harm suffered by the child was at the hand of the mother.

Child Neglect

Child neglect is characterized by a lack of basic resources in the home and a failure of the parent to provide the essential elements supporting the health and safety of a child. Neglect is the most common form of child maltreatment, but it receives less attention in the criminal justice system because it is often handled by social service departments, and most cases do not result in criminal charges. More recently, a variety of political and economic forces have changed the way we handle a number of child neglect issues. More cases are being brought before family courts in the hope that early intervention may prevent more serious crimes by either the parent or the child.

Single, female-headed homes are recognized in the literature as the most at-risk for child neglect. The ability of a mother to cope with personal problems is viewed as the distinguishing trait between neglectful and non-neglectful environments. Defining neglect as specific behavior, though, is difficult. Experts argue about what specifically constitutes neglect and what does not, while the legal side of the issue appears no easier. Attempts to balance due process rights and the concept of equal treatment under the law have included the right of individuals to be free from interference in family matters. In challenges to various state laws on child neglect, the courts have made it clear that there must be adequate notice about what is allowed and what is not, and that this notice must be clear to a reasonable person. Thus, courts have ruled in some instances that statutes that ban "conduct detrimental" to a child are too vague, as are prohibitions against exposing the child to an "injurious environment." The courts have also ruled that simply requiring that a parent provide a "proper home" for a child constitutes a statement that is too vague. What the courts have found as acceptable language is a reference to requiring "proper maintenance and care" for the child as well as "proper parental control." Other terms that have been found constitutionally valid include the prohibition against "endangering without justifiable cause." This means that a mother might justifiably appear to be speeding and driving recklessly if, for instance, she were rushing a child in a diabetic coma to the hospital.

Mothers also find themselves disproportionately at risk for charges of neglect related to disputes over the course of their children's prescribed medical treatments. In Michigan, a single mother caring for a disabled daughter was jailed after a standoff with authorities over allegations that she neglected to provide the proper medications to that child. Maryanne Godboldo believed she had the right to object to the antipsychotic drugs and to enlist holistic treatments that she felt were more appropriate (Williams, 2011). In a related case, a Massachusetts woman was sentenced to 8 to 10 years for withholding at-home chemotherapy treatments from her disabled, autistic son. A remorseful Kristen LaBrie, who cared for the child alone, explained that the side effects were so severe and he seemed to be in so much pain that she could not bear putting him through the suffering (Lavoie, 2011).

Drug-Endangered Children

Recently, a new term in the abuse and neglect literature, "a drug-endangered child," appears to have helped create a new social problem. This term was originally used to describe the health and safety threats encountered by children exposed to drug manufacturing sites. According to the website of the Office of National Drug Control Policy, the risks include:

- inhalation, absorption, or ingestion of toxic chemicals, drugs, or contaminated foods that may result in nausea, chest pain, eye and tissue irritation, chemical burns, and death
- fires and explosions
- abuse and neglect
- hazardous lifestyle (presence of booby traps, firearms, code violations, poor ventilation)

Better detection to identify and target raids on suspected meth labs, enhanced sentences for crimes related to meth labs where children were present, and public education campaigns about the dangers of exposure to environments where meth is produced appear to have been effective in reducing the injuries children receive in these cases. Information from the El Paso Intelligence Center's (EPIC) National Clandestine Laboratory Seizure System states that over 1,000 children were either injured at or negatively impacted by methamphetamine labs during

2008. According to EPIC, that number is two-thirds lower than in 2004 (report generated February 3, 2009).[1]

Looking through the website for the Office of National Drug Control Policy and the links to various legislative initiatives as well as varying state policies, it appears that the term now has been greatly expanded. The meaning of drug-endangered children now includes any negative effects children might suffer, from neglect to death, if a parent is in any way past or present connected to controlled substances or alcohol abuse. In Texas, for example, the Texas Alliance for Drug-Endangered Children uses the term broadly to include any harm suffered by a child when a parent, family member, caregiver, or guardian is under the influence of drugs or alcohol or has possession of drugs or a history of drug possession. On their website you will see accounts of a mother arrested for driving while intoxicated (DWI) while a child was in the car; a couple arrested because they could not explain an infant's serious head injuries, and the report's focusing on the fact that the mother had previously lost custody of a child and the father had a prior drug conviction; and a young girl forced into prostitution by her mother and grandmother because at the time of the investigation one of the women was found to have a small amount of heroin in her possession (see http://www.texasdec.org/). Not to say that these are not serious offenses, it is true that these cases were already and quite effectively identified as neglect, abuse, and child endangerment. In the past, our system was quite capable of charging, convicting, and punishing these offenses. Criminal and child custody procedures already allowed for consideration of the defendant's history of substance abuse when cases were being evaluated. Only the use of the term "drug-endangered" has really changed. Still, with the new term comes new attention, new laws, new money, training, specialized units, and data keeping.

Interventions and Treatments

The tendency once was to remove children from dysfunctional homes, but in the 1970s and 1980s there was more emphasis placed on trying to treat and reunite families. By the 1990s, another shift was seen, and officials became concerned about classifying and making more customized decisions based on each family's circumstances. However, this process was time-consuming and expensive, and while some cases received more detailed study, other children were fast-tracked into foster care or adoption systems. The quick pursuit of hearings to terminate parental rights meant that children could be placed into permanent settings while a parent was in jail, prison, or even in drug treatment. As Martell explains:

> The Multi-Ethnic Placement Act (PL 103–382) of 1994, amended in 1996, attempted to reduce the length of time children spend in out-of-home care

---

[1] See more information at http://www.whitehousedrugpolicy.gov/enforce/dr_endangered_child.html

and ensure that race, culture or ethnicity is not used to deny placement to a child . . . the Adoption and Safe Families Act of 1997 (PL 105–89), was enacted to swiftly move children in foster care into permanent placements by clarifying the circumstances under which reasonable efforts to reunify were not required and establishing firm timelines for showing a reduced likelihood of maltreatment, and for making decisions regarding permanent placements (2005, p. 20).

Of course, policies such as these probably have a disparate impact on women who are more likely to be the custodial parent of children "swiftly" moved into foster care.

Deadbeat Parents and Child Support

Another avenue to aid families at risk would be to increase efforts to track down nonsupporting parents, "deadbeat dads" as they have been called. Any contribution, it would seem, toward the more than $106 billion owed to custodian parents (Cancian, Meyer, & Han, 2011) would reduce the economic and, thus, personal stress felt by the mostly single mothers. In Florida the number of deadbeat cases added to the rolls of the Department of Revenue has grown by more than 100,000 in the last five years to almost 800,000 (Douglas, 2009). Close to 40% of those did not make any payments in the year 2008. This impacts 1 million children — close to 25% of all minors in that state (Douglas, 2009).

Although initiatives such as sweeps and garnishing wages and income tax refunds have been high profile lately, critics argue that attempts are only periodic and piecemeal. Women report being on telephone hold for hours and eventually fronting money themselves to have their exes served to suit in civil court. One recounts sending $10 to a search company that found her deadbeat ex within 30 days when the state had been unable to do so in five years (Gerdeman, 2004).

A strong or sustained system of recourse must be available for women, and it needs to be user friendly and responsive. Most women who interact with the child support system are frustrated by the red tape and ineffectiveness of that system. One of the problems, though, is that you have to spend money to get money back. In Massachusetts, officials estimate that the state spends $52 million each year just trying to recoup child support (Gerdeman, 2004). Still, research consistently reports that stepped-up enforcement efforts pay off (Cancian, Meyer, & Han, 2011). Cancian, Meyer, and Caspar (2008) report from an experiment in Wisconsin that fathers in arrears are more likely to make payments when all monies are sent directly to the family instead of being encumbered by the government to pay for services rendered to the child, such as happens with Medicaid and TANF (Temporary Assistance for Needy Families).

Today, Texas is one of the states, along with California, Ohio, and Pennsylvania, that ranks highest in retrieving child-support payments. The amount of accumulating debt is due both to the lower income earning potential of many of these fathers and to the fact that a growing number of these men owe support to multiple families (Cancian, Meyer, & Han, 2011). The threat of jail may be the best incentive. In Pennsylvania anyone receiving cash assistance must comply with measures to identify paternity. When paternity is contested, a genetic testing process may be court-ordered (Pennsylvania Department of Public Welfare, 2012). In some states, agencies even attempt to find employment for nonworking deadbeats.

Over time, faster, more effective searches to locate suspects and their financial assets have resulted from increased computerization of court records. Douglas (2009) explains that across the country, various measures are used to pressure payments. Professional licenses, such as those for carpenters, electricians, doctors, and lawyers can be suspended (Sherry, 2009). Holds can also be put on passports or car registrations, driver's licenses can be revoked, and liens can be attached to real estate titles. Most importantly, the type of funds, besides wages and bank accounts, that can be seized for nonsupport include the following:

- Workers' compensation claims
- Settlements from personal injury and civil rights lawsuits
- Tax refunds
- Lottery winnings
- Inheritances
- Unused sick and vacation time from retired employees (from city jobs)

Minnesota, one of the states that appears to be most successful in obtaining child support, has indicated that roughly 73% of the total $615 million that they collected in 2007 was from garnishments from salaries or automatic disbursements such as those listed above (Rosario, 2008). In a number of jurisdictions across the country, websites post deadbeat dad lists in order to seek public help in locating some of the most egregious offenders. The Internet appears to have changed the landscape for tracking down and attempting to expose those who owe and perhaps increasing the collection of support money in the process.

Most jurisdictions see the fiscal necessity of enforcing child support payment as a way to reduce government expenditures, but there are still some going in the opposite direction. According to a report by a state news service in Wisconsin (April 26, 2011), Republican Governor Scott Walker cut $4.25 million in child-support enforcement aid that had been used to pay the salaries for collection investigators. More than one-third of the children in Douglas County, Wisconsin, for example, are currently dependent upon those officers to enforce child-support payments. The seven workers there are responsible for more than 3,300 cases, averaging caseloads of 475 for every investigator. News sources note that another collateral effect of those cuts is that the state will lose federal grant monies associated with that program which means an additional $8 million in losses. As the report indicates, prior to the cuts, Wisconsin had been one of the top states in collecting child support ($900 million in 2009). Critics argue that funds for enforcement of child support are essential to help families reduce reliance on welfare and other forms of government aid.

Matricide

When a 17-year-old Houston high school class president was alleged to have put out a contract hit on his mother, the media searched through the family's history for any type of explanation. As a single parent, Pakistani immigrant Tabassum Khan worked hard to support her family and to provide her son with all the advantages of a middle-class American teen life. Still, that young son stood look-out outside the apartment as she was stabbed to death by another male student, himself an African immigrant. The assailant would later receive just $1,000 for the murder. According to culture conflict theory, her dedication to maintaining caring discipline and control may have interfered with her teenage son's perceived need for autonomy and status among his peers. Subculture theorists would see that the youth's more immediate gratification and hedonistic pursuits would clash with the mother's attempt to restrict his activities and oversee his future (Feldman, 2010).

Examining over 20 years of data on children who kill their parents, Heide and Frei conclude that "Matricide, the killing of mothers by their biological children, is a very rare event" (2010, p. 3). Overall, a mother is much less likely to be killed by an adolescent child, and most matricide involves a White adult son killing his mother. Consequently, White women are more likely than women of other races to be victims of matricide. Hispanic youth had the lowest rates of killing parents or stepparents, although they represented a significantly higher proportion of overall homicides committed. Juvenile daughters are the least likely to commit matricide. As Heide and Frei explain:

> In 2005, of 14,680 total homicide victims, 123 were identified as mothers and 118 as fathers slain by their biological children, together representing less than 2% of all homicide victims and approximately 3% of homicides in which the victim-offender relationship was known (2010, p. 3).

Ironically, the availability of guns that many women keep in the home for protection seem to provide a weapon that can be used against them. Adam Lanza, the young man who killed 26 children and adults at the Sandy Hook Elementary School in Connecticut, began his deadly shooting spree by killing his mother with her own firearm (Freedman, 2013). Another mother who achieved notoriety for winning the right to carry her Glock to her daughter's soccer games was killed just after that in a murder/suicide by her husband in their Pennsylvania home. Police noted that the parole officer and his wife, who ran a day-care operation out of the house, had a number of handguns, rifles, and shotguns as well as several hundred rounds of ammunition on hand. As the author of one news story argues, women appear to have been exploited by the gun industry's marketing strategies and led to believe that owning weapons will reduce their vulnerability (Freedman, 2013).

Heide and Frei (2010) examined homicide data from 1976 to 1999 that included the deaths of 2,436 mothers and 3,122 fathers. They found that fathers were more likely to be killed than mothers, and daughters were more likely to kill mothers than were sons:

> Daughters were the killers in 16% of the matricide incidents and 13% of the patricide incidents over the 24-year-period. The involvement of females in parent killings appears to be a relatively stable phenomenon. A similar analysis restricted to single-victim, single-offender incidents involving parents slain during the 10-year period 1977-1986 revealed the same level of female involvement in the killings of fathers (13%) and slightly lower participation in the killing of mothers at 14% (Heide & Frei, 2010, p. 4).

Research indicates that most men who kill their mothers do so when suffering a serious episode of mental illness and in the context of a preexisting and long-term dysfunctional relationship. Some of these perpetrators later describe the mother as either too domineering or too ambivalent and the offense as "either liberating to maintain their masculinity or as protection against extreme emotions triggered by their mothers' behavior" (Heide & Frei, 2010, p. 7). Information about daughters who kill their mothers is similar to that of men in that serious mental illness, personality disorders, and alcohol dependence are often involved.

Women as Victims of Elder Abuse

The term "granny battering" was first used in the 1970s. Prior to this time, elderly victimization was virtually ignored. Granny battering brought to light the many issues of victimization and violence against the elderly, particularly elderly women. Even so, a standard definition of elder abuse has yet to be formulated. Defining and identifying elder abuse are critical for serving the needs of the 36 million persons in this country who are now 65 years of age and older. By 2030, that number is expected to double (Bulman, 2010). And, if reported rates of elder abuse remain consistent at just under 2%, there would be 1.2 million victims.

Gerald Lancaster was a former marine and retired engineer, 84 years of age, who spent most of his time drinking and arguing with his wife. When he fired a shot as his wife left the home, Houston police were called, and a short time later an HPD SWAT team was deployed. During the 6-hour stand-off, Lancaster mostly slept, even after a tear gas canister was deployed (Lezon, 2010). Later, following his arrest, he was asked how long he'd been married, and his reply was "too damn long." Lancaster's case highlights the problems for elderly couples with physical and mental health impairments, namely habits that mix fighting with alcohol and weapons. Lancaster claimed to have "enough guns to take down the whole (expletive) army if I wanted to" (Lezon, 2010).

In 1988, Pillemer and Finkelhor estimated that only 1 in 14 cases of elder abuse appeared to be officially reported to authorities. Although it has not been determined whether those estimates still hold, recent results from a national random sample of adults aged 60 or older indicate that 4.6% reported emotional abuse, 1.6% indicated that they were physically abused, just over 5% claimed neglect, and that same amount said they were victims of financial abuse (Acierno et al., 2009). Another study that interviewed both in person and using a booklet filled out independently indicated that 9% of the elderly reported experiencing verbal abuse (Laumann, Leitsch, & Waite, 2008). As with other forms of crime, attempts to increase reporting have been made through educational/awareness campaigns and the passage of mandatory-reporting laws. The majority of elder abuse victims in domestic settings were female. However, there was no gender difference between the perpetrators, with males at 47.4% and females at 48.9%. According to Payne (2005), adult children are the most likely perpetrators of elder abuse and, as the NCEA (2013) adds, spouses and other family members are the second most likely perpetrators. In a recent study, Amstadter et al. (2011) found that women victims of elder abuse are more likely to be those who need assistance with daily activities, and offenses are more likely to be perpetrated by family members who were living with them. Older women who report being both physically and verbally abused within the last year, researchers have found (Baker et al., 2009), have higher mortality risks than women who do not report abuse.

One strategy for addressing this growing problem is to identify perpetrators who are at risk for engaging in elder abuse. Several studies have noted that because of language deficits, elderly immigrant women may have trouble accessing assistance when they are mistreated by husbands, children, or their spouses. Although bruising is one of the indicators of abuse in these cases, medical analysis must differentiate carefully between accidental bruising, to which the elderly are prone, and intentionally inflicted injuries. Experts indicate that abusive bruises are often larger, with most measuring 2 inches or larger in diameter. And, as one study determined, victims of physical abuse "were much more likely to have bruises on the head and neck, especially the face, and on the posterior torso. Researchers also noted significant bruising on the right arm, perhaps because people raised their arms in an attempt to block an attacker" (Bulman, 2010). Although physical neglect and financial exploitation promptly come to mind, institutional abuse is also relatively common (Payne, 2005, p. 6).

In taped testimony shortly before she died, Helen Love, a then 75-year-old grandmother, described how she was pummeled by a staff member because she soiled herself while a resident at a Sacramento, California, nursing home. She was choked, and her neck, wrists, and hands were broken. The perpetrator pleaded guilty to elder abuse and served one year in jail for the fatal assault (Associated Press, 2002).

Examining the court ruling in *People v. Heitzman* (1994), it is obvious that California statutes did not adequately identify who could be held responsible when neglect of the elderly led to death. In that case, daughter Susan Heitzman may have known that her father was suffering from dehydration, malnutrition, and bed sores that led to septic shock, and perhaps she even had the duty to report his condition while he was living with her brothers. Because she was not his legal caretaker, the court ruled that she could not be held accountable for his death.

Social workers readily admit that resources and services designated specifically for elderly victims are sparse, as this group did not historically appear to have as great a need of domestic violence intervention as their younger couple counterparts. Thus, elderly domestic violence victims are more likely to remain in abusive relationships due to financial need, shame, and family loyalty (Nelesen, 2003).

According to the NCEA (2005), which has been collecting data on reports of elder abuse since 1986, it is very difficult to track elder victimization. There is no uniform reporting system in place, and further, there is no national center for data dissemination. Still, interest in this area of crime prevention has been growing. The University of California at Irvine has instituted an Elder Abuse Forensic Center, and San Bernardino County, California, has been operating an Elder and Dependent Adult Abuse Prosecution Family Violence Unit in the District Attorney's Office since 2000 (Berson, 2010).

Reducing Family Crime

In terms of policy, more needs to be done to address issues related to poverty and the gaps in services that allow families to slip through the cracks when it comes to health and safety. Attempts should be made to standardize child support policies across the country and to increase child support enforcement. Some states appear to be very effective at minimizing the problems of deadbeat dads, such as Mississippi which is reported to bring in $9.45 for every dollar it spends on enforcement. States like Minnesota fare worse when every dollar spent on enforcement yields only $4.05 in payments (Rosario, 2008). The varying size of officer caseloads from manageable to unreasonable to impossible around the United States may be one of the factors related to cost effectiveness.

Because of the number of households that are the responsibility of single mothers, a disproportionate amount of family crime will center on female offenders or victims. When you add female children to that number, the gender-related risk of involvement in domestic violence increases. Those crafting strategies for reducing crime within families must be aware of the different roles played by family members, the expectations others in the family have for them, and the pressures that are assumed with those roles.

Thinking back to our criminology theory, we remember that power-control theory, developed by John Hagan, argues that gender relations within a family are the basis for the way power is used. As with many other conflict-based theories, economic disadvantage and the inability to control resources such as finances and job status create imbalances in the home that directly influence parenting. For power-control theory, there are two opposing types of families. One is more traditional in its orientation toward parenting and is patriarchal. This means that it is father-centered, and the man of the house makes most important decisions as a by-product of his role as primary breadwinner.

In this arrangement, mothers are weaker in power and more likely to defer discipline and child control issues to the father. Girls are more suppressed and restricted in terms of acceptable behaviors, while boys are given more freedom. Not only are boys allowed greater latitude in their routines, but there is also greater tolerance for delinquency and experimentation.

An egalitarian family model reflects more contemporary orientations where the mother's career may earn her status and income that equal or even surpass that of her husband. In this arrangement, daughters are given more equal consideration when it comes to curfews, outside activities, and experimenting with deviant behaviors. Where parents have equal status in the workforce and share parenting responsibilities, they are less likely to be able to implement hypocritical or double standards in their treatment of their daughters. In these arrangements, daughters are as likely as sons to engage in delinquent behaviors.

Educational interventions such as court-ordered parenting classes seek to assist clients in implementing reasonable and meaningful rules at home, as well as effective techniques for enforcing them. Programs and resources must continue to be directed toward helping parents, particularly single parents, develop adequate socialization skills in their children. As social control theorists have pointed out, children must be consistently disciplined if bonding to parents, schools, and other institutions reflecting traditional value structures is to occur. In the past, programs such as Big Brothers and Big Sisters, YMCA and YWCAs, and Girl Scouts and Boy Scouts served in this role, as did community sports teams, 4-H clubs, and church groups. From the research of the subculture (gang) theorists and social disorganization theorists of the Chicago School Era came the idea that single mothers needed community resources and programming in order to provide mentoring and supervision that they could not always provide on their own.

Critical Thinking Questions

1. Over time the state has swung from trying to fix dysfunctional and high-risk families to taking children out of these homes, often permanently. What are some viable strategies for and alternatives to both child safety and family preservation in these cases?

2. Mothers who harm their children are some of the most vilified offenders in our society. How would you develop reasonable sanctions for this group, considering both equitable punishment and rehabilitation?

3. Child neglect is a very broad term. How would you arrange various child neglect offenses on a continuum of seriousness from low to high?

Books, Websites, and Media Resources

Baby Moses Laws: http://fire.lacounty.gov/programsevents/SpecialProgramsSafeSurrender.asp
Child Support: http://www.deadbeatlocators.com/ and https://www.childwelfare.gov/can/
Dugard, J. L. (2012). *A stolen life: A memoir*. New York: Simon & Schuster.
National Center on Elder Abuse: http://www.ncea.aoa.gov/_
Salcido, C. (2009). *Not lost forever: My story of survival*. New York: William Morrow.
Spencer, L. (2007). *Shattered dreams: My life as a polygamist's wife*. New York: Center Street.

Popular Films

Changeling (2008), Angelina Jolie.
Precious (2009), Gabourey Sidibe and Mo'Nique.

References

Acierno, R., Hernandez, M., Amstadter, A., Resnick, H., Steve, K., Muzzy, W., & Kilpatrick, D. (2010). Prevalence and correlates of emotional, physical, sexual, and financial abuse and potential neglect in the United States: The National Elder Mistreatment Study. *American Journal of Public Health*, 100(2), 292-297.

Amstadter, A., Cisler, J., McCauley, J., Hernandez, M., Muzzy, W., & Acierno, R. (2011). Do incident and perpetrator characteristics of elder mistreatment differ by gender of the victim? Results from the National Elder Mistreatment Study. *Journal of Elder Abuse & Neglect*, 23, 43-57.

Associated Press. (2002, March 5). Abuse in nursing care focus of report. *Los Angeles Times*, p. A9.

Baker, M., LaCroix, A., Wu, C., Cochrane, B., Wallace, R., & Woods, N. (2009). Mortality risk associated with physical and verbal abuse in women aged 50 to 79. *Journal of the American Geriatrics Society*, 57, 1799-1809.

Berson, S. (2010). Prosecuting elder abuse cases. *NIJ Journal*, 265, 8-9.

Bulman, P. (2010). Elder abuse emerges from the shadows of public consciousness. *NIJ Journal*, 265, 1-7.

Cancian, M., Meyer, D., & Caspar, E. (2008). Welfare and child support: Compliments, not substitutes. *Journal of Public Policy and Management*, 27, 354-375.

Cancian, M., Meyer, D., & Han, E. (2011). Child support: Responsible fatherhood and the quid pro quo. *The ANNALS of the American Academy of Political and Social Science*, 635, 140-162.

Cheng, C., Fowles, E., & Walker, L. (2006). Postpartum mental health care in the United States: A critical review. *Journal of Perinatal Education*, 15(3), 34-42.

Crawford, S. (2010, April 24). Mother who killed baby is no longer free. *Dallas Morning News*, p. B1.

Donnelly, D. (2010). How far have we come since 2000? Nebraska's youth need help. *University of Miami Law Review*, 64, 771-808.

Douglas, M. (2009, January 15). State's chasing more deadbeat parents. *Tampa Tribune*, p. 1.

Duara, N. (Associated Press). (2010, September 20). Woman in acid hoax pleads not guilty to theft charges: 28-year-old is ordered to live in a mental health facility until trial. *Houston Chronicle*, p. B4.

Feldman, C. (2010, January 31). Confessed hit man details a chilling plot in the brutal slaying of classmate's mother. *Houston Chronicle*, p. A1.

Freedman, D. (2013, February 10). Marketing assault: Selling women on guns. *Houston Chronicle*, pp. A27-A28.

Gerdeman, D. (2004). Deadbeat dads: Who pays? *The Patriot Ledger*, p. 1.

Heide, K., & Frei, A. (2010). Matricide: A critique of the literature. *Trauma, Violence, & Abuse, 11,* 3-17.

Kindschi Gosselin, D. (2003). *Heavy hands: An introduction to the crime of intimate and family violence* (2nd ed.). Upper Saddle River, NJ: Prentice Hall.

Korosec, T. (2006, February 16). Pastor blames demons, not mental illness. Defense accuses him, husband. *Houston Chronicle,* p. B1.

Laumann, E. O., Leitsch S. A., & Waite, L. J. (2008). Elder mistreatment in the United States: Prevalence estimates from a nationally representative study. *Journal of Gerontology B Psychol Sci Soc Sci.,* 63(4), S248-S254.

Lavoie, D. (2011, April 16). Mother who withheld son's meds gets prison. *Houston Chronicle,* p. A4.

Lezon, D. (2008, May 1). Spring mom gets 15 years for son's needless surgeries — Prosecutors say she fabricated her children's illnesses to solicit money. *Houston Chronicle,* p. B2.

Lezon, D. (2010). Quarrel leads to gunshot and a SWAT standoff. *Houston Chronicle,* p. B2.

Martell, D. R. (2005). *Criminal justice and the placement of abused children.* New York: LFB Scholarly.

Mayes, S. (2011, May 14). "Extreme Makeover" family in Oregon finds mother under "medical child abuse" scrutiny. *The Oregonian.* Retrieved from http://www.oregonlive.com/clackamascounty/index.ssf/2011/05/clackamas_county_a_case_of_med.html

National Center on Elder Abuse. Online at www.ncea.aoa.gov

Nelesen, D. (2003, August 30). Violence in the home — unwanted guest. *San Diego Union Tribune,* p. A7.

Oberman, M. (2003). Mothers who kill: Cross-cultural patterns in and perspectives on contemporary maternal filicide. *International Journal of Law and Psychiatry, 26,* 493-514.

Payne, B. (2005). *Crime and elder abuse: An integrated perspective* (2nd ed.). Springfield, IL: Charles C. Thomas.

Pennsylvania Department of Public Welfare (2012, August). *Pennsylvania Child Support Handbook.* Harrisburg, PA: Bureau of Child Support Enforcement, Pennsylvania State Collection and Disbursement Unit.

People v. Heitzman, 9 Cal. 4th 189, 886 P.2d 1229, 37 Cal. Rptr.2d 236 (1994).

People v. Phillips, 122 Cal App 3d 69, 175 Cal Rptr 703 (1981).

Pillemer, K., & Finkelhor, D. (1988). The prevalence of elder abuse: A random sample survey, *The Gerontologist,* 28(1), 51-57.

Resnick, P. (1969). Child murder by parents: A psychiatric review of filicide. *American Journal of Psychiatry, 126,* 325-334.

Rosario, R. (2008, June 7). Dakota County says it just can't find deadbeat parent. Try Florida. *St. Paul Pioneer Press.* p. B2.

Sherry, V. N. (March 15, 2009). Epidemic of child support deadbeats, Court-orders ignored. *Staten Island Advance,* p. A1.

Shipley, S. L. (2007). Perpetrators and victims: Maternal filicide and mental illness. In R. Muraskin (Ed.), *It's a crime: Women and justice* (4th ed., Chap. 5, pp. 66-102). Upper Saddle River, NJ: Prentice Hall.

States News Service. (2011, April 26). Republicans make it harder to go after dead beat dads. Madison, WI.

Susman, T. (2011, April 14). Mother drowns herself and 3 of her children. *Los Angeles Times,* p. AA1.

Tovino, S. (2010). Scientific understandings of postpartum illness: Improving health law and policy? *Harvard Journal of Law and Gender, 33,* 99-173.

Whitely, G. (2006, May 18). The devil and Doyle Davidson. *Dallas Observer,* p. B6.

Williams, C. (2011, May 22). Mother battles Michigan over daughter's medication. *Associated Press.*

Female Drug Offending

Introduction

Female drug offenders have typically been treated in the same way as males in the war on drugs. However, unique aspects of gender-related issues, including prostitution, childbearing, and primary responsibility for child rearing, have evolved to make the issues affecting these women socially, legally, and politically controversial. Some of the measures to combat drug use are new, but many theorists argue that the forces at work in this scenario are simply traditional avenues of gender oppression (Boyd, 1999). Feminists have used the double victimization scenario to describe women as harmed by both drugs and a sexist and patriarchal system of justice.

Although it is still unclear why some people are more likely to become drug dependent than others, we do know the reasons people give for using drugs and the effects that various drugs have on the body over time. Researchers point out that women are more likely to abuse legal prescription drugs and illegal drugs and to be controlled by the men in their lives who may also be involved in the use and sale of drugs. These factors all contribute to a more complex view of female offending that must be understood within the context of a male-dominated society.

Women drug offenders, like men drug offenders, primarily abuse drugs and sell some to support their use, but they rarely have major roles in drug dealing networks. As Fagan's (1994, p. 210) research found, "Women sellers hold positions within drug-selling organizations that are skewed toward lower status roles and away from management-ownership status."

It is important to note that defining drugs as criminal and, subsequently, defining related policy decisions about how to "handle" the drug crime problem are integral to understanding both criminal drug use and those who are deemed to be offenders. Any notion of women drug users or abusers as a type of criminal is a product of these decisions. In other words, "women" drug offenders are primarily different from men based on the way society defines drug abuse, expresses concern about drug abuse, and enacts policies oriented toward prevention or suppression. In order to understand this, one must first have a sense of the history of drug abuse as a social problem in this country.

In the United States, the Civil War represented a major turning point in drug use. Before that point, opium was available in common trade.[1] A derivative of opium, morphine, became available as an injectable form of painkiller that was widely used during the Civil War. This medical usage of morphine created the nation's first major drug epidemic (as long as one ignores alcohol and tobacco use), and addiction was called the "soldier's disease." From there, morphine usage became widespread among the nation's households. Goode (1999) even states that the common addict of the period could be characterized as a middle-class, white female. However, studies of the problem and attempts at rehabilitation focused on prostitutes and showgirls who often frequented opium dens (Fagan, 1994). These were the women sent to prison as the nation confronted the vices of the early twentieth century in a broad-based strategy of eugenics, confinement, moral instruction, and training for employment.

In the mid-1970s, New York State was one of the first in this country to pass strict drug laws, called the Rockefeller Drug Laws. As Shelden (2006) explains, prior to that time "only 400 women were in prison and only 100 were in for drugs. By 2004 about 3000 women were in prison (40% for drugs); almost 87% of the women in for drugs were either black or Latina." Although many states soon followed suit, one of the federal government's major weapons in the war on drugs was the 1988 *Anti-Drug Abuse* Bill. This legislation allowed for increased sentences for drug-related offenses, allocated additional resources and equipment for law enforcement interdiction efforts, and created an asset forfeiture system much like that developed under the RICO (Racketeer-Influenced and Corrupt Organization) statutes a few years earlier (Miller & Selva, 1994). Ironically, in both organized crime and large-scale drug operations, women played little or no significant leadership role and did not profit in any real sense from its operation. Despite the consistency of the evidence on this matter, women—particularly poor, minority women—still appear to suffer the same harsh consequences of the laws as the men in their lives.

Women as Drug Offenders

Today there are over 1 million women under the supervision of the criminal justice system in this country (Bloom, Johnson, & Belzer, 2003).

---

[1] In point of fact, the United States supported Great Britain's efforts to cultivate, distribute, and sell opium to China in the two "Opium Wars" of 1839-1842 and 1856-1860. In both wars, the British forced China to legalize the sale of opium.

Overall, women have a 1 in 56 lifetime chance of being incarcerated, with the risks much higher for Blacks and Hispanics than Whites (Bonczar, 2003). Two-thirds of all females in state custody are serving sentences for non-violent offenses (West & Sabol, 2011). Looking at felony drug convictions in 2006, women ended up with a somewhat larger share (35%) than men (33%) (Department of Commerce: Economics and Statistics Administration, 2011). In 2009, 14% of those who were arrested by the DEA were women. Overall, women represented 20% of the DEA's methamphetamine arrests. Of every 10 females arrested by that agency, the breakdown would be two for methamphetamine, two for cocaine, and two for marijuana (Motivans, 2011).

Lest one think that these arrests are primarily for serious drug crimes, about 83% of women's total drug abuse violation arrests in 2010 were for drug possession/use. Of those arrested for drug sale and manufacturing, only 18% were female (Snyder, 2012). Moreover, women are not arrested as drug "kingpins" or major traffickers, the ostensible focus of the war on drugs. Instead, women are primarily arrested for drug use, drug possession, and minor selling of drugs. The research reveals that women are simply "holders," or in domestic relationships with dealers, that household responsibilities keep them from assuming more active roles in trafficking, and that female users often perform dealing activities only until more fixed measures of obtaining drugs for their habits can be obtained (Fagan, 1994).

If the corporate world allegedly has a glass ceiling for women executives, the drug world has an iron one: women are simply not counted among major distributors and traffickers. Instead, women are often legally in the roles of constructive possessor, aiding and abetting, or co-conspiring, all of which carry harsh penalties (Goldfarb, 2002). They are used by males for such purposes as carrying and distributing drugs, hiding the male's own stash, and maintaining the laundered gains of drug dealing (e.g., property purchased with drug proceeds and placed under the woman's name).

Approximately 25% of female state prisoners were serving drug sentences at the end of 2010 (Carson & Sabol, 2012), which represents a decline of almost 10% over the last decade. Jails also hold a disproportionate number of women for nonviolent drug and property crimes (Bloom, Johnson, et al., 2003). It should also be noted that drug use is commonly associated with women's criminal behavior in general. In a large national study it was reported that prisoners who were mothers were more likely to be serving time for a drug-related offense than prisoners who were fathers. Prisoners who were mothers were also more likely to have used drugs in the 30 days leading up to their commitment offense (Mumola, 2000). Further, according to 2003 government Arrestee Drug Abuse Monitoring (ADAM) data, at the time of arrest, close to 70% of arrested females tested positive for drugs, usually cocaine and marijuana. In addition, roughly 35% of the adult females arrested could be classified as involved with heavy drug use and at risk for dependence (Zhang, 2003).

The Impact of the War on Drugs

The war on drugs, originally intended as a strategy to break up large drug distribution and trafficking networks, is most likely the reason that the percentage of women incarcerated for a drug offense rose dramatically in the period from 1986 (12%) to 1991 (33%). And, in the decade that followed between 1990 and 2000, the number of women incarcerated in prisons in this country increased 125% (Kruttschnitt & Gartner, 2003).

Chesney-Lind (1997) refers to the war on drugs as a war on women (see also Bloom, Chesney-Lind, & Owen, 1994). The concept of a war, particularly a gender-based conflict, was furthered by the mid-1980s emergence of a "crack epidemic" among the poor. Media reports projected the image of the "crack mother" into mainstream crime coverage and began a prosecution frenzy, not only on drug charges but on a new range of crimes for exposing children, and even fetuses, to the effects of a woman's addiction (Humphries, 1999).

In an essay entitled "How the drug war targets women," Criminologist Randy Shelden (2006) writes that the mandatory sentences enacted in the 1980s meant more women would be sent to prison. In many cases, what were traditionally mitigating circumstances, such as being a single parent without prior convictions or a history of violent crime, no longer insulated women, even first offenders, from harsher sentencing decisions. He explains:

> Arrests on drug charges for women reflect their secondary status in the big world of illegal drug dealing (estimated to be around $500 billion yearly). Figures show that women are "overrepresented among low level drug offenders" and are "not principal figures in criminal organizations or activities." Regardless, they receive sentences that are similar to "high level" drug offenders (Shelden, 2006).

So what were these women doing to get these severe sentences? Shelden continues:

> A New York State study (1998) found that a total of 63 percent of women sent to prison were convicted of the lowest level drug offenses, what are called felony classes C-E. Another study notes that women most often serve as "mules" (those who carry drugs for the drug cartels and other high level dealers) for boyfriends or lovers, often doing so because of threats to their lives.

Finally, there is the possibility that female mules or couriers are carrying large amounts of drugs, which would explain their severe sentences when caught. Shelden anticipates this possibility as well:

> Still another report notes that "Just as male counterparts, female couriers are small time players in economy controlled by narco dictators, drug lords and barons, military and intelligence agencies, the police, organized crime, and so on." The report notes that "male couriers are able to realize a greater share of profits, unlike females who are paid a flat rate, tricked or simply coerced into

trafficking in drugs." Many of these women have been used by drug-dealers "as decoys for smugglers on their flight who pass easily through customs with large quantities of cocaine or heroin" (Shelden, 2006).

The American Civil Liberties Union sponsored research that resulted in a report entitled "Caught in the net: The impact of drug policies on women and families" that chronicles the impact aggressive drug policies have had in our society. They point to the Sentencing Project and the U.S. Bureau of Justice Statistics' data indicating that between 1986 and 1999, the number of women serving prison time in this country increased over 888% (Lapidus et al., 2005.).

One of the ironies of the "skyrocketing" rate of female incarceration as a result of the crackdown on drugs, Shelden (2006) explains, is that "women are indeed very small cogs in the illegal drug market, with many getting involved as a means of supplementing income in the face of unemployment, low-wage and unstable jobs, lack of affordable housing, and cuts to social programs such as child care, social assistance, and health care." Often their role is "limited to answering telephones or living in a home used for drug related activities." In addition, Rigert (1997) reports, a Minneapolis newspaper study of over 60,000 federal drug cases determined that "men were more likely than women to offer evidence to prosecutors in exchange for shorter sentences, even if the information placed others, including the women in their lives, in jeopardy." One would imagine those who play incidental roles in any criminal organization rarely have any information useful in bargaining with prosecutors; thus women are more likely to receive full prosecution and severe sentences precisely for being organizationally ignorant.

Although federal laws were amended by the early 1990s to allow judges to make special considerations for certain cases, it was highly unlikely that women would qualify for such an option. The criteria needed to deviate from the mandatory minimums were as follows:

1. the defendant has no prior record;
2. the defendant did not use violence or possess a weapon;
3. there was no death or serious bodily injury;
4. the defendant was not an organizer, leader, manager, or supervisor of others; and
5. the defendant truthfully provided the government all information and evidence.

As a product of fear for their own or their families' safety or because they lacked sufficient inside information, women would rarely turn against co-offenders or risk being viewed as a snitch.

Laws developed to reduce access to illicit substances have not only had disparate effects upon women but also unintended consequences for families. Probation and parole officers, social workers, and child protective service case-workers are constantly challenged by the lack of gender-responsive strategies available to address parenting, job, and personal skills development, as well as addiction and mental health needs. To be effective, interventions must be coordinated with all relevant agencies including the courts, corrections, treatment providers, public health, housing, child welfare, and community outreach centers.

Interaction between Drug Offending and Women's Lifestyles

Unfortunately, studies of female drug offenders, like those of female offenders in general, tend to focus almost exclusively on those incarcerated. This means that many functioning drug users, undetected by the system, are missing from the databases providing our knowledge of female drug users. This creates a bias in our information and, consequently, in the policies and programs derived from analysis of the known offenders.

Even the data on incarcerated women offenders tend to be ignored by policy makers. Data on female prisoners indicate that about two-thirds of all of the women in prison have minor children (Glaze & Maruschak, 2008). The majority of these women are single, custodial parents who are five times more likely than men to live on some type of supplemental assistance (such as Temporary Assistance for Needy Families [TANF], or unemployment). Approximately 70% of mothers report living on less than $1,000 per month (Kruttschnitt, 2010). There is also evidence these women have a higher incidence of being under the influence of drugs at the time of their offense than men. Thus, it is difficult to consider female drug offenders without including the way that social values, laws, and policies impact their children as well.

Sources of Interaction

As a consequence of contemporary social values and perhaps political pressures, judges and prosecutors are more likely to find alternatives to incarceration less appropriate for mothers who commit crimes while under the influence. Feminists have long argued that as primary caregivers, women bring more attention to themselves in the legal system and subsequently suffer more serious condemnation than men who are fathers. Throughout the criminal justice process, drug offenses become intertwined with perceptions about the proper role of women, prostitution, lifestyle, conditions of the home, care of the children, and potential fetal health risks which appear both to complicate and to enhance the punitive aspects of sentencing dispositions (Belknap, 2001; Boyd, 1999).

The issue of drug use/abuse cannot realistically be viewed in isolation, as a simple behavior or lifestyle. Instead, one must analyze the many social and economic problems in effect including marginalized employment, discrimination, single parenthood, poverty, lack of access to medical and mental health care, domestic violence, and historic sexual victimization. All increase the risk factors for women being drawn into the criminal justice system (Department of Commerce: Economics and Statistics Administration, 2011). It often is difficult to establish any temporal sequence or any consistent cause-and-effect relationships between these factors. Instead, they function more as coexisting variables that may aggravate and enhance each other as children are drawn into the network. In addition, any of the issues outlined in Chapter 1 that remain untreated could become more serious over time or more difficult to resolve as the number of children increases.

Drugs and Social Issues

Although women remain a small percentage of those involved in the courts, they represent a group that may be more amenable to treatment. Some researchers have indicated women stay longer in programming, exhibit higher levels of commitment to abstinence, and have a greater ability to self-regulate behavior controls. Even though these women report higher levels of satisfaction with the rehabilitation process (Laudet & Stanick, 2010), they also seem more vulnerable to stress related to parenting. As Van Voorhis (2012, p. 127) indicates, "a key risk factor for women's recidivism, especially in community settings, is parental stress exhibited by women who have little financial and emotional support in raising their children and who experience difficulties with child management."

Virtually all drug-court programs, supervised-release agreements, and other diversion contracts require that offenders hold regular jobs. For women, particularly those who are single parents, the ability to balance the scheduling demands of work and a family, transportation issues, and the often break-even nature of working and paying for adequate child care is a daunting task. Add to that the pressures of paying supervision fees and the court costs associated with their criminal convictions and it often seems like a vicious and self-defeating cycle.

Research has consistently found that women are more likely than males to succeed on parole (McShane, Williams, & Dolny, 2002) and that their substance abuse history is less of a risk factor for predicting failure than the histories of males (Bonta, Pang, & Wallace-Capretta, 1995). Women are also more likely to be revoked from parole and probation for technical reasons than for new offenses. The use of technical grounds often implies that parole officer discretion is operating and that personal interpretations of a client's behavior are being used in making the decision to seek revocation. Norland and Mann (1984) found that when men violated for technical reasons, those charges were likely to be absconding or failure to work. In the case of female clients revoked for technical reasons, the charges were more often absconding and having "improper associates." The difficulty with revoking a parolee for having improper associates is that it is usually a moralistic judgment call. Interviews with officers led Norland and Mann to conclude that women consume more of the officers' time and seek more emotional support. It has been suggested that having a higher service need may actually predispose supervising officers against the female client.

As Holtfreter, Reisig, and Morash (2004) argue, poverty factors, specifically unemployment and financial problems, seem to place women in higher-risk categories for recidivism when assessed with traditional instruments like the

LSI-R. In fact, when they controlled for poverty status in their analysis, these risk instruments failed to predict recidivism among female offenders. The link between poverty and involvement in the criminal justice system has been a major theoretical issue for both conflict and feminist criminologists.

Feminists argue that the female drug offender is symptomatic of the "pink-collar ghetto" status of women that lingers in today's society. Unemployed and underemployed, low-paid, unskilled women employees suffer the hopelessness of the dead-end nature of work and seek to escape the pressures of single parenting while trying to make ends meet by long hours and difficult negotiations of hours, transportation, and child care.

The hopelessness of this position creates a situation in which women, particularly poor, minority women, are more likely to be attracted to drug use and criminal activity. Data consistently show that women of color are more likely to be prosecuted and incarcerated, lose custody of their children, have their parental rights terminated, and have their pregnancies monitored and regulated by health and law enforcement systems. For women drug offenders, economic issues are common and profoundly related to their lifestyle choices — even the decision to sell drugs is frequently related to the need to bolster family income.

Drugs and Criminological Theories

There are a number of sociological and psychological approaches to studying the female drug offender, particularly in reference to victimization and abuse. Arguably, this group of women would be at greater risk of violence both inside and outside of the home as they continually find themselves in high-risk places, situations, and relationships. Criminological theories such as routine activities, lifestyle, rational choice, conflict, and feminist perspectives would all see different roots of the problem. They would also suggest varied methods of treatment in the areas of diagnosis, prioritization of therapeutic goals, family reconciliation plans, and style of intervention used.

Bednar (2003) comments on the difficulty in unraveling the relationship between domestic violence and substance abuse, particularly as both violent and substance-abusing families seem to exhibit intergenerational transmission of dysfunctions. Studies have consistently indicated that female offenders are more likely to report not only more addiction problems but also more childhood trauma such as physical and sexual abuse, post-traumatic stress disorders, homelessness, and physical and mental health disabilities than males (Messina, Grella, Cartier, & Torres, 2010). In supervision as well as in treatment, therapists must deal with frequent crises, low self-esteem, and the dynamics of blaming, forgetting, feeling isolation, and losing control. And as researchers note, the victimizations that women experience earlier in life may lead to greater criminal involvement.

Some experts argue that substance abuse therapies like domestic-violence treatment programs should separate clients by gender, as men and women may have different circumstances contributing to their dysfunctional lifestyles.

For these clients, different law enforcement, sentencing, and treatment plans might be more appropriate (Bloom, 1999; Shearer, 2003). This concept has been termed "gender-responsive treatment" (GRT). Conflict and feminist perspectives have claimed that the failure to adopt gender-specific strategies is part of the patriarchal social structure that pervades not only our responses to female drug use but our theoretical consideration of it as well (Goode, 1999).

Access to Treatment

Officials often use evaluative criteria in determining who should be directed to drug treatment, particularly when there are not enough treatment programs, beds, or funds available to serve all those in need. Motivation and the desire to be in treatment is one of those factors, and given the consequences of losing one's children and one's freedom, women are most often eager to be involved in rehabilitation programs.

One of the major criticisms of drug prevention and treatment programs is that they have operated with a "unisex, one-size-fits-both-sexes mentality" (Califano, in Barrett, 2003). To be more effective, the design of such efforts should consider differing risk factors as well as patterns of use and abuse in women over time. Ideally, the goal would be to address as many of the social and personal problems contributing to substance abuse as possible. What we find in reality is that programs are more likely to address only the most critical health issues and to react in ways that do not promote the maintenance of the independent family unit.

Many of the more intensive drug treatment programs are residential, and it is a challenge to find any of these willing to accept children (Miller, 2002), which limits the options available to single parents. Other criticisms of drug treatment programs are that they are difficult to attend because of transportation problems, they are too short, and they do not offer enough transition services to needed social resources such as housing, skills development, jobs, and assistance with child care. Many programs require health insurance to subsidize the costs of drug treatment which some women may not be able to obtain, or obtain quickly enough to avoid discouragement. Spotty employment, poor record keeping, and frequent moves may make eligibility status hard to verify.

Drug courts are perhaps a viable option for female offenders but have been dominated by male offenders (Belenko, 2001) and, at least in their first decade, were not particularly successful (Nolan, 1998; Hoffman, 2000). Even now, though there is greater acknowledgment of drug court success, the factors that create that success are still in question (Nored & Carlan, 2008) and are even less likely to be known for women than men. Unfortunately, many women do not receive comprehensive drug treatment until they are incarcerated, and even at that time, there is competition for limited programming resources.

A number of gender-responsive treatment programs have been developed over the past decade and have had some promising results. In one evaluation, participants were divided randomly into two groups, one with traditional drug treatment and another with a GRT format. Comparisons at intake, 6 months, and 12 months after treatment found that while both groups had similar mental health outcomes, the GRT group "had greater reductions in drug use, were more likely to remain in residential aftercare longer, and were less likely to have been re-incarcerated within 12 months after parole" (Messina et al., 2010, p. 97).

Treatment for AIDS

Research indicates that women drug users, particularly those who engage in prostitution for drugs, are more likely to contract HIV/AIDs than men who engage in similar high-risk behaviors (Freeman, Rodriguez, & French, 1994). Female inmates also have higher rates of HIV and AIDS than men with about 2.5% of female jail inmates and 3.5% of female prison inmates classified as HIV-positive (Hammett, Harmon, & Maruschak, 1999). And, as Mahan (1996) explains, women entering prison have higher rates of HIV infections, which are exacerbated by the low level of medical services available in most institutions.

There are many possible strategies for reducing the spread of AIDS infections. According to officials, injecting drug use, one of the primary causes of AIDS, could be reduced by needle exchange programs and the use of safe injection facilities (that would replace crack houses where violence, victimization, and the spread of disease have been prevalent). Health officials also call for the provision of male and female condoms, onsite counseling and testing for HIV and hepatitis, the provision of alcohol and bleach, and screening for tuberculosis and other sexually transmitted diseases (U.S. Centers for Disease Control and Prevention, 2001).

Mental Health, Abuse, and Family Support Issues

As with drug courts and battered women's shelters, most drug treatment facilities and outpatient programs do not accommodate the mentally ill. Given the complex abuse histories of many women, it is often common to find severe personality disorders and dissociative illnesses whose treatment most professionals would argue takes precedent over drug treatment. In fact, drug use is often characterized as a symptom of these psychic disturbances and viewed as a coping mechanism, a strategy for dealing with pain and suffering that must be dealt with outside of normal drug treatment curricula.

Other drug treatment strategies may involve family therapy or periods during which the patient is guided in attempting to repair relationships damaged by drug use and criminal activity. Incarcerated women may have more difficulty using these techniques because of physical and resource limitations. With far fewer female prisons, there is a greater likelihood that children and other family members live too far away to visit or participate in treatment sessions. Foster and even custodial relatives may be unwilling to promote relationships between female prisoners and their children. Many children, particularly teenagers, are angry at their mothers for the pain and separation they are experiencing and cut off communications, which often causes the prisoner to lose hope and drop out of programming. At the same time, research has determined the risks for youngsters include abuse, emotional problems, school failure, and association with delinquent peers (Hoffmann, Byrd, & Kightlinger, 2010). With 1.7 million children coping with a parent behind bars, advocates are campaigning for more comprehensive, family-based approaches to drug treatment.

Policy Responses and Implications

Laws Affecting Female Drug Offenders

There are three areas of drug law with potential impact on women in ways that are different from their impact on men. Although most law equally affects men and women, as is the case with mandatory minimums, mandatory treatment, and asset forfeiture, other areas such as pregnancy and the termination of parental rights are directed almost exclusively at women.

Pregnancy

Data from 2009 reflect that over 13,000 babies were born exhibiting signs of drug withdrawal (Associated Press, 2012). Hospital reports indicate that this finding has increased in the last decade from about 1 per 1,000 infants to 3 per 1,000. According to Mahan (1996), laws regulating pregnant female drug users fall into three categories: those addressing the use of narcotics itself (such as delivering a controlled substance to a minor), those criminalizing more general behaviors such as fetal endangerment and fetal abuse, and those regulating the conduct of informants such as health care workers who come into contact with pregnant women who may be abusing drugs.

Drug war rhetoric exploited the concept of illicit drug use and fetal abuse. One highly sensational report claimed that pregnant crack-cocaine users were delivering over 100,000 extremely damaged "crack babies" a year. The first studies (Chasoff, Hunt, & Kletter, 1986; Riley, Brodsky, & Porat, 1988) reporting on the negative effects of maternal use of crack failed to control for various other drugs (such as alcohol and tobacco), unhealthy behaviors, and socioeconomic factors. Subsequent medical studies have responded with reliable indications that pregnancy issues related to crack cocaine were misrepresented and exaggerated (Bauchner et al., 1988; Hurt et al., 1997; Zucherman & Frank, 1992). They also demonstrated that the negative effects were approximately the same as those derived from tobacco use during pregnancy (Jacobson et al., 1994; Zucherman, Frank, & Hingson, 1989). Research has indicated that given intensive prenatal care, even serious cocaine users show significant improvements in fetal health and development (Youchah & Freda, 1995). Regardless of the research, drug policy makers have continued to repeat the crack-baby claims and politicians have used the hysteria to support criminal laws specifically focusing on pregnant women with drugs found in their systems.

In *Ferguson v. City of Charleston*, the Supreme Court struck down a local policy that allowed women receiving prenatal care to be surreptitiously screened for drugs and arrested if the tests were positive. A local hospital had advertised the prenatal care program for those on welfare and then, at the urging of the prosecutor's office, reported any evidence of drug use. The justices refused to find a "special needs" exception when the intent of the test appeared to be the furthering of prosecution. Such a search was deemed unreasonable, as the patient had not consented to that type of procedure (Leslie, 2001). Further, it appears that the Court echoed the sentiment of research that associated prosecution for substance abuse with avoidance of prenatal medical care and social services, resulting in potentially harmful behavior by pregnant women (Coles, 1990; Koren et al., 1992; Poland et al., 1993).

Changes in Texas law illustrate how prosecutors interpret legislation that the courts must subsequently review and rule on, which is often a lengthy process for an adjudicated defendant. As Sagatun-Edwards explains:

> In 2004, Texas made it a felony to smoke marijuana while pregnant, with a prison sentence of 2 to 20 years.... Likewise, state lawmakers recently amended Texas law to redefine the term "individual" to mean "a human being who is alive, including an unborn child at every stage of gestation from fertilization to birth...." In one county, the district attorney interpreted the civil child abuse law to mean that physicians were required to report all pregnant drug-abusing women to local law enforcement officials. This resulted in the arrest of over a dozen women who allegedly used an illegal drug while pregnant. However, in 2005, the Texas attorney general concluded that the county district attorney's interpretation of the Texas law was wrong, and that physicians were not required to report (Sagatun-Edwards, 2007, p. 352).

In New York, a judge ordered a couple, both drug-addicted and living in the streets, to stop having children after the woman was forced to give up her fourth child. Although arguably both parents could be jailed if the woman, Stephanie, becomes pregnant in contempt of the court, it is the status of the woman as pregnant that is the basis for the punitive sanction (Dobbins, 2004). Many hailed the judge's ruling as significant in its attempt to ensure that children have caring parents and a home, but others saw it as a direct infringement on human rights. Ironically, two weeks before the Family Court's ruling was handed down, it was already determined that Stephanie was pregnant again.

On the other hand, there is little political concern about an estimated 12,000 infants who are born each year with symptoms related to fetal alcohol syndrome (Kelly, 2003). This condition appears to pose more serious, long-term effects than cocaine exposure. It is important to note, however, that there is disagreement about what the term "fetal alcohol syndrome" specifically means. There is also disagreement about the degree of impairment that is directly attributed to alcohol use versus other behaviors associated with alcohol, use such as poor diet, lack of prenatal monitoring, and poverty. Similarly, the effects of smoking tobacco during pregnancy do not seem to create social concern, even though there is substantial evidence of various types of harm to the fetus and even an increased risk of diabetes (Montgomery & Ekborn, 2002).

In an attempt to address social concerns about the perceived "costs" of a social problem like drug use in pregnancy and perhaps to justify expenditures on treatments and interventions, researchers have attempted to quantify the amount of money related to the various types of substance abuse. The direct and indirect economic costs can be substantial[2] but not necessarily different from those presented by alcohol or tobacco.

Asset Forfeiture and Zero-Tolerance Policies

Originally designed as a way to undermine the advantages of wealthy drug lords, asset forfeiture laws have become what critics describe as an overused mechanism for harassing and intimidating the poor. Over the years, the courts' tolerance for liberal asset-forfeiture policies has resulted in many law enforcement agencies becoming dependent on the supplemental resources provided by confiscated funds. According to Miller and Selva (1994), the result was that law enforcement agencies tended to engage more in asset hunting than in traditional strategies for reducing drug trafficking. In 1999, the total of U.S. government civil asset forfeitures was $957 million (Gibson & Huriash, 2000).

When female drug offenders, and women who live with men who are targeted for drug-related arrests, are faced with asset forfeiture, they may lose not only their homes but also access to transportation, work, and a secure environment for their children. One of the unintended consequences of these harsh policies is the impact on non-drug-offending family members, particularly children who may even end up in foster care. For example, the California Safe Streets and Anti Terrorism Act was initially written with strict measures to confiscate the property of suspected gang members. However, the likelihood of mothers and caretakers losing their homes and assets was brought to the attention of lawmakers and the measure was not passed until these provisions were removed. Zero-tolerance policies relating to drug use in public housing also affect women in the same way and endanger the stability of living arrangements for family members.

Termination of Parental Rights

Family law has traditionally decided cases based on the principle of *parens patriae*, which asserts the state's ultimate right to exercise an urgent interest in the welfare of the child and fulfill its duty to protect that child. Under this doctrine the court will determine the "best interests of the child," which more recently has been through the assistance of a guardian or advocate who would speak on the child's behalf. With the passing of the *Uniform Marriage and Divorce Act*, the relevant factors used in making custody decisions include specific health concerns, and this is

---

[2] See, for instance, http://www1.spa.american.edu/justice/publications/babies.pdf

where the dangers of exposure to drugs and drug use are weighed (Chinnock, 2003).

Women under evaluation for possible termination of parental rights are often assessed in terms of "cumulative environmental risk" to their children. Thus, officials may weigh any number of home factors including the physical and mental health of the parents; amount of space and cleanliness of the living areas; ability to provide meals, adequate clothing, schooling, and health care; presence of physical and mental health risks; weapons; drug use; and potential sexual victimization.

The *Adoption and Safe Families Act of 1997* (Public Law 105-89) limits the time between the placement of a child in foster care and the processing of the petition to terminate a parent's rights. Goldfarb (2002) argues that this will likely speed up the rate at which female drug offenders, particularly those who are incarcerated, will lose their children. Given the connection between physical and sexual abuse, subsequent mental problems, and substance abuse, there is a strong likelihood that a mother's drug conviction, paired with a history of previous abuse, will result in a termination of parental rights.

Besinger et al. (1999) examined the cases of over 600 children removed from their homes for maltreatment. Almost 80% of the caregivers in those cases were known to be substance abusers. Overall, though, it may be easier for officials to find neglect than actual maltreatment as a basis for terminating parental rights. Parents who are involved in a drug-centered lifestyle may neglect their children by leaving them unattended for hours at a time and leaving them without food. In other cases, exposure to the passive smoke of marijuana or other drugs such as cocaine, methamphetamine, or heroin may be considered abuse or maltreatment.

Media attention surrounding the presence of children in homes used as methamphetamine labs has led to changes in child protection policies and laws in many states. The highly toxic and potentially explosive chemicals used in the manufacturing process have caused a number of deaths and injuries, particularly in younger children. In California, Bureau of Narcotics Enforcement agents are required to contact social workers whenever children are found at a methamphetamine lab. Authorities are also encouraging child advocates to test clients for drugs and other health-related risks, as well as for evidence of child endangerment (Weikel, 1996).

Mandatory Minimum Sentences and Harsher Drug Laws

Harsher sentences for drug offenses, part of the drug war policies, have impacted women in direct and indirect ways. First, sentences for all types of drug-related crimes have increased. Incidents involving even smaller quantities of drugs are now charged as felonies, and subsequent offenses yield longer prison terms. And, a wider net has been cast over persons further removed from the actual criminal event, as by relationship and association others are drawn into the web of prosecution. For example, under the Rockefeller Drug Laws in New York, a judge must impose 15 years to life for anyone convicted of selling two ounces or more or possessing four ounces or more of cocaine or heroin. As the Families Against

Mandatory Minimums organization explains, many others who are caught in a nonviolent, low-level, addiction-related criminal pattern are also required to serve lengthy prison terms, and only the prosecutor, not the judge, is allowed to make placements in drug-treatment alternatives.

Under the California Street Terrorism and Enforcement Act, mothers whose children have been involved as gang members engaged in drug sales, or who have unknowingly benefitted from the profits of those drug sales, may be faced with criminal charges. All of these recent criminal enhancements and punitive sentencing measures have had a disparate impact on people of color. African American women appear to have been incarcerated for drug offenses at a much higher rate than White females (Harrison & Beck, 2002) and appear more likely to have been reported to child welfare agencies for prenatal drug abuse, although reported use rates were similar (Common Sense for Drug Policy, 2004; Sandy, 2003).

Conclusions

Women drug offenders are disproportionally represented in the criminal justice system. At the same time, they are overwhelmingly on the lower end of the drug seriousness spectrum. In many cases, their offenses are the product of roles undertaken in a male-dominated culture—as holders and purveyors of male drug property and paraphernalia. They have also been criminalized because of association with male drug users and sellers (especially gang members) and because of pregnancy. Much of this has less to do with an actual offense than with society's fear of a questionable drug epidemic and an overreaction to and politicization of that fear.

The reality of our drug concern has been that those guilty of minor drug offenses, and we have seen that women are overrepresented in that regard, have been given longer mandatory sentences normally reserved for serious and violent crimes. Meda Chesney-Lind (1997) is not far from the truth with her statement that the drug war is a war against women, primarily because it is women who have borne the brunt of harsh sentencing for minor drug offenses.

Politicians continue to focus on illegal drug use rather than the myriad other social problems plaguing our communities. Although smoking causes more deaths each year than alcohol, AIDS, cocaine, heroin, homicide, suicide, auto accidents, and fire accidents combined (National Institute on Drug Abuse, 2012), the pursuit of illegal drug offenders dominates our political and criminal justice system agenda. Despite the fact that alcohol is more likely to be related to serious birth defects than cocaine, laws continue to be devised that, purposefully or not, target poor, inner-city women.

Critics argue that the failures of the drug war should lead us to adopt more humanistic approaches, such as harm reduction efforts that involve treatment and education. From methadone to clean needles to prevention programs and a range of subsidized therapies, the suggestions contain the core elements of family-based, multi-agency, long-term neighborhood-level interventions. The lack of gender-specific services remains a serious defect in the rehabilitation and treatment field. As women appear to have different antecedents to drug use, patterns of substance abuse, barriers to treatment, and relapse triggers (Bloom, Owen, & Covington, 2003), many have advocated for more appropriate intervention strategies designed to create more effective outcomes.

Critical Thinking Questions

1. Should there be separate drug intervention strategies for women and for men? Why or why not?

2. Feminists argue that the "war on drugs" was a war on women. Do you agree? Why or why not?

3. What changes would you suggest for drug laws, enforcement policies, and treatment that would do more to reduce drug demands and support the needs of families?

Books, Websites, and Media Resources

http://www.aclu.org/files/images/asset_upload_file431_23513.pdf
http://www.drugabuse.gov/publications/topics-in-brief/prenatal-exposure-to-drugs-abuse
Drug Abuse Treatment Outcome Studies (DATOS): http://www.datos.org/
Families Against Mandatory Minimums: http://www.famm.org/

Popular Films

28 Days (2000), Sandra Bullock.
Traffic (2000), Michael Douglas, Benicio Del Toro, and Catherine Zeta-Jones.
When a man loves a woman (1994), Meg Ryan.

References

Associated Press. (2012, May 1). Newborns dependent on opiates rising. Houston Chronicle, p. A4.

Barrett, D. (2003, February 8). Females more vulnerable to addictions, study finds. Associated Press. Houston Chronicle, p. 2A.

Bauchner, H., Sucherman, B., McClain, M., Frank, D., Fried, L. E., & Kayne, H. (1988). Risk of sudden infant death syndrome among infants with in utero exposure to cocaine. Journal of Pediatrics, 113, 831-834.

Bednar, S. G. (2003). Substance abuse and women abuse: A proposal for integrated treatment. Federal Probation, 67(1), 52-57.

Belenko, S. (2001). *Research on drug courts: A critical review, 2001 Update.* New York: National Center on Addiction and Substance Abuse, Columbia University.

Belknap, J. (2001). *The invisible woman: Gender, crime and justice* (2nd ed.). Belmont, CA: Wadsworth.

Besinger, B. A., Garland, A. F., Litrownik, A. J., & Landsverk, J. A. (1999). Caregiver substance abuse among maltreated children placed in out-of-home care. *Child Welfare, 78,* 221-239.

Bloom, B. (1999). Gender-responsive programming for women offenders: Guiding principles and practices. *Forum on Corrections,* 11(3), 22-27.

Bloom, B., Chesney-Lind, M., & Owen, B. (1994). *Women in prison: Hidden victims of the war on drugs.* San Francisco, CA: Center on Juvenile & Criminal Justice. .

Bloom, B., Johnson, J., & Belzer, E. (2003, September/October). Effective management of female offenders. *American Jails* 4(17), 29-33.

Bloom, B., Owen, B., & Covington, S. (2003). *Gender-responsive strategies: Research, practice and guiding principles for women offenders.* Washington, DC: National Institute of Corrections.

Bonczar, T. (2003). *Prevalence of imprisonment in the U.S. Population, 1974-2001.*Washington, DC: Bureau of Justice Statistics.

Bonta, J., Pang, B., & Wallace-Capretta, S. (1995). Predictors of recidivism among incarcerated female offenders. *Prison Journal, 75,* 277-294.

Boyd, S. (1999). *Mothers and illicit drugs: Transcending the myths.* Toronto, Ontario, Canada: University of Toronto Press.

Carson, E. A., & Sabol, W. J. (2012, December). *Prisoners in 2011.* Washington, DC: U.S. Department of Justice, Bureau of Justice Statistics.

Chasoff, I. J., Hunt, C., & Kletter, R. (1986). Increased risk of SIDS and respiratory pattern abnormalities in cocaine-exposed infants. *Pediatric Research, 20,* 425A.

Chesney-Lind, M. (1997). Patriarchy, prisons, and jails: A critical look at trends in women's incarceration. In M. D. McShane & F. P. Williams (Eds.), *The Philosphy and Practice of Corrections* (pp. 71-87). New York: Garland.

Chinnock, W. F. (2003). No smoking around children: The family court's mandatory duty to restrain parents and other persons from smoking around children. *Arizona Law Review, 45,* 801-821.

Common Sense for Drug Policy. (2004). *Drug war facts: Impact of the drug war on families.* Retrieved from http://www.drugwarfacts.org

Department of Commerce, Economics and Statistics Administration (2011). *Women in America: Indicators of social and economic well-being.*Washington, DC: Office of Management and Budget.

Dobbins, B. (2004, Sunday, May 16). Judge tells couple to stop having children. *Houston Chronicle,* A, p. 8.

Fagan, J. (1994). Women and drugs revisited: Female participation in the cocaine economy. *Journal of Drug Issues, 24,* 179-225.

Ferguson v. City of Charleston, 121 S.Ct. 1281 (2001).

Freeman, R., Rodriguez, G., & French, J. (1994). A comparison of male and female intravenous drug users' risk behaviors for HIV infection. *American Journal of Drug and Alcohol Abuse,* 20(2), 129-157.

Gibson, W., & Huriash, L. (2000, April 11). Drug cops may be reined in: Congress is likely to make it harder for the government to take money, homes, cars and other items in drug cases. *Orlando Sentinel,* p. A1.

Glaze, L., & Maruschak, L. (2008, August). *Parents in prison and their minor children.* Bureau of Justice Statistics Special Report. Washington, DC: Bureau of Justice Statistics.

Goldfarb, P. (2002). Counting the drug war's female casualties. *Journal of Gender, Race and Justice, 6,* 277-296.

Goode, E. (1999). *Drugs in American society*(5th ed.). Boston: McGraw-Hill.

Hammett, T., Harmon, P., & Maruschak, L. (1999). *1996-1997 update: HIV/AIDS, STDs and TB in correctional facilities.* Washington, DC: National Institute of Justice.

Harrison, P. M., & Beck, A. (2002). *Prisoners in 2001.* Bureau of Justice Statistics Bulletin. Washington, DC: Office of Justice Programs.

Hoffmann, H., Byrd, A., & Kightlinger, A. (2010). Prison programs and services for incarcerated parents and their underage children: Results from a national survey of correctional facilities. *Prison Journal*, 90, 397-416.

Hoffman, M. B. (2000). The drug court scandal. *North Carolina Law Review*, 78, 1533-1534.

Holtfreter, K., Reisig, M., & Morash, M. (2004). Poverty, state capital, and recidivism among women offenders. *Criminology & Public Policy*, 3, 185-208.

Humphries, D. (1999). *Crack mothers: Pregnancy, drugs and the media*. Columbus, OH: Ohio State University Press.

Hurt, H., Malamud, E., Betancourt, L., Braitman, L. E., Brodsky, N. L., & Giannetta, J. (1997). Children with in utero cocaine exposure do not differ from control subjects on intelligence testing. *Archives of Pediatrics & Adolescent Medicine*, 151, 1237-1241.

Kelly, S. J. (2003). Cumulative environmental risk in substance abusing women: Early intervention, parenting stress, child abuse potential and child development. *Child Abuse & Neglect*, 27, 993-995.

Koren, G., Gladstone, D., Roberson, C., & Robieux, I. (1992). The perception of teratogenic risk of cocaine. *Teratology*, 46, 567-571.

Kruttschnitt, C. (2010, Summer). The paradox of women's imprisonment. *Daedalus*, 139(3), 32-42.

Kruttschnitt, C., & Gartner, R. (2003). Women's imprisonment. *Crime and Justice*, 30, 1-81.

Lapidus, L., Luthra, N., Verma, A., Small, D., Allard, P., & Levingston, K. (2005) *Caught in the net: The impact of drug policies on women & families*. Washington, DC: American Civil Liberties Union; Break the Chains: Communities of Color and the War on Drugs; and the Brennan Center at NYU School of Law.

Laudet, A. B., & Stanick, V. (2010). Predictors of motivation for abstinence at the end of outpatient substance abuse treatment. *Journal of Substance Abuse Treatment*, 38(4), 317-327.

Leslie, H. (2001). *Ferguson v. City of Charleston*: A limitation on the "special needs" doctrine. *Loyola Journal of Public Interest Law*, 3, 93-104.

Mahan, S. (1996). *Crack cocaine, crime and women*. Thousand Oaks, CA: Sage.

McShane, M., Williams, F. P., III, & Dolny, H. M. (2002). Do standard risk prediction instruments apply to female parolees? *Women & Criminal Justice*, 13, 163-182.

Messina, N., Grella, C., Cartier, J., & Torres, S. (2010). A randomized experimental study of gender responsive substance abuse treatment for women in prison. *Journal of Substance Abuse Treatment*, 38, 97-107.

Miller, A. F. (2002). Substance abuse treatment for women with children. In H. T. Wilson (Ed.), *Annual editions: Drugs, society and behavior*(17th ed., pp. 210-213). Guilford, CT: McGraw-Hill/Dushkin.

Miller, J. M., & Selva, L. H. (1994). Drug enforcement's double-edged sword: An assessment of asset forfeiture programs. *Justice Quarterly*, 11, 314-335.

Montgomery, S. M., & Ekborn, A. (2002). Smoking during pregnancy and diabetes mellitus in a British longitudinal birth cohort. *British Medical Journal*, 324, 26-27.

Mumola, C. (2000). *Incarcerated parents and their children*. Washington, DC: U.S. Department of Justice, Bureau of Justice Statistics.

National Institute on Drug Abuse (2012). What are the medical consequences of tobacco use? Retrieved online, 2 January 2014 from http://www.drugabuse.gov/publications/research-reports/tobacco-addiction/what-are-medical-consequences-tobacco-use

Nolan, J. L. (1998). *The therapeutic state*. New York: New York University Press.

Nored, L. S., & Carlan, P. E. (2008). Success of drug court programs: Examination of the perceptions of drug court personnel. *Criminal Justice Review*, 33, 329-342.

Norland, S., & Mann, P. J. (1984). Being troublesome: Women on probation. *Criminal Justice and Behavior*, 11, 115-135.

Poland, M. L., Dombrowski, M. P., Ager, J. W., & Sokol, R. J. (1993). Punishing pregnant drug users: Enhancing the flight from care. *Drug and Alcohol Dependence*, 31, 199-203.

Rigert, J. (1997, December 15). Some win fight with depression, others lose. *Minneapolis Star Tribune*.

Riley, J. G., Brodsky, N. L., & Porat, R. (1988). Risk for SIDS in infants with in utero cocaine exposure: A prospective study. *Pediatric Research, 23,* 454A.

Sagatun-Edwards, I. (2007). Legal and social welfare response to substance abuse during pregnancy: Recent developments. In R. Muraskin (Ed.), *It's a crime: Women and justice* (4th ed., Chap. 21, pp. 346-362). Upper Saddle River, NJ: Prentice Hall.

Sandy, K. (2003). The discrimination inherent in America's Drug War: Hidden racism revealed by examining the hysteria over crack. *Alabama Law Review, 54,* 665-693.

Shearer, R. (2003). Identifying the special needs of female offenders. *Federal Probation, 67*(1), 46-51.

Shelden, R. (2006). How the drug war targets women. Retrieved from http://www.shelden-says.com/Com-sixty-seven.htm

Snyder, H. N. (2012, October). *Arrest in the United States, 1990-2010.* Washington, DC: U.S. Department of Justice, Bureau of Justice Statistics.

U.S. Centers for Disease Control and Prevention. (2001, May 18). Update: Syringe exchange programs—United States, 1998. *Morbidity and Mortality Weekly Report, 50,* 385.

Van Voorhis, P. (2012). On behalf of women offenders: Women's place in the science of evidence-based practice. *Criminology & Public Policy, 11,* 111-145.

Weikel, D. (1996, Sunday, April 7). Meth labs: How young lives are put in peril. *Los Angeles Times,* pp. A1, A18-19.

West, H. C., & Sabol, W. J. (2011). *Prisoners in 2009.* Bureau of Justice Statistics Bulletin—Revised. Washington, DC: Office of Justice Programs.

Youchah, C., & Freda, M C. (1995). Cocaine use during pregnancy and low birth weight: The impact of prenatal care and drug treatment. *Seminars in Perinatology, 19,* 293-300.

Zhang, Z. (2003). *Drug and alcohol use and related matters among arrestees.* Chicago: National Opinion Research Center, Arrestee Drug Use Monitoring Program.

Zucherman, B., & Frank, D. (1992). "Crack kids": Not broken. *Pediatrics, 89,* 337-339.

Zucherman, B., Frank, D. A., & Hingson, R. (1989). Effects of maternal marijuana and cocaine use on fetal growth. *New England Journal of Medicine, 320,* 762-768.

8

Women and Corrections

Introduction

If you were to observe an early American reformatory for women, you might have been struck by the simplicity of the treatment and the dormitory nature of the surroundings. A director of the Framingham, Massachusetts, Reformatory for Women was said to have remarked that they did not release a woman until she could bake bread. Katherine Davis, a pioneering women's superintendent, wrote an article entitled "The Fresh Air Treatment for Moral Disease" (Harris, 1988) that seems to be linked to more modern notions of taking delinquents out to rural wilderness camps for interventions.

Framingham State was one of the first prisons built for women in the United States, and it is now one of the oldest operating in this country. During its first year in 1877, writer Cristina Rathbone tells us, more than half of the 246 women there were incarcerated just for being drunk. She goes on to describe the population at that time:

> A third were prostitutes. Seventy-six were petty thieves or shoplifters, . . . thirty-one were vagrants. Six, that first year alone, were convicted for "being stubborn." Ten for being lewd and for "cohabitation." Three were in for something called "simple fornication" and only two for assault. Just one woman was there for attempting murder; one also, for breaking glass. One for being idle, one for begging, and one for "committing" an abortion (Rathbone, 2005, p. 24).

The historical data on the Framingham facility are typical of that era. Prison records from across the country find women held for being pickpockets or "sneaks," for crimes of confidence, and for offenses against chastity (common night walking), forgery, or shoplifting.

The Female Prison Population Today

Women today represent about one quarter of those arrested for crimes in this country and also one-quarter of those on probation (Davidson, 2009; FBI, 2011). According to Walmsley (2009), female incarceration rates worldwide are similar with women representing 2 to 9% of inmates in at least 80% of prison systems. This is another good indication of the stability of the gender gap discussed in Chapter 2.

Overall, statistics indicate that the growth of the female prison population has outpaced that of their male counterparts in almost all areas of the country. According to one report (Women's Prison Association, 2009), the number of females serving state prison sentences increased 832% in the period from 1977 to 2007, while the men's state prison population increased 416%. Data also indicate that in mountain states such as Colorado, Montana, and Idaho, women represented over 10% of the incarcerated population, while the national average is still about 7% (Guerino, Harrison, & Sabol, 2011, p. 14). Drugs are often cited as the reason for the dramatic increases across the south and west. The highest per capita incarceration rate for women is in Oklahoma (129 per 100,000 residents, though Mississippi runs a close second at 107 for every 100,000 residents (AP, May 21, 2006).

As a rule, in this country, males are more likely to be incarcerated (943 per 100,000) than females (67 per 100,000) (Guerino et al., 2011). Of females at risk for incarceration, data indicate that Black women are more likely to be incarcerated than either Hispanic or White women. Data from 2010 show that Black, non-Hispanic females were three times more likely to serve time in prison than women who were White or non-Hispanic (Guerino et al., 2011). When you examine the backgrounds of female offenders, you will find that most were raised in a single-parent household and at the time of their incarceration had been raising young children alone (Bloom, Owen, & Covington, 2004; Glaze & Maruschak, 2008; La Vigne, Brooks, & Schollenberger, 2009; Mackintosh, Myers, & Kennon, 2006). About half had a family member with an incarceration history. A significant number of women had been physically or sexually abused or had come from a background of poverty and neglect (Lombardo & Smith, 1996; O'Brien, 2001).

In 2005, there were over 3,200 persons on death row in the United States, including 52 women (Snell, 2006). Today, women represent about 8% of those incarcerated (including federal and state prison populations) and 12.7% of the jail population (Minton, 2012). The number of women in prison appears to be growing faster than the number of men, and federal prison increases are greater than those of the individual state prisons. In fact, recent data from the Bureau of Justice Statistics indicate that the number of women incarcerated decreased slightly between 2008 and 2009, which they attributed mostly to declines in the number of women in state custody (Guerino et al., 2011).

The profile of adult female offenders has also changed over the years. In 1975 women were primarily incarcerated for larceny, forgery, embezzlement, and prostitution. By 1995, offenses were more likely to be drug related or larceny. The percentage of women incarcerated for a drug offense rose dramatically in the period from 1986 (12%) to 1991 (33%) (U.S. Dept of Justice, 1994), most likely as a consequence of the war on drugs in the 1980s. Still, more recent data indicate that drug offenses now have dropped to 26% of women serving more than one year of incarceration. Property offenses make up another 30%, and crimes of violence constitute the greatest percentage of that group at 36% (Guerino et al., 2011).

Female Facilities: When Less Is Less

Because there are far fewer female inmates than male, there are also far fewer facilities for them to be housed in. This means that units are more likely to be generalized and house a wider range of offenders than do male facilities. Specialized male units have been developed to meet special needs and to consolidate the provision of services as well as allow staff to become more experienced in handling certain types of inmates. For example, in the Texas Department of Corrections, there are separate male units for developmentally disabled offenders, the mentally ill, the shorter-term prisoner, the lifers and the very old, the very young, para- and quadriplegics, and so forth. Yet in Texas and across the country, there are no counterparts to these perhaps more appropriate classification models in female facilities. Consequently, the interactions of so many diverse female offender types in the same facility are often difficult not only for staff to manage but for inmates to adjust to.

One of the hardest adjustments for females in prison is that in many states there is no separate housing for mentally ill offenders. As George (2010) indicates, daily problems arise when mentally ill prisoners are blended into the general population:

> Then there was Lorna, an unmedicated paranoid schizophrenic who was housed with a series of blameless elderly ladies all of whom (according to Lorna) were dedicated to destroying her property, stealing from her, and urinating in her shampoo when she left the room. When Lorna was finally removed, the entire wing heaved a collective sigh of relief. Not even the officers had been able to ignore it when she popped out of her room one night and smeared used sanitary pads over the walls of the bathroom (George, 2010, pp. 40-41).

Today, a number of treatment programs inside institutions attempt to directly address substance abuse, mental health, and family reunification planning. Drug treatment initiatives such as therapeutic communities (i.e., the KEY program in Delaware) or residential efforts (the Forever Free program in California, for example) do offer a separate housing area for the few who meet the criteria for these programs, thus facilitating re-entry into the community. In addition to work release initiatives, many offer anger management, relapse prevention, and parenting instruction that may allow women to regain custody of their children upon their release (NIJ, 2005).

A Female Inmate Subculture

It can be said that prison culture is not shaped solely by inmates; rather it is also a product of interactions with both administrative style and correctional officers. Criminologist Barbara Owen (1998) uses the term "in the mix" to describe the complex and challenging cultural context that female inmates must survive both outside prison and while incarcerated. From her three years of observational research and 294 inmate interviews at the Central California Women's Facility (CCWF), she concluded that pre-prison experiences, such as patriarchy and socioeconomic disadvantage, not only contribute to female criminality but also affect the nature of the prison climate. This "pain of life" shapes their choices and resistance to change, as criminality is a way of survival that also influences their adaptation to prison and the prison culture itself. This is a much broader view of a prison subculture than the model proposed by Gresham Sykes (1958), where only the "pains of imprisonment" and the deprivations of the immediate environment were thought to define the motivations and behaviors within the male prisoner experience.

For Owen (1998), the prison culture of female inmates served three functions: (1) to negotiate the prison world with a "juice" approach (successfully and uneventfully getting work done) and to gain respect and reputation; (2) to develop styles of doing time by adhering to the convict code; and (3) to avoid the "mix," which refers to not being involved in trouble (i.e., hustling and conflicting with other inmates or staff, or becoming involved in drug use).

Former lifer, Erin George (2010) explains the stresses of trying to avoid some types of inmate conflicts, particularly through the unsettling randomness of roommate assignments she encountered living in the general population (GP):

> I had a series of semipsychotic roommates. One of them, Shandra would scream at me if I tried to open my storage bins while she was sleeping. And because she seemed to sleep 20 hours out of 24 . . . I was yelled at a lot. . . . Delilah was a master of the passive-aggressive. . . . She amped up her attacks quickly after I moved in. Fingernail clippings would appear in my water cup. My radio was accidentally brushed off my desk. Appointment slips or mail that was slipped under the door by an officer while I was asleep would disappear before they reached me. Delilah was the only roommate that I've ever actually feared. She possessed a volatile combination of religious mania and sociopathy that is only exacerbated by close confinement (George, 2010, pp. 40-41).

Greer (2000) feels that mistrust best explains why many female inmates are reluctant to form friendships in prison. Her research found that a number of women saw their counterparts in the subculture as self-serving and manipulative, particularly in terms of seeking out economic benefits. Still, Owen (1998) observed that "play families" among inmates, as a distinct aspect of women's prison culture, reflected their need for "emotional, practical, and material" attachment (p. 134). Family ties in the free world could support them throughout the prison term, whereas "losing family" was described as one of the "hardest things" about serving time (p. 126).

Mothers as Prisoners

The concept of children being cared for in the prison by the mother is not new. In English prisons of the 1700s, mothers were permitted to keep their children with them despite the harsh and unsanitary conditions. This practice continued until the 1850s when only those actually born in prison were allowed to be raised there. As the evolution of penal philosophy considered separate rehabilitative initiatives for women, reformers such as Elizabeth Fry were able to establish mother/child programs in a number of institutions (Craig, 2009). Though this idea was not adopted by early American prison officials, most states have utilized at least parts of this concept over the years.

In a Massachusetts institution from 1858 until 1958, women were allowed to keep their children with them. Volunteer nurses helped with the children during the day while the mother worked, and then the mother cared for her own child throughout the evening. Children remained with their mothers up until anywhere from 18 months to three years (Boudouris, 1985).

Today there is tremendous variation across the states in how the issue of incarcerated mothers is treated. New York is one of the most progressive in terms of programs that are oriented toward preserving bonds between a mother and her children despite incarceration. There are three prisons in that state that have nurseries, and Bedford Hills, the oldest of the facilities, hosts a summer camp where children can spend days with their mothers while staying with host families in the area at night. That program has been a model for innovative treatments that include parenting classes, prerelease unification efforts, and halfway houses upon release:

> Sister Elaine Roulet, 67, a Catholic nun who has been director of the Children's Center at Bedford Hills for 28 of its 96 years, says no baby has ever been hurt in the nursery. "The babies don't know they are in prison," she says. "The babies know that they are with the person who is significant, and that's where they should be." What is a crime is "to snatch the babies from their mothers" (Meyer, 1997, p. A5).

Advocates argue that the highly supervised programs provide a training ground where mothers learn not only parenting and prenatal care, but the responsibility of working in the day-care facility, completing education requirements, and earning high school and vocational degrees. According to Meyer (1997, p. A5):

> Each baby costs the state $4,000 per year ... (which is) cheaper than foster care. ... The babies can stay 18 months. Gina Worley, 37 and the mother of

twins, is serving 3.5 to 7 years at Taconic for criminal possession of a controlled substance. Impregnated by a rapist, Worley says, she kept her children so they would not go through the emotional, physical and sexual abuse she did in the foster care system.

The California-based Family Foundations Program combines supportive social service assistance for inmates with young children including parent training. Programs like this also exist in Kansas, Georgia, Nebraska, Texas, and Missouri. For the same cost as regular incarceration, women are supervised as they learn to effectively parent their small children; receive treatment, education, and skills training; and maintain highly disciplined schedules. It is the intent of the state to break the cycle that has had generations of children following their mothers into lives of delinquency and crime (http://www.cdcr.ca.gov/Adult_Operations/FOPS/index.html). Data seem to indicate that children whose parents are incarcerated are more than six times more likely to eventually end up in the justice system than other children (Mehren, 1996).

Currently, about 70% of women prisoners have one or more children under the age of 18. In California the number is closer to 80%. A clear majority of these women had custody of their children prior to their incarceration and most were single mothers (Mackintosh et al., 2006). About half of the children will be able to stay with a grandparent while their mother is incarcerated, some will go to the father or another relative, and about 10% will enter foster care.

Visiting Incarcerated Mothers

For a number of reasons, imprisoned mothers can find the in-prison visits of their children to be a particularly stressful event. Although the mothers strongly desire to see their children, there are possible detrimental effects associated with the visit. First, some parents do not want their children to see the negative aspects of prison. According to Stanton (1980, p. 65), one mother was angered because her ex-husband brought the child to see her in jail. In her mind, the purpose was to humiliate her in front of the child and to make the child embarrassed about her because her ex planned to marry and seek permanent custody of the child.

Second, even if they do overcome their reservations about children visiting in the prison setting, the children's caretakers or guardians frequently will not bring them to prison despite the mother's wishes. Often this is because the visitation experience itself is so frustrating. As one visiting sister explained, "The day would begin at 9:00 AM and it would take hours to get to the prison and fill out all the papers. Sometimes we wouldn't get into the visiting room until 2:00 PM. Since we couldn't take in any food, we'd have to eat from the vending machines in the prison. Sometimes it cost forty or fifty dollars to visit" (Coralia G. in Bloom & Steinhart, 1993).

Sometimes guardians who are trying to win the affection of the child encourage the separation (Stanton, 1980, p. 65). Finally, some children react very emotionally when the visit ends and cry and resist leaving their mother, making the visit very traumatic for both parties and difficult for the mother to attempt again. This is more likely the case when visits were short and no contact is allowed (Stanton, 1980). When measuring mothers' reactions to child visits in a jail, Stanton (1980, p. 56) found that 38% of the mothers were positive and 36% were negative about the visits, the rest were somewhat ambivalent. Women were more likely to be positive about younger children's visits and more apprehensive about the bad example or image it symbolized to older children. The author concludes that "visits appear to be more important in reassuring school-age children about their mom's welfare."

Mothers may also keep in touch with their children by writing letters and through phone calls. In a study of incarcerated mothers, letters were identified as the main form of contact, followed by phone calls, and only 28% said that their main contact was through visits. Over 50% said that they never had a visit with their children during their incarceration (Bloom & Steinhart, 1993). This may be because grandparents or other older relatives do not have cars, or the money, or the time to arrange visits that may involve travel to facilities hours away from their homes. Baunach (1979, p. 121) concludes that when mothers lose contact with their children through incarceration, it may heighten their understanding of their own behavior and its effects on their children. This may be especially true for mothers who have been involved in drugs or alcohol for prolonged periods. In many cases, incarceration provides them with a chance to step back and take stock of the experiences their children have endured.

According to Stanton (1980), incarcerated mothers often have very unrealistic and ideological perceptions of their roles and exaggerate their maternal anxiety and concern. Many prison managers do not approve of children spending increased amounts of time with their mothers or having babies live in with them because the prisoners already have enough personal and adjustment problems in prison. Still, many correctional administrators, judges, and policy makers express concern at the rate at which children of female offenders ended up behind bars themselves and continue to look for effective interventions.

One such intervention, the Girl Scouts Behind Bars Program has been implemented in a number of states. The program, as Elizabeth Mehren (1996, p. 1) of the *Los Angeles Times* explains, represents "a steady wave of social awareness measures that include troops for homeless girls, pregnant teens, the daughters of migrant workers and girls in foster care." At California's Norco facility, mothers are required to first complete a course in parenting before they can participate. Alabama's Tutwiler Prison also allows boys to take part in this program as the Girl Scouts have amended their rules to include them (Johnson, 2001). Girls Inc., another large organization that was formerly known as the Girls Clubs of America, also has branched into juvenile justice intervention.

Most prison visitation regulations have strict guidelines about the terms of child visits. Because the ratio of supervisors to inmates and visitors is higher when children are present, it represents an additional expense for the institution. In most cases, the child must be a natural offspring or stepchild of the prisoner, cannot be a child for whom the prisoner's parental rights have been terminated, and must be accompanied by a family member or guardian (although no one with a prior incarceration record is likely to be approved for visits). Further restrictions and the right to bar certain people from visiting if they represent a legitimate risk to the orderly operation of the facility still remain in the discretionary power of wardens.

Some of the most difficult aspects of prison visitation for prisoners and their families to adjust to are the lack of privacy, the inability in many instances to have any physical contact, and the fact that visitors are all subject to searches. Many inmates reject the process of visitation because it often means long waits for visitors in holding areas before prisoners are brought out, and there is a high likelihood of subjecting their loved ones to humiliating pat downs. As Belbot and Hemmens (2011) explain, visitors may be required to submit to a strip search or body cavity search if officials have a reasonable suspicion that the visitor is carrying or transferring contraband. Both correctional officer observations and informant tips may be used to meet the standard of reasonable suspicion:

> Visitors may be searched both when they enter the prison and when they are leaving it, in order to prevent the flow of contraband either into or out of the prison. If a visitor does not wish to be searched, he or she may refuse and simply leave without entering the institution. By entering a prison, visitors implicitly consent to being searched before they leave the prison (Belbot & Hemmens, 2011, p. 95).

For inmates, the various conditions that give rise to the various types of searches are well known and are a normal part of their institutional lives. This is not true for visitors and can be an unpleasant experience.

Cross-Gender Pat Downs and Strip Searches

Although there is no expectation of privacy within a prison, the courts have periodically heard cases regarding the way searches are carried out and under what conditions. As a rule, pat-down searches and body-cavity observations can be done routinely and randomly, and the court requires only that they be carried out according to reasonable written policies that fit the security needs of the institution. No particular degree of suspicion need be met to instigate one of these searches, and this is also true for the use of equipment such as scanners and metal detectors or the use of scientific tests such as drug and alcohol screens. In order to justify a digital body-cavity search, because of its more severe level of intrusion, Belbot and Hemmens (2011) explain, a reasonable suspicion must be present.

The need for various levels of searches to ensure the proper order and safety of an institution is well substantiated by the courts, but cross-gender searches are more controversial. Limited staffing resources have simply not allowed administrators the ability to assign all women to the more intrusive searches of females or all men to the searches of males. In many rulings, judges have made the determination that the female employee's right to have equal opportunities in corrections supersedes most inmate concerns about privacy in the conduct of searches. With male institutions vastly outnumbering female facilities, it would be constitutionally unreasonable to not allow women to assume all the same responsibilities as male officers, particularly as assignments in the more danger-ous, high-security areas are critical to promotion in the field. In fact, prison administrators have effectively argued in court that prohibiting adult magazines with frontal nudity is permissible as it serves a number of safety and security goals within an institution including reducing the amount of sexual harassment female officers may encounter (*Mauro v. Arpaio*, 188 F. 3d 1054, 1999).

Usually, however, wardens are able to make special arrangements when exi-gent circumstances exist. For example, when female inmates with histories of abuse and sexual assault are further traumatized by being touched by males, or in the case of religious prohibitions against females touching males, only same-sex correctional officers can be assigned. The idea of assigning female officers to pat down or strip-search Muslim men has recently become more problematic as it represents a freedom of religion issue and is something that may be interpreted as actionable under the *Religious Land Use and Institutionalized Persons Act* of 2000.

Female Prison Subculture: Reality versus Film Fantasy

In three classic studies of women in prison, similar findings formed the basis of what has been called the female inmate subculture. Ward and Kassebaum (1965), Giallombardo (1966), and Heffernan (1972) agreed that distinct fea-tures of the female incarceration experience differentiated it from the experi-ences of institutionalized males and were deserving of their own, separate analysis (Owen, 1998). These early researchers postulated that "prison culture among women was tied to gender role expectations of sexuality and family; and prison identities were at least partially based on outside identities and experi-ences" (Owen, 1998, p. 4). Owen argues from her research two decades later that little has really changed. "Personal relationships with other prisoners, both emotionally and physically intimate, connections to family and loved ones in the free community . . . and commitments to pre-prison identities continue to shape the contemporary prison culture" (Owen, 1998, p. 4).

The concept of female inmates developing pseudo-families is well documen-ted in the literature. Bowker (1981) believed that this was because women had stronger family instincts and felt the void of losing family more strongly than men; consequently, he felt that women were compelled to fill those needs with relationships developed inside prison. This fits with the general model proposed by Gresham Sykes (1958) that focuses on what he called the "pains of impris-onment." The loss of normal heterosexual relationships that Sykes refers to might serve as a basis not only for the creation of lesbian partnerships but also for much broader family-like kinship groups. This also is consistent with a deprivation model of the prison environment in which a loss of outside identities forces inmates to create new roles and relationships in order to function effectively within the unusual (for them) prison setting. As Mann (1984, p. 188) explains the prison pseudo-family: "Kinship relationships vary in size dependent upon the family network and the number of 'relatives' in the family. The basic dyad, of course, consists of the parents. Then there are children, aunts, uncles, grandparents, cousins, in-laws, and the like."

Early women's prison scholar Giallombardo (1966) found that family units may be interracial, may include up to 100 members, and may involve switching from one family group to another. As Propper (1981, p. 155) notes, not all kinship groups center on sexual relations: "Participation in make-believe families seems to be less motivated by a desire for sexual gratification than by a need for security, companionship, affection, attention, status, prestige and acceptance."

Feminist critics argue that some of the more distinctive features of female prison subculture have also fed stereotypes and exploitation, particularly in popular Hollywood films. According to Cecil (2007):

> With taglines such as "Women's prison U.S.A. — Rape, Riot, Revenge! White hot desires melting cold prison steel" (Corman & Demme's 1974 *Caged Heat*); "Women so hot with desire they melt the chains that enslave them" (Corman & Hill's 1972 *The Big Bird Cage*); and "Their bodies were caged, but not their desires. They would do anything for a man — or to him" (Corman & Hill's 1971 *Big Doll House*), one can imagine what must be imprinted in the minds of viewers. These "babes-behind-bars" films perpetuate highly sexualized images of female prisoners. . . . Very little factual representation is contained in these films. It is Hollywood, after all; they do not necessarily seek to educate — instead they aim to titillate (Cecil, 2007, pp. 304–305).

Medical Issues Inside

Overall, experts note, women entering prison today are less healthy than those incarcerated ten years ago (Lanier & Zaitzow, 2007). Part of the difference may be explained by the fact that current intake procedures probably provide more medical screening and personal/social history taking than in the past. As a class of prisoners, females experience medical problems that either appear in substantially higher rates than their male counterparts, such as mental illness and breast cancer, or they have unique needs that men do not, such as a number of critical reproductive services. As has been noted in testimony to legislators in many states and at the federal level, there are substantial gaps in the continuum of medical care afforded female prisoners. This includes everything from prevention and routine screening to diagnosis, treatment, medical rehabilitation, and recovery. As Elsner (2006) explains, one prison in the south determined that 70% of women who should have been receiving mammograms according to standard medical guidelines, did not. He documents the unfortunate case of one of their inmates who had medical problems:

> It took Sherrie Chapman two years to convince authorities at the California Institution for Women in Frontera that she needed an urgent mammogram and examination after she felt a lump in her right breast in 1991, her lawyer said.

By 1995, she required an immediate radical mastectomy and the removal of four lymph nodes (Elsner, 2006, p. 136).

One would suppose that Chapman's surgery would have provided sufficient evidence of her medical problems and, at the very least, overcome the prison authorities' previous reluctance to take her condition seriously. Unfortunately, that was not the case as correctional officers continued to be unsympathetic during her chemotherapy, resulting in frequently missed appointments. As a result, she lost her left breast in 1997.

Even this was not the end, as Chapman found lumps in her neck. Elsner (2006) quotes her attorney, Cassie Pierson, as saying "Sometimes they would send her out for tests — but usually she would call and tell me that the prison doctors didn't seem concerned. 'You've just got swollen glands; don't worry, they're not cancerous.' They were cancerous." Chapman died from her cancer in 2002 at the age of 45.

The treatment of pregnant inmates has also been criticized by human rights activists across the country. Of particular concern is the policy of using restraints, handcuffs, or shackles on women in labor when a prisoner is moved anywhere outside of high-security housing. Because there are fewer women prisoners relative to men, there are fewer medical services available in their housing units. This means that transportation and security escorts must be arranged for any of the more serious medical procedures. The costs and complications associated with arranging such appointments means that they are less likely to be offered, which is often a great risk to the inmate's health. Consequently, a number of "equal treatment under the law" suits have been filed on behalf of female inmates in regard to medical care.

In addition to reproductive health care needs, women who are incarcerated have disproportionately high rates of HIV. It is estimated that women in prison have HIV-positive rates that are twice that of incarcerated men and 35 times that of non-incarcerated women. Most HIV cases can be traced to high-risk behaviors such as intravenous drug use and unprotected sex with men who are intravenous drug users (Lanier & Zaitzow, 2007). HIV inmates are also more likely to be infected with hepatitis C, which is also likely to be contracted with intravenous drug abuse. Female inmates with compromised immune systems related to these diseases do not have the same housing resources that are sometimes found in male prison populations. The ability to avoid other sick and contagious inmates is critical for the well-being of immune-suppressed patients. Prisoners with AIDS are two times more likely to become sick than persons with AIDS on the outside (Lanier & Zaitzow, 2007).

Because inmates have no control over their own medication regimens, there are often interruptions (and even terminations) during a full course of a prescribed medicine. This has been identified as one of the main causes of the development of drug-resistant strains of many viruses. As this is a possible health crisis for everyone, we all have a stake in the provision of more appropriate and thorough medical treatment in prison. Experts argue that a perfect time to offer education and training in basic health care and disease prevention is while women are incarcerated.

Women in Immigration Detention

Under international standards of care, persons detained because of their immigration status are expected to be provided the same level of medical services as a country's general population. However, in this country, as in many others, immigration hearings, which are part of a civil administrative process, not a criminal one, have become stalled in a lengthy incarceration limbo. Although the average time that an immigrant detainee is held is about 38 days, many languish far longer with more serious health consequences for the inmates. This situation has recently been addressed by a number of human rights groups.

According to a report issued by Human Rights Watch (2009) and another by the Florida Immigrant Advocacy Center (2009), women in immigration detention facilities in this country face significant physical and mental health risks. Barriers to obtaining critical services include "inadequate communication about available services, unexplained delays in treatment, unwarranted denial of services, breaches of confidentiality, and failure to transfer medical records. When women were denied services, complaint mechanisms were ineffective" (Human Rights Watch, 2009). Shortages of qualified medical staff, inadequate outside oversight, unsanitary and overcrowded facilities, and retaliation and other forms of abusive behavior by detention personnel have also been noted. Texas detention centers were included in the nine facilities that made up the Human Rights Watch study.

Today women make up 10% of the daily population of over 300,000 immigrant detainees in the custody of the federal ICE (Immigration and Customs Enforcement) agency. Women are currently held in four different types of facilities: service processing centers, contract detention facilities run by private companies, intergovernmental service agreement facilities such as beds in state and local jails, and Federal Bureau of Prison facilities. Most women detainees (67%) are housed in state and local jails under intergovernmental service agreements, which may be because of the rapid increase in the demand for housing females. This means that detainees who are being held on warrants only addressing their immigration status are mixed in with criminal populations who may have serious histories of substance abuse, violence, predatory behavior, and mental illness. This exposes these women to a much higher risk of victimization than if they were housed only with other immigration-only detainees.

Community Corrections

Perception of Women as Difficult Clients

For years, female offenders have been processed through a criminal justice system dominated by authorities who may not understand the gender-related differences between the caseloads. Because women represent a significantly smaller percentage of the community corrections population, they have had fewer services and resources available to them on a regular basis. In addition, women have been subjected to discrimination and stereotyping concerning their roles and abilities. Attitudes and perceptions impact relationships and no doubt influence the probability of success in alternative forms of supervision and release (McShane & Krause, 1993).

In the past, research studies have indicated that women, as is the case with men, are more likely to be revoked from parole and probation for technical reasons than for new offenses. The use of technical grounds often implies that officer discretion is operating and that the officer is using personal interpretations of the client's behavior in making the decision to seek revocation. Norland and Mann (1984) found that men whose parole was revoked for technical reasons were likely either to have absconded or to have failed to work. On the other hand, female clients were more often revoked on technical charges for absconding and having improper associates. The difficulty with charges such as "improper associates" is that it is usually a moralistic judgment call; there may be no real consensus about what "improper" is. Interviews with officers led Norland and Mann (1984) to conclude that women consume more of the officers' time and seek more emotional support, which officers may find disruptive to their schedules. In addition:

> Women's problems under supervision tend to be of a different nature from the problems men acknowledge. Women's problems of adjustment are believed by agents to be beyond their interest and competence. . . . These contingencies make it convenient to "sacrifice" women probationers. As a result, these females tend to be perceived as troublesome cases (Norland & Mann, 1984, p. 127).

What Norland and Mann and several other researchers have pointed out is that officers seem to view their relationships with clients as necessarily brief and shallow. Understandably, officers claim they cannot take the responsibility for solving all of the clients' problems. When officers make statements about how they wish their clients would develop independent skills, they may also be reflecting their own inability to relate to and assist those who require more personal support (McShane & Krause, 1993, p, 387).

Women on Parole

Predicting Risk for Female Parolees

Much work has gone into constructing parole risk-prediction instruments to better assign and manage caseloads. Parole risk prediction has been largely an actuarial process. This means that large data sets are compiled using as many known cases as possible describing a range of offender traits. From this information, general predictions are formed that people with factor *x* or *y* may be more likely to recidivate. These odds or chances are then applied to the individual under consideration, and his or her risk is based on prior information about other similar offenders.

Another feature of parole prediction is that, historically, all instruments have been male oriented. This is primarily the case because males have traditionally constituted over 90% of all parolees. Thus, instruments constructed on general parole samples or populations have been based on factors derived from male behaviors or characteristics due to their overwhelming presence in the data. However, as the raw numbers of parolees have increased, not only have the numbers of females increased, but their percentage of the total population has as well.

Between 1986 and 1996, the average annual increase in the number of parolees was about 8%. Today, approximately 73% of all prisoners receive some type of community supervision upon discharge, and almost 50% of those will fail. Most of those who fail will return to prison, but only about one in eight will arrive with a new conviction (Bureau of Justice Statistics [BJS], 1996). As of 2010, there were over 840,000 persons on parole, of whom 12% were females (Glaze & Bonczar, 2011, p. 43).

The fact that the percentage of women making up the parole population has increased from 8 to 12% in the last ten years suggests that efforts are now overdue for an examination of variables in risk instruments and a determination as to whether the predictability of those instruments differs by gender. A growing body of literature now argues that separate risk-prediction systems may be needed for female offenders both for institutional and for community supervision purposes (Burke & Adams, 1991; Craddock, 1994; Fowler, 1993; Gehring, Van Voorhis, & Bell, 2010; Van Voorhis, 2012; Van Voorhis, Wright, Salisbury, & Bauman, 2010).

Gender Differences in Parole Recidivism

The first issue is whether female parolees have differential recidivism rates. Although examining parole recidivism by gender is not a common form of analysis, a few studies have been conducted. Most have found significant differences between the rearrest rates of males and females on parole (Hoffman, 1982). A study by Williams and Dolny (1998) determined that females are more likely than male offenders to succeed on parole even though they need more interventions and services than the parole population at large. Female parolees are also faced with significant barriers that might negatively impact their successful return to the community (Schram, Koons-Witt, Williams, & McShane, 2006). Parolees are most often released to their former neighborhoods which may mean that they return to inner-city areas and crime-prone areas plagued with problems like drug dealing, gangs, poverty, and unemployment. That being the case, it is even more important to examine risk-prediction factors for a potential gender effect (Williams & McShane, 2012).

Gender and Parole Prediction Instruments

Some research studies suggest that current instruments of risk assessment are not necessarily or automatically valid for female offender populations. For example, the questionnaire developed for the Canadian Prison System was not effective in predicting recidivism when used with samples of female and native offenders

(Nuffield, 1989). As with other special populations, some of the traditional risk variables have been found to lack predictive efficiency. For example, in a Canadian study, researchers found that age at the time of parole and age at admission to the penitentiary were associated with reconvictions in a three-year follow-up on female offenders (Bonta, Pang, & Wallace-Capretta, 1995). In addition, variables usually predictive of recidivism in male populations such as history of juvenile delinquency, weapons-related offenses, and drug/alcohol abuse, were not good predictors for recidivism for female parolees.

There are two basic approaches to gender-based risk prediction. The first approach is to design a separate instrument for women that would consider the variables that appear to be related to risk of recidivism based on research findings for male parolees. Such an approach would require separate research to locate predictive variables for female parolees, the development of a separate prediction instrument, and a validation study of the prediction instrument. The second approach is to make adjustments to traditional, male-based scales by using gender-based comparative risk differences to adjust female risk levels. In this instance, the adjustments might theoretically vary according to each jurisdiction's recidivism rate. The problem here is that the resulting "prediction" would be based on females' average rates of risk for all offenses. Offense-specific recidivism rates might produce substantially different results, leading to improper prediction in the aggregate. Of course, creating different rates for each offense type would require both an original study and a validation study which would be very cumbersome and time consuming. Thus, of the two approaches, the first may be more efficient and produce more useful results in the long run.

It would seem logical to conclude that, in each jurisdiction, validation studies would have to determine the applicability of any instrument to women eligible for parole. Because studies of females are typically based on small samples, it may be necessary to add in-depth interviews to provide additional information useful for developing more effective instruments. For example, Bonta, Pang, and Wallace-Capretta (1995) used interviews with women as an alternative data source and found higher recidivism rates among women who reported that they usually relied on illegal sources of income or welfare as opposed to legitimate employment.

The McShane/Williams Study

In research conducted in California in the late 1990s, this text's author, with Frank Williams and Michael Dolny (McShane, Williams, & Dolney, 2002; Williams & McShane, 1997, 2012), attempted to determine whether females differed from males in their success rates on parole. If so, there would be an even greater justification for analyzing female parolees separately. Because female parolees are reincarcerated at a different (lower) rate, there is some reason to believe that predictors may vary or may show a differential effect. We therefore turned to a comparison of the prediction variables for males and females.

Based on previous research findings, the variables that were hypothesized to be important were:

- marital status,
- propensity for violence,
- drug commitment offense,
- alcohol-related commitment offense,
- significant history of gang involvement,
- employability at release,
- family and/or friends with drug problems,
- family and/or friends with alcohol problems, and
- family, spouse, or close relatives with criminal histories.

In regard to the first issue, female parolees in our research study were more likely to succeed on their first year of parole than males by about 12%. Slightly more than half of females had not violated parole in comparison to about 41% of male parolees. This higher success rate suggested that for females, the use of a risk-prediction instrument created with a predominantly (90%) male parolee population might be inefficient or inadvisable.

A search for alternative predictors of female parolee success yielded three potential variables (propensity for violence, employability at release, and family and/or friends with alcohol problems). When these variables were added to the risk-prediction model built on the general parole population (90% male), not only was there no improvement in predicting parole success for females, but the classification accuracies were worse than in the original model. In short, the female-specific risk-prediction instrument was slightly inferior to the model developed primarily on males.

We concluded that the use of the generic risk-prediction instrument does no special harm to female parolees. Although these results can be technically applied only to the population on which the research is based, the combination of a large female subsample, a large general sample, and the large size of the state's parolee population serve to suggest that other jurisdictions are likely to have similar results. Our answer to the question of whether risk-prediction instruments derived from a general population may be applied to female populations is a qualified "yes." We found little negative effect as a result of using these specific instruments with female parolees. Keep in mind that there are potential differences in different versions of the instrument. Thus, we believe it is likely that standard risk-prediction instruments, and in particular actuarial instruments, do little harm to female parolee populations. However, each parole jurisdiction should carefully examine its own existing instrument before assuming that the "little harm" argument applies. In addition, the use of what is referred to as "dynamic" instruments (those based on continual evaluation of the parolee while on parole) may produce different results, especially those with factors accounting for the stability of the parolee's family life and residence/employment status.

Candace Kruttschnitt (2010) argues that legislative reforms should consider that while women may be at risk to reoffend, given their problems with unemployment and substance abuse histories, their offenses are less serious and less violent than those of men. She reasons that this should be taken into consideration in deciding what "risk" really means. Risk-prediction instruments usually focus on the "risk" of a parolee either returning to prison or generically reoffending (though most instruments use the former definition of risk). Thus, "risk" is not what most people think; it is effectively the probability of an event happening and does not include the concept of harm. Others have used the concept of "stakes" to differentiate between those for whom the social costs and dangers associated with reoffending, such as pedophiles, are greater instead of just the simple probability or risk that some offense/event will occur.

Women Who Marry Prisoners

It seems like a topic from an Oprah or even a Jerry Springer show: *Murderers and the women who love them.* Despite the tabloid nature of the topic, the reality of relationships between women and prisoners is much less dramatic or sordid. Media accounts tend to make the women look needy or afraid of face-to-face human contact, hiding in the safe romanticism of loving from afar, or secretly flirting with bad boys who, in a perfect world, will never be released. However, the bottom line is really that many of these relationships are just like any others across America. With over 2.5 million persons incarcerated in the United States, many of them young, it should be obvious that some of those people will search for someone, find someone, and fall in love.

Neither male nor female prisoners have access to the Internet, but they have family and friends who might post their invitations for them, so that women who are searching the Internet for male "pen pals" can initiate a postage correspondence. It would also seem highly unlikely that someone outside would fail to recognize a prison address system, and most departments would make it a disciplinary offense for an inmate to misrepresent his or her identity in correspondence. Of course, we are likely to hear about the most extreme cases, where couples push for state-sponsored artificial insemination or an inmate secretly dates 14 different women, getting each of them to send him substantial amounts of money each month. Those, however, are not the typical relationships and paint a stereotypically weak picture of the average woman who is in a relationship with an inmate. What you are less likely to see in the media stories is a couple regularly visiting, making plans, writing letters, and celebrating anniversaries in their journals. One of those women is Carole Santos, and if you were to read about her marriage to long-term prisoner Michael Santos, you might find her quite normal, not much different from you and me.[1]

The correctional literature has always indicated that settling down and marrying has positive effects on the parole outcomes of male prisoners, particularly

---

[1] For her story see http://www.businessinsider.com/michael-santos-on-getting-married-in-prison-2013-9

because they have a good chance of meeting through Internet dating women who have no criminal history. The same is not true for women. In fact, data indicate that women being released from prison, especially into poor, socially disorganized neighborhoods, have little chance of being romantically involved with a man who does not have a criminal history (Leverentz, 2006).

Perhaps the structure and operation of corrections systems in this country doom women offenders to continually come into contact with criminogenic men. First, most systems require that prisoners be released to the county where they committed their original crime and received their conviction. Most often they move back in with family members or friends with gang and criminal associations. Reporting to probation and parole is required in the county of offense origin, and few are ever given permission to transfer away. This precludes ever making a clean start. Second, spending considerable amounts of time in waiting areas for appointments in drug court, drug rehabilitation treatment, parole and probation supervision offices, and so forth, means that they are constantly in contact with other offenders (ironically, even though that contact is officially prohibited). Alcoholics Anonymous (AA) and 12-step programs are other places that male and female offenders begin relationships that are seldom healthy or productive.

Toward More Gendered Corrections

The number of women offenders in the criminal justice system has risen disproportionately faster than the number of men (Guerino et al., 2011). The attention of feminist reformers and researchers has been instrumental in elevating the visibility of this relatively small group. As a consequence, we now have increasingly stronger evidence that women both come into the criminal justice system from different pathways than men and have different needs as they leave the system (Visher & Travis, 2003). Developing best practices and programs and then implementing them with caring staff appear to be our best hope for the successful reintegration of women into their families and communities.

Critical Thinking Questions

1. Discuss the barriers to more creative and innovative programming for female inmates, particularly in regard to maintaining contact with their children.

2. If you were a probation or parole officer, would you have a preference for the gender of your caseload? If not, why not? If so, what gender and why?

3. What would a reasonable and constitutional policy on inmate marriage be? Would this policy treat male and female prisoners differently?

Books, Websites, and Media Resources

George, E. (2010). *A woman doing life: Notes from a prison for women.* New York: Oxford University Press.

Harris, J. (1988). *They always call us ladies.* New York: Zebra Books.

Immigration: www.hrw.org/en/news/2009/03/17/us-immigration-detention-neglects-health

The National Institute of Corrections: http://nicic.gov/

Rathbone, C. (2005). *A world apart: Women, prison, and life behind bars.* New York: Random House.

Women in jail: https://www.bja.gov/Publications/Women_Pathways_to_Jail.pdf.

Women in jail and post-release reintegration: http://www.urban.org/UploadedPDF/411902_women_outside_houston.pdf

Popular Films

Brokedown Palace (1999), Claire Danes.

What I Want My Words to Do to You (2004), Glenn Close, Rosie Perez, and others.

References

Baunach, P. (1979). The families of inmate mothers: Perceptions of separation from their children. Paper presented at the National Institute of Mental Health's Conference on Incarcerated Parents and their Children. Bethesda, MD.

Belbot, B., & Hemmens, C. (2011). *The legal rights of the convicted.* El Paso, TX: LFB Scholarly Publishing.

Bloom, B., Owen, B., & Covington, S. (2004). Women offenders and the gendered effects of public policy. *Review of Policy Research, 21,* 31-48.

Bloom, B., & Steinhart, D. (1993). *Why punish the children?* San Francisco: National Council on Crime and Delinquency.

Bonczar, T., & Glaze, L. (1999). *Probation and parole in the United States, 1998.* Washington, DC: Bureau of Justice Statistics.

Bonta, J., Pang, B., & Wallace-Capretta, S. (1995). Predictors of recidivism among incarcerated female offenders. *The Prison Journal, 75,* 277-294.

Boudouris, J. (1985). *Prisons and kids: Programs for inmate parents.* Alexandria, VA: American Correctional Association.

Bowker, L. H. (1981). Gender differences in prisoner subcultures. In L. H. Bowker (Ed.), *Women and crime in America* (pp. 409-419). New York: MacMillan.

Bureau of Justice Statistics. (1996). *Correctional populations in the U.S.* Washington, DC: U.S. Department of Justice.

Burke, P., & Adams, L. (1991). *Classification of women offenders in state correctional facilities: A handbook for practitioners.* Washington, DC: National Institute of Corrections.

Cecil, D. (2007). Looking beyond *Caged Heat:* Media images of women in prison. *Feminist Criminology, 2* (4), 304-326.

Craddock, A. (1994). *Inmate classification.* Research Triangle Park, NC: Research Triangle Institute, Center for Social Research & Policy Analysis.

Craig, S. (2009). A historical review of mother and child programs for incarcerated women. *The Prison Journal, 89* (1), 358-538.

Davidson, J. T. (2009). *Female offenders and risk assessment.* New York: LFB Scholarly Publishing.

Elsner, A. (2006). *Gates of injustice: The crisis in America's prisons.* Upper Saddle River, NJ: Pearson.

Federal Bureau of Investigation. (2011). *Crime in the United States, 2010.* Retrieved from http://www.fbi.gov/about-us/cjis/ucr/crime-in-the-u.s./2010/crime-in-the-u.s.-2010/about-cius.

Florida Immigrant Advocacy Center (2009). *Dying for decent care: Bad medicine in immigration custody.* Miami FL: Author.

Fowler, L. (1993). *Classification of women offenders.* Columbia, SC: South Carolina Department of Corrections.

Gehring, K., Van Voorhis, P., & Bell, V. (2010). "What works" for female probationers? An evaluation of the Moving On Program. *Women, Girls, and Criminal Justice,* 11 (1), 6-10.

George, E. (2010). *A woman doing life: Notes from a prison for women.* New York: Oxford University Press.

Giallombardo, R. (1966). *Society of women.* New York: John Wiley.

Glaze, L. E., & Bonczar, T. P. (2011, November). *Probation and parole in the United States, 2010.* Washington, DC: Bureau of Justice Statistics.

Glaze, L. E., & Maruschak, L. M. (2008, August). *Parents in prison and their minor children.* Bureau of Justice Statistics Special Report. Washington, DC: Office of Justice Programs.

Greer, K. (2000). The changing nature of interpersonal relationships in a women's prison. *Prison Journal,* 80, 442–468.

Guerino, P., Harrison, P. M., & Sabol, W. J. (2011). *Prisoners in 2010.* (NCJ 236096). Washington, DC: U.S. Department of Justice, Bureau of Justice Statistics.

Harris, J. (1988). *They always call us ladies: Stories from prison.* New York: Scribners.

Heffernan, E. (1972). *Making it in prison: The square, the cool, and the life.* New York: John Wiley.

Hoffman, P. B. (1982). Females, recidivism, and salient factor score. *Criminal Justice and Behavior,* 9 (1), 121-125.

Human Rights Watch (2009). *Detained and dismissed: Women's struggles to obtain health care in United States immigration detention.* New York: Author.

Johnson, B. (January 14, 2001). Young scouts join mothers behind bars. *Los Angeles Times,* p. A27.

Kruttschnitt, C. (2010, Summer). The paradox of women's imprisonment. *Daedalus,* 32-42.

Lanier, M., & Zaitzow, B. (2007). Living and dying with HIV/AIDS: The inside experience of women in prison. In R. Muraskin (Ed.), *It's a crime: Women and justice* (Chap. 22, pp. 363-378). Upper Saddle River, NJ: Prentice Hall.

La Vigne, N. G., Brooks, L. E., & Schollenberger, T. L. (2009). *Women on the outside: Understanding the experiences of female prisoners returning to Houston, Texas.* Washington, DC: Urban Institute, Justice Policy Center.

Leverentz, A. (2006). The love of a good man? Romantic relationships as a source of support or hinderance for female ex-offenders. *Journal of Research in Crime and Delinquency,* 43, 459-488.

Lombardo, V. S., & Smith, R. (1996). A model program for female offenders. *Corrections Today,* 58 (6), 92-95.

Mackintosh, V., Myers, B., & Kennon, S. (2006). Children of incarcerated mothers and their caregivers: Factors affecting the quality of their relationship. *Journal of Child and Family Studies,* 15 (5), 581–596.

Mann, C. (1984). *Female crime and delinquency.* Tuscaloosa: University of Alabama Press.

Mauro v. Arpaio, 188 F. 3d 1054, 1999

Mehren, E. (May 31, 1996). Badge of honor; They're scouts complete with uniforms and badges, yet they are like no others. *Los Angeles Times,* p. 1.

McShane, M., & Krause, W. (1993). *Community corrections.* New York: MacMillan.

McShane, M., Williams, F. P., III, & Dolney, H. M. (2002). Do standard risk prediction instruments apply to female parolees? *Women and Criminal Justice,* 13, 163-182.

Meyer, L. (August 14, 1997). Babies behind bars sustain maternal tie. *Los Angeles Times,* p. A5.

Minton, T. D. (2010). *Jail inmates at midyear 2011: Statistical Tables* (NCJ 237961). Washington, DC: Bureau of Justice Statistics.

National Institute of Justice. (2005, July). *Reentry programs for women inmates* (NCJ 208703), National Institute of Justice Journal, 252. Washington, DC: Office of Justice Programs.

Norland, S., & Mann, P. (1984). Being troublesome: Women on probation. *Criminal Justice and Behavior,* 11, 115-135.

Nuffield, J. (1989). The "SIR Scale": Some reflections on its applications. *Forum on Corrections Research,* 1 (2), 19-22.

O'Brien, P. (2001). Just like baking a cake: Women describe the necessary ingredients for successful reentry after incarceration. *Families in Society: The Journal of Contemporary Human Services,* 82, 287-295.

Owen, B. (1998). *"In the mix": Struggle and survival in a women's prison.* Albany: State University of New York Press.

Propper, A. (1981). *Prison homosexuality.* Lexington, MA: D.C. Heath.

Rathbone, C. (2005). *A world apart: Women, prison and life behind bars.* New York: Random House.

Schram, P., Koons-Witt, B., Williams, F. P., III, & McShane, M. (2006). Supervision strategies and approaches for female parolees: Examining the link between unmet needs and parolee outcome. *Crime & Delinquency,* 52, 450-471.

Snell, T. (2006, December). *Capital punishment, 2005.* Washington, DC: Bureau of Justice Statistics, U.S. Department of Justice.

Stanton, A. M. (1980). *When mothers go to jail.* Lexington, MA: Lexington.

Sykes, G. (1958). *The society of captives.* Princeton, NJ: Princeton University Press.

U.S. Department of Justice. (1994). *Women in prison: Survey of state prison inmates, 1991.* Washington, DC: Bureau of Justice Statistics.

Van Voorhis, P. (2012). On behalf of women offenders: Women's place in the science of evidence-based practice. *Criminology and Public Policy,* 11 (2), 111-145.

Van Voorhis, P., Wright, E., Salisbury, S., & Bauman, A. (2010). Women's risk factors and their contributions to existing risk/needs assessment: The current status of gender responsive assessment. *Criminal Justice and Behavior,* 37 (3), 261-288.

Visher, C., & Travis, J. (2003). Transitions from prison to community: Understanding individual pathways. *Annual Review of Sociology,* 29, 89-113.

Walmsley, R. (2009). *World female imprisonment list* (8th ed.). London: Kings College London, International Centre for Prison Studies.

Ward, D., & Kassebaum, G. (1965). *Women's prison: Sex and social structure.* Chicago: Aldine.

Williams, F. P., III, & Dolny, H. M. (1998). *Risk/stakes assessment and supervision practices: Analysis and results.* (Main Report, Vol. 1). Sacramento, CA: California Parole and Community Services Division.

Williams, F. P., III, & McShane, M. (1997). *Predicting parole success.* Sacramento, CA: California Parole and Community Services Division.

Williams, F. P., III, & McShane, M. (2012). Female parole absconders. *Southwest Journal of Criminal Justice,* 8 (2), 112-131.

Women's Prison Association (2009). *Quick facts: Women & criminal justice–2009.* Retrieved online, January 2, 2014 at http://www.wpaonline.org/pdf/Quick%20Facts%20Women%20and%20CJ_Sept09.pdf

Issues in Female Delinquency

Introduction

Elisabeth Mandala lived many roles in her short life. At 18 she was a Sugar Land, Texas, high school student, a stripper at a nightclub, and someone who joked about becoming a coyote or human smuggler. During a trip across the border in a rental car, Elisabeth was beaten to death along with two Mexican nationals with criminal contacts. In retrospect, many of her friends could not believe the light-hearted girl who enjoyed riding horses and participating in social clubs would have such a secret side. But excitement, danger, and trouble were the types of characteristics Walter Miller saw in delinquent boys who were inner-city, first-generation American youth. Although so much has changed since subculture theorists first analyzed ways the stress to achieve conflicted with the perceptions of blocked opportunities, for many youth today the frustrations are perhaps the same. In fact, law enforcement authorities readily acknowledge that drug cartels lure young people into high-risk activities with the promise of fast money, cars, and notoriety. Elisabeth was not poor and had financial support from her large family, but she seemed to crave a more dramatic lifestyle. Even though she was a serious college prep student, she engaged in Internet fraud schemes, adding more dimensions to her mysterious persona (Knight, 2010).

Ashley Benton, on the other hand, was a girl who was constantly in trouble. The teen from Houston, Texas, had family problems as well as a history of disruptive behavior that had her living with her grandmother off and on in attempts to straighten out her life. Her school disciplinary violations ranged from fights to weapons. She made dangerous gang friends. Acquaintances said her life had too much drama:

> She seemed confused about race. Sometimes she said she was black. But she was white. There might have been other identity issues, too. Sometimes she was all girlie-girl. And sometimes she swaggered like she was bigger and badder than any punk boy. "She wanted to prove herself," the boy said. "She wanted to prove to somebody she could take down any dude" (Peralta & Feldman, 2006, p. A1).

What Ashley eventually proved was that she could buy a knife, go up against a young man with a baseball bat, and kill him (Peralta & Feldman, 2006). After joining in a confrontation in the park between gang members, she fatally stabbed MS-13 member Gabriel Granillo. After her first trial ended in a mistrial, the prosecution offered her a reduced charge and deferred adjudication. She pleaded guilty and moved away from town.

In stories like those of Ashley and Elisabeth, we see teens who in so many ways are normal but whose unpredictable behavior and perhaps bad choices put them into statistical groups that are not typical for adolescent girls. In fact, we might even argue, they seem more like delinquent boys. Are girls really becoming more delinquent, or are we just hearing more stories about some uncommon or outlier behavior?

Female Delinquency by the Numbers

Almost 15% of females arrested in the United States are under the age of 18, and about 4% are under the age of 15 (FBI, 2011). By 2006, young females accounted for about 30% of the over 2 million youth arrests each year. This is a significant increase over the 20% of arrests they represented during the 1970s (Chesney-Lind, 2011). Although the percentage of offenses attributed to girls appears to be increasing over those of their male counterparts, it is important to note that most arrests are under Part II of the Uniform Crime Report. This means that the offenses are not the more serious Part 1 Index offenses but instead are such things as running away, curfew violations, disorderly conduct, and drug use. The public seems to focus on homicide and gang violence, but it is important to note that vehicle crashes, suicide, and unintentional injuries are the other more common causes of death among youth.

Today over 12 million children live in poverty, which is defined as a family of four living on $19,000 per year or less. Ten million households do not maintain a bank account, a number of these families deal with a debt collector, and the children are more likely to live through a bankruptcy than a divorce. These factors are important when we look at risk for becoming delinquent. As a report by Hawkins, Graham, Williams, and Zahn indicates:[1]

---

[1] See the entire report at http://www.ncjrs.gov/pdffiles1/ojjdp/220124.pdf

For girls, the key risk factors for delinquency and incarceration are family dysfunction, trauma and sexual abuse, mental health and substance abuse problems, high-risk sexual behaviors, school problems, and affiliation with deviant peers. . . . Physical abuse and sexual abuse contribute to male and female involvement in delinquency . . . but female delinquents are more likely than their male counterparts to have been abused (Hawkins et al., 2009, p. 4).

Williams (2010) also notes similar risk factors for teens who become caught up in prostitution. Researchers estimate that girls now reach puberty even earlier than in the past with the average at 12.5 years of age. Consequently, the criminal justice system has had to deal with much younger victims and offenders than ever before. As Williams explains, these young girls have case files containing many of the elements of life risks we noted in the chart in Chapter 1:

> A review of the family background and experiences of many prostituted teens reveals a long history of highly destructive families fraught with violence and dysfunction. Many of the teens have been in numerous foster care settings or have lived on the streets or with no permanent home for months and even years . . . . Their experiences and survival based coping skills suggest a successful strategy of care and support of these youth may be achieved only through the development of meaningful partnerships between the youth and social services (Williams, 2010, p. 303).

Much of the literature on the early juvenile justice system demonstrates the court's preoccupation with status offenses, particularly in sanctioning what was inferred as sex-related behaviors of girls. Today, running away is a much more common arrest for girls. In 2006, there were more than 38,000 arrests for running away recorded for girls and only 1,000 arrests for prostitution. Although girls were less likely than boys to be apprehended and adjudicated, they were more likely to be detained and institutionalized for status offenses (Chesney-Lind, 2011; Chesney-Lind & Shelden, 2004). This was true even though self-report studies showed males as likely, if not more likely, to be involved in status offenses (Canter, 1982). Obviously, the juvenile courts were practicing a double standard for acceptable behavior. This double standard was obvious in the theories of delinquency popular in the early to mid-1900s.

Historical Approaches to Girls in Need of Supervision

In almost every juvenile delinquency textbook, the author traces the juvenile court and other interventions on behalf of the best interests of the child back to the early American (approximately 1875) case of Mary Ellen Wilson. The Society for the Prevention of Cruelty to Children is alleged to have been associated with the need to assist abused and neglected children, like Mary Ellen. Mary Ellen's torment was reported by a neighbor, and she was taken to court bearing the scars of frequent beatings. She was inadequately dressed against the cold and seriously undersized for her age. Apparently, placed into servitude at the age of one year and six months, she was later removed from this early form of foster care, and the woman at whose hands she had suffered was prosecuted and jailed. Mary Ellen eventually went to an institution for dependent children (Costin, 1991).

Although Costin (1991) argues that Mary Ellen's plight was illuminated to some degree by the contrast between laws protecting animals and the lack of the same for children, there was, in reality, a more complex evolution of rights and charities:

> Public concerns about cruelty to children was heightened by the powerful women's rights movement of the 1870s and its attention to a variety of social justice reforms — woman suffrage, reform of the patriarchal family system by granting equality within the structure of the family, "protected childhood," banishment of punitive corporal punishment, prevention of sexual exploitation of young girls and single women, the temperance movement, and action against family violence (Costin, 1991, p. 220).

Nonetheless, Costin adds, it was not apparent that women or children were making steady strides in the quest for equality under the law. Courts were blamed for not being sensitive to the problems facing poverty-stricken women and children in a male-dominated society. "One such obstacle was the rise of judicial patriarchy, which significantly expanded judicial power in family life" as well as the way issues of child protection became "a powerful organization for coercive social control of poor, immigrant families, those headed largely by women" (Costin, 1991, p. 220). At that time, it was often considered in the best interests of the child to remove them from homes that did not measure up to middle-class standards of care.

Another case that illustrated the power the courts assumed when it came to intervening in family issues related to delinquency is *Ex Parte Crouse*. In that case, a mother complained about the unruliness or incorrigibility of her daughter who then was committed to the Philadelphia House of Refuge by a justice of the peace. Her father filed a *habeas corpus* petition to remove her, arguing that such a process of institutionalization was unconstitutional. The court denied his writ and proffered that the government has the right to intercede and remove a child from a home where the situation might lead to criminal behavior. The ruling explained "may not the natural parent, when unequal to the task of education, or unworthy of it, be superseded by *parens patriae*? . . . parents' rights of control are natural, but not unalienable."[2]

Much of the popular and academic literature of the time blamed delinquency on defects in the character of the parent. In most cases, this singled out the mother because, as was common back then, poor immigrant women were often raising children alone through the fateful intervention of the father's

---

[2] For more commentary on this case, see http://www.sheldensays.com/Ex%20Parte%20Crouse.htm

drinking, death, or desertion. As we see again in *Crouse*, the judges believed that children should also be removed from the home when "the moral depravity or otherwise of the parent or next friend in whose custody such infant may be, such parent or next friend is incapable or unwilling to exercise the proper care and discipline over such incorrigible or vicious infant." The key accusations here are that a parent might be "morally depraved" which might mean that he or she gambled or drank or was noted not to be attending church. The wording also indicates that the court could find a parent unwilling or incapable of providing what the courts perhaps have determined to be "proper care."

At this same time, the early part of the 1900s, the new field of psychology had popularized the idea that childhood development progressed in critical stages and that appropriate habits and responses were needed at each of the important steps. There was concern that mothers must be trained to recognize and encourage the child's normal progression through these stages. This led to increased importance being placed on education for women, particularly in fields related to home health and home economics.

Dysfunctional and Criminogenic Families

Delinquency has long been linked to the criminogenic influence of hereditary traits such as feeblemindedness, intemperance, and immorality. In the once popular field of eugenics, experts advocated sterilizing young women who appeared to be of "inferior breeding" so that they would not produce offspring prone to crime or dependent on the state. Books such as *The Jukes* (1877) by Richard Dugdale and *The Kallikaks* (1913) by Henry Goddard traced the generations of deviants and offenders who seemed to descend from young women who bore illegitimate children who were, in their opinion, destined for poorhouses and jails.

Perhaps when we look at film and literature images of the crime-prone family we see cunning, street-savvy, even evil, masterminds. Mafia daughters, drug-cartel girlfriends, and the familia of the gangbanger appear smart, dangerous, and more sophisticated in their criminal enterprises. These popular media depictions are far from the reality of the dysfunctional family that often ends up in the courts today.

Recently, in a scenario not too dissimilar from *Ex Parte Crouse*, a south Texas woman was brought before the court because she confined her daughter to a closet every day after school. The situation sounds like a simple case of child abuse, but the context is actually very complex and demonstrates the way a severely dysfunctional family is addressed by the criminal justice and child protective services systems. Leticia Ines, 41 years old, argued that her daughter's mental health and behavior problems created risks within the family, as the daughter attempted to stab her brothers (Associated Press, 2011). Although not physically abused, the 13-year-old girl appeared underdeveloped and malnourished. After missing scheduled court appearances because she did not have a phone to receive notifications, the mother served time in jail while the children entered foster care. Officials admit the woman seemed to lack parenting skills and the ability to deal with the child's special needs. Now homeless and jobless, the mother who speaks little English defended her actions by saying that she did not want her daughter sneaking out of the house and that she, herself, often slept too soundly to monitor her.

Delinquent Girls in the Justice System Today

In 2008, the Office of Juvenile Justice and Delinquency Prevention sponsored a study to more accurately assess the differences between young women and men in victimization and offending. The report concluded that girls may experience higher levels of depression and hopelessness than males. The propensity to get into fights may be associated with more disadvantaged neighborhoods where there is a greater likelihood of being victimized (Zahn et al., 2008). When girls get into fights, it is often over sexual reputation, to gain status among their peers, and even in self-defense when they experience sexual harassment. Young women are more likely to fight with their parents, often in response to perceptions of being overcontrolled, or as a way of rejecting sexual abuse. School violence may be initiated by a young woman as a result of poor relationships with teachers and the feeling that they are being labeled or stigmatized (Vito & Kunselman, 2012).

Other forms of juvenile justice data indicate that the number of girls in the system is rising faster than the number of boys. Government reports include the following:

> [G]irls in the 21st century comprise over one quarter of all delinquency cases, nearly a 100 percent increase over the past 20 years . . . . Increases in female caseloads as well as the proportions of girls' cases petitioned to juvenile court have outpaced boys. Between 1985 and 2002, the number of delinquency cases being referred to juvenile courts involving girls increased by 92 percent compared to a 29 percent increase for males . . . . Girls have also become an increasing proportion of juveniles in custody. Between 1991 and 2003, girls' detentions rose by 98 percent compared to a 29 percent expansion seen in boys' detentions . . . girls' commitments to facilities increased by an alarming 88 percent between 1991 and 2003 while boys' commitments only rose by 23 percent . . . . Girls are also proportionally more likely to be admitted to training schools or groups homes, whereas boys are more likely to receive day treatment (Pasko, Okamoto, & Chesney-Lind, 2011, p. 418).

The findings detailed above mean that not only are girls being exposed to the justice system in greater proportion than ever before, but they are being processed deeper into the system with potentially more negative, long-term effects. Impacting on education, career preparation, and family ties, these effects may perpetuate delinquency and increase the probability of future high-risk behaviors.

Theory and Research on Female Delinquency

A number of criminological theories have focused primarily on delinquents though few have addressed female delinquency specifically. If we go back to the chart we used in Chapter 1, we can see that children growing up in socially disorganized areas, in environments of poverty, substance abuse, and crime, like their mothers, have fewer life chances or pathways to success. Based on research that focused on girls being held as "wards" in the California state system (CYA), Bloom, Owen, Deschenes, and Rosenbaum (2007) explain how these disadvantages play out:

> Seventy-six percent of female CYA wards in the 1960s and 89 percent of female CYA wards in the 1990s had family members who had been arrested . . . . nearly one-half of the respondents reported that their father had been incarcerated and one-fourth reported that their mother had been incarcerated. About three-fourths of the girls in the 1960s had at least one family member with a criminal record, and half of the time it was the girls' mothers . . . . The girls reported that 71 percent of their parents fought regularly with the children. Family conflict over alcohol was noted in 81 percent of the families; 34 percent of the fathers were known alcoholics, as were 31 percent of the mothers . . . although records were not being kept on domestic violence unless a specific charge was filed, in the 1960s a number of the known fathers had spent time in jail for fighting with their wives. Nearly one-third of the parents of the CYA wards in the 1960s had histories of mental illness (Bloom et al., 2007, p. 798).

It was these mothers who were primarily the focus of subculture theories.

Subculture Theory

Subculture theories prominent during the 1940s and 1950s emphasized the social environment in which delinquent boys sought status and peer relationships. Early gang theories identified lower-class boys, first- and second-generation immigrants, and children of single mothers living in socially disorganized areas as having the highest risk for joining gangs. Subculture theory, particularly the work of theorists Albert Cohen, Walter Miller, and Richard Cloward and Lloyd Ohlin, has been used to explain gang membership as well as the various activities of gangs. These theories basically argue that lower-class youth are unable to compete with middle-class youth for status and legitimate opportunities because of factors associated with their poor socioeconomic backgrounds. These lower-class boys become frustrated and disengage from traditional American achievements and activities. The mother's dependence on what seemed to be a series of live-in boyfriends does not supply the types of role models that young boys are able to identify with. The subculture, peers, or somewhat older neighborhood youth provide a relatively "safe" environment within which they can practice masculine behaviors. The boys within a group share similar values and attitudes. Consequently, life within a subculture, or gang, affords many youths the ability to experience belonging, success, and even outlets for their frustration in terms of competition with other gangs, as well as daring and often violent exploits. Illegal enterprises such as burglary and drug sales may not only fund their lifestyle, but may provide leadership roles and status during one's career inside the gang.

Today, officials estimate that between 20 and 40% of gang members are now females. Symbols of membership include certain styles and colors of clothing, as well as preferred methods of makeup and speech. Although the likelihood of a girl joining a gang tends to be correlated with higher levels of life stress, young women are more likely to decrease violent gang activity upon their first pregnancy. This desistence would be consistent with the subculture theory argument that as girls are confronted with alternate identities, values, and priorities, the ability of the subculture to continue to meet their needs would be reevaluated. Even those who have gang-involved family members would be receiving different messages from relatives about expectations for the young woman to conform to the more traditional maternal role.

Females and Gangs

Most of the literature on female gangs makes the specific point that law enforcement agencies have not taken female gang membership seriously and view females as only a shadow of male gang activity. Since gangs have been in existence, female gang members have been viewed as satellites of male gang members, causing a gap in our knowledge about young girls who are at risk of becoming involved in the gang life and developing a pattern of criminal behavior (Moore & Hagedorn, 2001).

Research today estimates that female gang members make up about 10% of all those reported to be in gangs, although they seem to be actively involved for shorter periods of time overall than males (Champion, Merlo, & Benekos, 2013). A number of researchers have noted that females seem to form in either auxiliary gangs, autonomous gangs, or mixed gangs. In auxiliary gangs, females are subordinate to their dominant male gang unit. Even though a few females may operate independently of the male gang member's authority and set out rules for other female gang members, they are still lower in status and subservient to males.

In a study of the national school-based Gang Resistance Education and Training (G.R.E.A.T.) program, researchers found that the girls in gangs seemed to commit criminal offenses with less frequency than their male counterparts, and they seemed to commit the same types of offenses. If you include all delinquent conduct, events broader than just those involving crimes, girls in gangs were two to five times more delinquent than nongang boys. G.R.E.A.T. program data on young female Hispanic gang members also seems to indicate that "peers influenced their decision to join, especially when parental supervision was absent or inadequate" (Vito & Kunselman, 2012, p. 374).

Further information about Latina gang members and the types of affiliations they have with male gangs can be found in a study by Karina Rodriguez (2010).

She reported that "Females are expected to conduct duties within the gang (e.g., act as lookouts, weapon and drug carriers, and lure gang rivals into rival territories for an ambush). Historically, females were part of auxiliary gangs and had the role of girlfriends, sex objects, or mules to the male gang members" (Rodriguez, p. 19). In an autonomous gang, there would be no connection to a controlling male gang or influence by its members. This would be an independent, all-female gang. In a mixed gang, however, females have more shared responsibilities with a related male gang and have higher status and control over the operation of their own female gang members. As Rodriguez (2010) explains, the young women may serve as communicators or go-betweens with the men's rival gangs or carriers of messages to prisons and jails as visitors. Still, under this arrangement, females remain as the girlfriends and sexual property of their corresponding male gangs.

In a study of girl gang members committed to the CYA, Rosenbaum (1996) found her subjects to be much more violent than earlier studies from the 1980s suggested. Her conclusions were that the young women were motivated to prove themselves to male peers. Eager to enhance their reputations, they actively assume more aggressive and violent roles. Rosenbaum finds less support now for the "accessory" role and theorizes that anomie, frustration, and reactions to surrounding deprivations may be keys to understanding female gang member behavior.

Differential Association and Female Delinquency

In a manner that is not inconsistent with subculture theory, Edwin Sutherland's differential association theory argues that crime is learned within the context of close personal relationships. In intimate communication, the values and attitudes that are compatible with rule breaking are transmitted. It was suggested that individuals may be exposed to a variety of different relationships in everyday life, many of them prosocial and conforming, such as those with teachers, coaches, and grandparents. However, it is thought that those relationships with the most intensity, that last the longest, and that occur with the most frequency will be the ones that are most likely to influence one toward violations of the law. Thus, Sutherland viewed the individual's potential behavior as a see-saw on which at any given time, the definitions or circumstances of any situation might be tipped in favor of committing a crime, if the forces favorable to that crime exert more weight. Although Sutherland would argue that males or females, young or old, rich or poor, learn crime in the same way, he also allowed that socially disorganized areas might have higher rates of crime based on the concentration of shared values favorable to law breaking. As Giordano and Rockwell (2000, p. 11) explain, marginal family environments do not provide the young person with what might be considered proper conforming social values and definitions for acceptable behavior. Relatives, friends, and associates of the parents seem to be poor role models, who instead offer a "united front of deviance." As the authors clarify:

In some instances, simple observation and repeated exposure to the behavior might be enough to normalize it, increasing the probability that the child eventually will enact the same or a generally compatible behavior ... (p. 12). Through direct and indirect learning processes, certain acts of law violation come to be seen as tolerable, acceptable, or even desirable behaviors (p. 21).

It has been suggested that perhaps differential association theory better describes why more females are not delinquent (Price & Sokoloff, 2004). Sutherland seemed to believe that even in the same neighborhoods and homes, girls are exposed to higher levels of supervision and care that may offset the pressure of friends and peer groups to disobey the law. According to the theory, a person resorts to deviant behavior when he or she feels that there are more factors favoring a deviant act than a conventional course of action. More specifically, that which convinces one to deviate from conformity is an excess of definitions indicating law breaking is acceptable or valued. Close friends and status groups have the power to pressure one toward the delinquent activity, but some theorists find that it may be less successful with girls. Perhaps girls have fewer but closer associates to whom they turn for guidance on acceptable behavior, and those may be less likely to advocate for higher-risk activity. Social control theory constructs a similar view when it suggests that parents raise girls with more restrictions and pro-social mandates.

Because it has been a much more difficult research task to determine whether delinquency in an individual manifests itself before the establishment of meaningful relationships in delinquent peer groups, we are left with questions about causal order. This means that we are not sure whether a delinquent seeks out delinquent friends or whether hanging around with delinquents could cause an otherwise law-abiding youth to become delinquent. Over time, researchers have attempted to clarify the nature of peer influence, particularly the way girls influence each other compared to the way boys might influence male peers. Also, in teen couples, the natures of male influence on females and female influence on males have been examined.

For both young males and females, associating with delinquent peers seems to correlate with early sexual encounters. Although other family structure and physical development factors may be influential, the role delinquent friends play in encouraging higher-risk behaviors has been found to be significant across a number of studies (Majumdar, 2002). Research also indicates that the importance of educational goals and achievements noticeably diminishes for girls who become sexually active early in life. Still other studies seem to suggest that this relationship might be reversed in that sexual precociousness may be a response to or result of reduced academic interests (Kierkus, 2009).

Social Control and Social Learning

Social control theory would argue that bonds girls form with their parents and with others who reflect traditional conforming gender roles serve to insulate them from the pressures to engage in more serious forms of delinquency.

Girls who are law abiding have established the meaningful bonds of attachments to parents and teachers and are involved in traditional activities that instill conventional values. Research over the years has demonstrated that girls are more adaptable to common socialization techniques such as praise, recognition, and the benefits of a positive reputation.

Social learning theory, built directly on differential association, is particularly relevant for delinquency because of its emphasis on how socially meaningful rewards are used to enforce behaviors both within the family and within peer groups. Relying on sociology's process of symbolic interaction and the reinforcement principles of behaviorism, the theory posits that learning takes place because of the strength of the values and attitudes associated with certain types of conduct. We learn from others the appropriate motives associated with certain types of actions, and we assess the risks, as well as the benefits, of engaging in deviant activity. Rewards increase the probability that a behavior will be repeated, and when delinquency or deviant behavior is more often rewarded, then one could expect those acts to be committed more frequently.

Both differential association and social learning theories have been used to explain smoking, drug, and alcohol use among young people. A number of studies have supported the roles of both parents and peers in establishing values favorable to substance abuse.

Factors Leading to Increased System Involvement

Female Delinquents and Drugs

In the late 1990s, DARE programs had been implemented in schools across the country, and youth readily admitted in surveys that drug use was one of the most important concerns they were facing. Although 75 to 80% of kids surveyed admitted to trying some form of drug, addiction and abuse are characteristic of only a very small percentage of those children. Drug use, according to the National Youth Survey, does not appear to be related to social class.

The American Correctional Association conducted a study of girls housed in detention centers and found that 60% were in need of substance abuse treatment. Of this group, more than half were addicted to multiple substances. As Chesney-Lind explains:

> They also reported that many of these girls took drugs (34.4%) or drank alcohol (11.4%) as a form of self-medication to make themselves feel better. In addition, a majority stated that they used alcohol (50%) and marijuana (64%) regularly. Of the girls who were substance dependent, most started using between the ages of 12 and 15 . . . evidence for females also indicates that substance abuse is highly correlated with disruptive behavior (2011, p. 81).

In a report from the National Center on Addiction and Substance Abuse, it was noted that there were significant differences in the way young men and women engaged in substance abuse. Girls, the report alleged, are more vulnerable to becoming addicted to cigarettes, alcohol, and drugs; they also become addicted faster than boys do while using less of the substances than their male counterparts. It is further argued that they then suffer the negative consequences more quickly and severely (Barrett, 2003). According to the study:

> Teenage girls often begin smoking and drinking to relieve stress or alleviate depression, while boys do it for thrills or heightened social status . . . . Researchers determined girls are also more likely to abuse substances if they reached puberty early, had eating disorders or were ever physically or sexually abused. Their likelihood of using cigarettes, alcohol or drugs also increases if their families move often. Another trouble period occurs when girls advance from middle school to high school or from high school to college (Barrett, 2003, p. A2).

Although the study did not find significant differences in the percentage of high school girls and boys who drink, girls were more likely to abuse prescription drugs (Barrett, 2003). Low self-confidence and negative self-assessments in comparison to peers were believed to create a risk factor that is greater in young girls. These findings have significant implications for prevention as well as intervention and treatment.

Zero Tolerance and the Creation of Delinquency

According to Randy Shelden, zero-tolerance policies have been responsible for widening the net of the juvenile justice system and increasing the number of youths being officially labeled as delinquents today. He cites examples such as a girl who gave a friend a Nuprin and was subsequently suspended for dealing drugs in school, and a 13-year-old Massachusetts girl who was expelled for having what might be considered a potential weapon in her handbag, an empty lipstick tube. Even though many of the behaviors he outlines are inappropriate and immature, it is questionable whether they should be labeled as "criminal."

As an example, Shelden relates a case reported in one newspaper article:

> [A] 14-year-old girl was handcuffed by the police and hauled off to the local juvenile court. Her "crime" was the clothes she was wearing: a "low-cut midriff top under an unbuttoned sweater," which was a "clear violation of the dress code." The school offered to have her wear a bowling shirt, but she refused. Her mother came in and gave her an oversize T-shirt, which the girl also refused to wear, saying that it "was real ugly." According to the story, the girl is one of the more than two dozen arrested in school this past October for such "crimes" as being "loud and disruptive," "cursing at school officials," and "shouting at classmates" and, of course, violating the dress code. Such "crimes" are violations of the city's "safe school ordinance" (Shelden, n.d.).

Fortunately, the juvenile court judge hearing the case was more reasonable than the school officials and noted that she "didn't come across as a major problem at all. She just wanted to show off a certain image at school."

A zero-tolerance philosophy coupled with more screening and detection on campuses, particularly with special units of school police and probation officers patrolling the grounds, suggests that it is much easier to be caught and punished today for even minor infractions of rules than was the case in the past. Court decisions have upheld the use of locker searches and hair-trigger suspension and expulsion policies. However, a 2009 U.S. Supreme Court decision drew a very clear line in the sand when it struck down the strip search of a 13-year-old girl, all over prescription-strength aspirin. (For those of you who use ibuprofen instead of aspirin, a prescription-strength ibuprofen equals two Advil tablets.) As Savage (2009, p. A1) explains, eighth-grader Savana Redding was suspected of giving another girl the pills:

> Savana said she knew nothing of the pills. Her backpack was searched. When no pills were found, Wilson sent her to a nurse's office, where she was told to remove her outer clothes and to pullout her bra and underwear to check for hidden pills. Nothing was found, and the school officials did not apologize when Savana's mother, April, confronted them over the strip search.

The justices ruled 8 to 1 that school officials went too far, with too little evidence. Justice Souter reasoned, "In sum, what was missing from the suspected facts that pointed to Savana was an indication of danger to the students from the power of the drugs or their quantity, and any reason to suppose that Savana was carrying pills in her underwear. We think that the combination of these deficiencies was fatal to finding the search reasonable."[3]

The U.S. Supreme Court has long been an opponent of strip-searching children in schools or anywhere else. Justice Stevens proffered that "it does not require a constitutional scholar to conclude that a nude search of a 13-year-old child is an invasion of constitutional rights of some magnitude" (*Safford Unified School District v. Redding*, 2009, p. 380) Still, the lone dissenter, Justice Clarence Thomas argued in support of strip-searching children. He said officials should have the power to ensure the health and safety of students in school, without judges second-guessing them. His colleagues, however, would go even further in their condemnation of the practice, often voting to uphold liability claims against schools engaging in strip searches. In 2004, Justice Sotomayor voted in favor of a lawsuit against Connecticut corrections officials who authorized a strip search of two girls in custody at a detention center (Savage, 2009). More recent claims against TSA officials and the random pat downs of young girls in airports will undoubtedly come before the courts.

The courts rationale has perhaps been influenced to some degree by expert testimony about potential damage that strip searches may do to young girls.

---

[3] See http://www.law.cornell.edu/supct/html/08-479.ZS.html

In fact, earlier case law specifically designates that officials must weigh the risks of intrusiveness in terms of "the age and sex of the student and the nature of the infraction" (*New Jersey v. TLO*, 1985). Emotional damage, inability to concentrate, and even subsequent dropping out of school have been effects noted. Savana Redding called the incident "the most humiliating experience" of her life and, as Lithwick (2009) notes, Savana herself dropped out of school.

Another phenomenon noted in the research is the effect of court processing called "bootstrapping." This occurs when court officials intentionally use more serious charges against a youth than those originally specified in order to increase the severity of outcomes that can be used, specifically placement in a detention facility. Pasko, Okamoto, and Chesney-Lind (2011) argue that charges such as contempt of court or violation of a valid court order almost guarantee that the youth will become eligible for institutionalization. Research has also indicated that girls fair worse under these practices than do boys, or other girls who are not issued these types of charges. Studies also seem to conclude that once girls have been in detention, they are more likely to be returned to detention — most likely in response to technical violations — than are boys (Pasko et al., 2011).

Bullying

As with many other types of delinquent behaviors, research seems to indicate that boys and girls process and cope with bullying differently. Most studies find that girls are bullied more frequently than boys and suffer more serious long-term effects such as depression, early pregnancy, and declines in achievement. Girls who come from families offering less emotional support and those who have lower self-esteem are more likely to both bully and be bullied (Totura et al., 2009). Conversely, girls who indicate that their homes are functional are also less likely to bully.

Among middle- and high-school youth, bullying takes on different forms. Girls are more likely to bully within their own social networks or friendship groups, which often makes it difficult for the victims to report or to avoid contact with their tormentors. As Besag (2006) indicates, because the victims and offenders are close, they have personal information about each other and they know phone numbers, passwords, social networking accounts, and various other ways to taunt each other publicly. Girls are more likely than boys to engage in rumors, character attacks and stealthy insults, less-direct gossip, and activity exclusion. Young females tend to become fixated on wrongs and retaliation, spending much more time worrying about bullying events than do boys (Totura et al., 2009).

Teachers report that the seemingly petty squabbles generated by female bullying take up much more of their time and have more negative effects than the less-frequent but more high-profile fighting events that boys engage in. Because the bullying of young girls is less overt, it is harder for school officials to determine when it is occurring and who the initiators are. Totura et al. (2009) explain that girls use covert attack skills to gain social status within their peer group, and that they respond more aggressively to more intense supervision and monitoring. This makes intervention difficult, yet the damage from verbal abuse and psychologically aggressive behavior can drive less emotionally stable girls to skip school and even contemplate suicide. In the last few years the media has highlighted a number of accounts of young girls taking their own lives as a result of the perceived hopelessness of a serious bullying episode.

Acting-Out Behaviors and Self-Harm

Although research based on general population samples of adolescents seems to indicate that some delinquent and acting-out behaviors such as self-mutilation may be more gender-neutral than originally thought, studies based on samples of juvenile teens in the justice system have identified specific gender differences. Eating disorders, suicidal gestures, and self-mutilation have been diagnosed in female delinquent populations much more frequently than in male delinquent populations. The reason for this may have to do with how the concepts are defined and whether or not they are even part of diagnostic screening for young men. More importantly, the dysfunctional family histories and victimization experiences of incarcerated young girls may be more clinically indicative of self-mutilation, suicide gestures, depression, and post-traumatic stress disorder.

National data indicate that Hispanic girls have a higher rate of suicide attempts (16%) than either White (11%) or Black (10%) adolescents. For all racial/ethnic groups, the rates of suicide attempts for girls exceed those of young men (7%). In a study of female teens on probation in El Paso, Texas, Cuellar and Curry (2007) found significant links between suicide attempts, self-mutilation, histories of physical and sexual abuse, as well as drug abuse and certain forms of delinquency, including violent offenses. One of the problems with the study, however, was that self-mutilation included any nonprofessionally created tattoo, something that is not traditionally linked to self-mutilation in other studies. The wider inclusion of amateur tattoos may have contaminated their results and made any conclusions about self-mutilation problematic.

Using a more traditional definition of self-mutilation, Turell and Armsworth (2003) looked at girls with a history of child sexual abuse and its correlation with self-mutilation. They found that child sexual abuse victims who self-mutilated were more likely to manifest dissociative disorders, depression, and eating disorders. These victims were also more likely to have been physically and psychologically abused within their childhood families. The researchers explain that "cutting," as self-mutilation is often called, can be a coping mechanism that helps the victims "survive and accommodate the secrecy, helplessness, and entrapment of the abuse" (Turell & Armsworth, 2003, p. 487). Cutting has also come to be recognized as a symptom of post-traumatic stress disorder. The acknowledgment of a number of celebrities, such as Angelina Jolie, Christina Ricci, and rocker Courtney Love, that they have engaged in cutting has made it a national issue. Even Princess Diana admitted that as a young woman, cutting was a way of dealing with other pain. Television shows like *Beverly Hills 90210* and *7th Heaven*, which were popular among teens, featured the story line as well. If it is, however, as some general-population youth surveys show, something that young males will do — why don't we hear the male stories as well?

Gender-Based Strategies for Delinquency Prevention

In a Maryland juvenile intervention for girls, teens gather around a table for their mandated participation in a Girl Scout program. Unlike scouting topics of the past, however, this session focused on abstinence and contraception. Part mentoring, part venting, the troop leader attempted to rally the participants for a frank discussion:

> "What are the possible side effects of not having sex?" asked Bobbie. "You get real cranky!" Alondra cried out. Merely getting together and girl-talking like this once a week shows the value of gender-specific intervention, Daniele said. "Girls need relationships, they need affiliation," she said (Mehren, 1996, p. A1).

What the juvenile justice worker in this program has known for some time has only become more seriously addressed by government officials in the last decade. As one program administrator reflected, "You can't continue to paint a wall pink and call it a girl's program" (Mehren, 1996, p. A1). In fact, most recognize that delinquency programs for young women cannot be one-size-fits-all:

> For some girls exposed to childhood risks, caring adults, school connectedness, school success, and religiosity helped to prevent certain forms of delinquency during early adolescence, but in other cases, these protective factors were not strong enough to mitigate the impact of the risks. This underscores the notion that one delinquency prevention program cannot be tailored to the needs of all girls who are at risk for delinquency (Hawkins et al., 2009, p. 10).

Unfortunately, government programming for delinquency remains fixated on interventions for young males. This is particularly obvious both from funding reports and from reviews of potentially promising programs. Both public and private funding initiatives are disproportionately geared toward services for boys (Pasko et al., 2011). Experts continue to strive for some more direct and, hopefully, individualized pathways that will lead girls in the system back into lives of productivity and self-esteem. Many of today's federal program priorities call for "gender-specific" initiatives, meaning that funding opportunities are geared toward efforts that are not just replications of traditional male-based strategies.

Throughout the literature there are continued references to the notion that young women are viewed as being more emotionally volatile in treatment and are perceived by social services staff as more stressful to deal with. In fact, much of William Glasser's Reality Therapy counseling techniques were developed around working with teen girls at an institutional setting in California. The idea of contracting for behavior and holding clients accountable for failures to follow through on prescribed treatment protocols were an essential part of his approach.

The literature also recognizes that the treatment needs of young women may be different from those of young men. Young women may have had no experiences living on their own and need more skills development for independent living. They may also require interventions for coping with prior domestic abuse and trauma as well as substance abuse. In some cases, young women may be less prepared for work with fewer marketable skills than their male counterparts and fewer opportunities for positions of unskilled labor. Literacy and academic placement programs, continuing education, and GED completion are also critical for rehabilitation and further delinquency prevention.

Another way to address delinquency prevention that would have a positive effect on young women is through legislation that decriminalizes certain types of conduct and enables or promotes treatment strategies. For example, both New York and California passed "Safe Harbor Acts" in 2008. This legislation requires that teens under the age of 16 who are arrested for prostitution be certified as a child in need of supervision, rather than processed as a delinquent. The intent was to use a system of safe houses to provide a range of health and counseling services that are less likely to be provided in an incarceration setting. Unfortunately, girls aged 16 and 17 are not eligible for this status, which suggests that some other measures might need to be developed to fill the gap that remains for them.

Critical Thinking Questions

1. How do you think male and female delinquency might have changed over the years, and what factors appear responsible for the shifts? Provide support for your answers from what you have read.

2. What could schools do to provide gender-based support for high-risk girls?

3. Which theories about female delinquency seem to best explain behaviors for which we have data? Why? What types of programs do you think would provide the most effective interventions?

Books, Websites, and Media Resources

Fisher, Amy (2004). If I knew then . . . iUniverse, Inc.
Girls and delinquency: https://www.ncjrs.gov/pdffiles1/ojjdp/228414.pdf
Office of Juvenile Justice and Delinquency Prevention: http://www.ojjdp.gov/programs/girlsdelinquency.html

Popular Films

Mi Vida Loca (1993), Angel Aviles, Seidy Lopez, and Jacob Vargas.
The Bad Seed (1956), Nancy Kelly, Patty McCormack, and Henry Jones.
The Girl with the Dragon Tattoo (2011), Rooney Mara.

References

Associated Press. (2011, February 16). Girl, 12, locked up after school for year. Houston Chronicle, p. B2.

Barrett, D. (2003, February 8). Females more vulnerable to addictions, study finds. Associated Press. Houston Chronicle, p. 2A.

Besag, V. (2006). Bullying among girls: Friends or foes. School Psychology International, 27, 535-551.

Bloom, B., Owen, B., Deschenes, L., & Rosenbaum, J. (2007). Developing gender-specific services for delinquency prevention. In R. Muraskin (Ed.), It's a crime: Women and justice (Chap. 49, pp. 792-819). Upper Saddle River, NJ: Prentice Hall.

Canter, R. J. (1982). Sex differences in self-report delinquency. Criminology, 20, 373-393.

Champion, D. J., Merlo, A., & Benekos, P. J. (2013). The juvenile justice system: Delinquency processing and the law (7th ed.). Upper Saddle River, NJ: Pearson.

Chesney-Lind, M. (2011). Gender matters: Trends in girls' criminality. In M. Maguire & D. Okada (Eds.), Critical issues in crime and justice (Chap. 6, pp. 79-94). Thousand Oaks, CA: Sage.

Chesney-Lind, M., & Shelden, R. (2004). Girls, delinquency, and juvenile justice, 2nd Ed. Belmont, CA: Wadsworth.

Costin, L. B. (1991). Unraveling the Mary Ellen legend: Origins of the "Cruelty Movement." Social Service Review, 65(2), 203-223.

Cuellar, J., & Curry, T. (2007). The prevalence and comorbidity between delinquency, drug abuse, suicide attempts, physical and sexual abuse, and self-mutilation among delinquent Hispanic females. Hispanic Journal of Behavioral Sciences, 29(1), 68-82.

Dugdale, R. L. (1877). The Jukes: A study in crime, pauperism, disease, and heredity. New York: Putnam's.

Federal Bureau of Investigation. (2011). Crime in the United States, 2010. Retrieved from http://www.fbi.gov/about-us/cjis/ucr/crime-in-the-u.s/2010/crime-in-the-u.s.-2010/about-cius

Giordano, P., & Rockwell, S. (2000). Differential association theory and female crime. In S. S. Simpson (Ed.), Of crime & criminality (Chap. 1, pp. 3-24). Thousand Oaks, CA: Pine Forge Press.

Goddard, H. H. (1913). The Kallikak family: A study in the heredity of feeblemindedness. New York: Macmillan.

Hawkins, S., Graham, P., Williams, J., & Zahn, M. (2009, January). Resilient girls — Factors that protect against delinquency. Washington, DC: Office of Justice Programs, Office of Juvenile Justice and Delinquency Prevention.

Kierkus, C. A. (2009). Sex, dating and delinquency. El Paso, TX: LFB Scholarly Publishing.

Knight, P. (2010, July 22). Over the Line; As Mexican drug cartels increasingly recruit American teens as runners, a Sugar Land teen goes across the border and ends up dead. Houston Press, pp. 1-5.

Lithwick, D. (2009, April 21). The Supreme Court is neither hot nor bothered by strip searches. Retrieved from http://www.slate.com/id/2216608.

Majumdar, D. (2002). Social and familial determinants of risky sexual behavior among adolescents. Doctoral dissertation, Bowling Green, OH.

Mehren, E. (1996, May 31). Badge of honor. Girl trouble: America's overlooked crime problem. Los Angeles Times, pp. E1, 4.

Moore, J., & Hagedorn, J. (March 2001). Female gangs: A focus on research. Juvenile Justice Bulletin. Washington, DC: Office of Juvenile Justice and Delinquency Prevention.

New Jersey v. T. L. 0., 1985.

Pasko, L., Okamoto, S., & Chesney-Lind, M. (2011). What about the girls? Gender, delinquency and juvenile justice in the 21st century. In D. Springer & A. Roberts (Eds.), *Juvenile justice and delinquency* (Chap. 20, pp. 415-442). Boston: Jones and Bartlett.

Peralta, E., & Feldman, C. (2006, December 4). How they struggled; The butterfly and the knife; In different parts of the city, two kids look for love and a safe place. *The Houston Chronicle*, p. A1.

Price, B. R., & Sokoloff, N. J. (2004). *The criminal justice system and women: Offenders, victims and workers* (3rd ed.). New York: McGraw Hill.

Rodriguez, K. (2010). *Latinas and gangs.* Unpublished master's thesis. Houston, TX: University of Houston, Downtown.

Rosenbaum, J. (1996). A violent few: Gang girls in the California Youth Authority. *Journal of Gang Research*, 3(3), 17–23.

Safford Unified School District v. Redding 557 U. S. 364, 129 S. Ct. 2633, 174 L.Ed.2d 354, 2009.

Savage, D. G. (2009, June 26). High court draws line on school strip-search. *Los Angeles Times*, p. A1.

Shelden, R. (n.d.). Introduction: Getting tough, zero tolerance and net widening. In *Resurrecting radical non-intervention: Stop the war on kids.* Retrieved from http://www.sheldensays.com/Res-one.htm

Totura, C., MacKinnon-Lewis, C., Gesten, E. L., Gadd, R., Divine, K., Dunham, S., & Kamboukos, D. (2009). Bullying and victimization among boys and girls in middle school: The influence of perceived family and social contexts. *Journal of Early Adolescence*, 29, 571–609.

Turell, S., & Armsworth, M. (2003). A log-linear analysis of variables associated with self-mutilation behaviors of women with histories of child sexual abuse. *Violence Against Women*, 9, 487–512.

Vito, G., & Kunselman, J. (2012). *Juvenile justice today.* Boston: Prentice Hall.

Williams, L. (2010). Provide justice for prostituted teens: Stop arresting and prosecuting girls. In N. Frost, J. Freilich, & T. Clear (Eds.), *Contemporary issues in criminal justice policy* (Chap. 19, pp. 297-306). Belmont, CA: Wadsworth.

Zahn, M., Brumbaugh, S., Steffensmeier, D., Feld, B. C., Morash, M., Chesney-Lind, M., Miller, J., Payne, A. A., Gottfredson, D. C., & Kruttschnitt, C. (2008). Violence by teenage girls: Trends and context. Girls study group, understanding and responding to girls' delinquency. Washington, DC: Office of Juvenile Justice and Delinquency Prevention.

Women Working in the Criminal Justice System

Historical Background

In a late nineteenth century book on occupations for women, Willard (1897) describes the profiles of several young women who stumbled into positions as deputy sheriff in the only way that seemed likely in those days, by accident. One, Florence Klotz, a deputy sheriff in Allegheny, Pennsylvania, was the daughter of the alderman. Although the jurisdiction had a constable, it turned out "he had an inconvenient way of being sick or invisible when he was wanted for duty" (p. 363). Desperate to have warrants, summonses, and subpoenas served, the alderman besieged his daughter to deliver them, and the community embraced her efficient performance of duty. From the accounts Willard relates, the young woman settled disputes, effected arrests, and quickly earned a reputation as one of the most reliable employees in the town. Still, Florence's evaluation is something you would never read in today's workplace. "She is the pet of the municipal court, and if she ever sent word for help the entire retinue of clerks, heads of departments, and underlings, would turn out to the rescue of Constable Florence" (Willard, 1897, p. 363).

Likewise, Lillie Fountain worked her way into a deputy sheriff position through an attempt to provide gender-appropriate matrons for women in the social services system. First a schoolteacher, Fountain went to work as an attendant and then a teacher in the State School for the Feeble-Minded. When a chaperone was needed for transporting a mentally ill woman, Fountain became the area's legal escort for the 90-mile trip to Kentucky's Insane Hospital near Louisville. The ability of women in early law enforcement to effectively work with juvenile offenders, female offenders, and mentally ill populations ensured that it would become their primary charge for many years.

The first woman police officer in Houston was hired in 1918. According to Thomas Johnson (1999), she should probably be considered the first female detective because she was assigned to Public Morale and Safety (a type of vice unit) and in that capacity she received the $5 stipend that those promoted beyond patrol earned. By the late 1920s, however, the Houston Police Department had moved toward employing women as matrons instead of for patrol work. In fact, then Chief McPhail was emphatic that "a woman on the police force is unnecessary" (Johnson, 1999, p. 4). Matrons worked exclusively with juveniles and female arrestees. Up through the 1950s more women were coming through the new training academy but not into patrol positions. The assignments that women received continued to be limited to serving as matrons in the jail, performing clerical duties, and dispatching.

In Houston, as in many other jurisdictions across the country at this time, the requirements for patrol officers included being 21 years of age or older, being 5′8′′ to 6′5′′ tall, weighing from 140 to 150 lbs, being a high school graduate or passing an entrance examination (that was given by the University of Houston), and being in good health. Good health meant not having asthma or diabetes, hay fever, a history of tuberculosis, or any physical defects or deformities. And, through the 1960s women who had young children were not eligible, although by 1969 they would be accepted after the youngest child was over one year old (Johnson, 1999).

Women in Law Enforcement

Introduction

When the President's Commission on Law Enforcement and Administration of Justice issued their 1967 report, they advocated the increased hiring of women. The authors pointed out that a major shift was needed in the criminal justice system's view of gender-appropriate roles. They cautioned, "Their value should not be considered limited to staff functions or police work with juveniles; women should also serve regularly in patrol, vice and investigative functions."

Still, progress was very slow and few accomplishments were seen in terms of gender equity. Quotas, instead of benefiting women, were used to limit the number of positions women were eligible to fill, usually 1% of the department's workforce (Balkin, 1988). In fact, minority males made much faster progress into the ranks of law enforcement at local, state, and federal levels.

When J. Edgar Hoover took over the FBI in 1924, he immediately demanded the resignation of two of the three women agents (Jeffreys-Jones, 2007). The third female quit four years later, and the agency went through the next four decades without any female representation in the ranks of special agents. Only after Hoover died in 1972 did things begin to change and women filtered in behind a small but growing number of minority males. Waves of lawsuits by Blacks, Hispanics, and women, coupled with the effect of more progressive leadership, finally began to bring about a more diverse workforce. Perhaps the most dramatic increases in minority employees came throughout the term of Director William Webster (1978-1987). During his tenure, the number of women increased from 147 to 787. And, by 2008, the FBI agent roster was 19% female (Jeffreys-Jones, 2007; Langton, 2010).

The career of Harris County, Texas, Sheriff's Deputy Effie Skinner spans this period where women faced substantial barriers to obtaining the higher-paying jobs of patrol officers as well as the period in which these barriers were overcome. As Turner (2010) explains, Effie had been a secretary in the Houston Police Department, but at 5 feet tall, she was 7 inches below the minimum height required to be a police officer. "Turning to the county, which had no such rule, Skinner enrolled in the sheriff's academy. Upon graduating, she donned the tailored knee-length skirt that female deputies were required to wear. She carried her pistol, handcuffs, and other police gear in a *tres chic* shoulder bag" (Turner, 2010, p. B3). When she attempted to work an after-hours, extra job she was turned down because of the uniform skirt. The business owner just could not believe she would be able to tackle a robber in such an outfit. Not to be rejected, Skinner was eventually successful in arguing for women to be similarly uniformed as their male counterparts. When Skinner retired in 2010 after 35 years, the department had over 300 women, roughly 13% of all deputies (Turner, 2010).

In addition to the President's Commission report of 1967, another of the main forces that helped women like Effie forge careers in the male-dominated criminal justice system was the 1972 *Equal Employment Opportunity Act*. In it, protections from the 1964 *Civil Rights Act* were extended, and vague arguments about "suitability" were challenged in court. The judiciary consistently struck down minimum height and weight requirements and any other criteria that were not logically defensible as a *bona fide* occupational qualification. Many departments modified their hiring practices according to affirmative action only after litigation and the implementation of consent decrees that put specific plans in place to diversify the ranks of law enforcement (Martin, 1991).

Women in Law Enforcement Today

In looking across the employment figures of federal, state, and local law enforcement agencies nationwide, there appear to be approximately 100,000 women serving as sworn officers (Langton, 2010). Women also represent close to 27% of all full-time law enforcement employees (FBI, 2011). And, according to the 2010 *Uniform Crime Report* published by the FBI, there are over 705,000 police officers in the United States of whom about 11.8% are women. However, that percentage is an aggregate figure, meaning that the number of women working in law enforcement is not evenly distributed across the states or within states. The largest numbers are found in large states such as California, Florida, and New York. In rural areas, the rates may dip down to 7% and, in large metropolitan areas, the numbers are closer to 18%. For example, only 2.6% of West Virginia State Troopers are women, and in Connecticut, the State Troopers are only 7% female. Iowa has over 235 police departments, the report notes, and 60% of those agencies have no female officers (Snow, 2010).

As the figures seem to indicate, the number of women in law enforcement varies among the different local, state, and federal agencies. According to one report, in local police departments, women constitute almost 12% of full-time sworn personnel (Reaves, 2010). Federal agencies that had few if any women in the 1970s have increased their numbers to significantly above the national average and by at least 15% by 2008. Women make up 10% of the U.S. Drug Enforcement Administration, 19% of the National Park Service Rangers, and 13% of the Bureau of Alcohol, Tobacco, Firearms and Explosives (Langton, 2010; Schiller, 2008). A recent study of women in federal law enforcement (Barratt, Thompson, & Bergman, 2011) acknowledged that although women may obtain jobs and careers in this field, many are unsure of promotion opportunities within the system. Female respondents indicated that they felt less accepted on the job, particularly in terms of supervisory roles, and that their work generated a certain amount of family/home conflict.

Many in the field acknowledge that barriers to raising the proportion of women in policing still remain. Economic disadvantage and primary child-care responsibilities make it difficult to complete prolonged unpaid training periods or academies where uniforms and weapons must be purchased out of pocket (Taylor et al., 2005). One of the avenues by which women often become interested in and recruited into careers in criminal justice is from prior military service. Today, across all branches of service, including reserves, women constitute about 16% of military forces. The Air Force has the highest percentage of females at almost 20%, with the Marines having the lowest numbers at 7.5%.[1]

Research on Women in Policing

Research indicates that women bring a number of benefits to policing. Although it may not reflect the entire gamut of performance, for administrators as well as community advocacy groups, the avoidance of complaints, lawsuits, and disciplinary action is an advantage for any agency. In addition, the stronger the presence of women in police departments, the fewer are the problems of sexual harassment and gender discrimination. Spillar, Harrington, and Wood (2000) conducted an analysis of civil lawsuits against the Los Angeles Police Department between 1990 and 1999, with a focus on liability costs. Their emphasis was on

---

[1] Current figures, including the number of female veterans by state can be found at http://www.womensmemorial.org/PDFs/StatsonWIM.pdf

potential differences in liability costs between male and female officers serving in a patrol capacity. The study titled *Gender Differences in the Cost of Police Brutality and Misconduct* found the following:[2]

> Female officers were involved in excessive force lawsuits at rates substantially below their male counterparts, and no female officers were named as defendants in cases of police officer involved sexual assault, sexual abuse, molestation, and domestic violence. Of the $66.3 million in judgments or out-of-court settlements paid out by the City of Los Angeles for which the gender of the officer(s) could be determined, $63.4 million (or 95.8%) was attributable to male officers' misconduct. In contrast, $2.8 million (or 4.2%) of total payouts were attributable to female officers' misconduct (Spillar et al., 2000, p. 1).

Of course, the lower payout amounts for female officers might be simply a product of their lower numbers. The raw dollar amounts need to be adjusted for the proportions of male and female officers. Here is what the report had to say about that:

> Although the overall ratio of male to female police officers and sergeants serving in a patrol capacity from 1990-1999 was 4:1, payouts on cases involving male officers' misconduct exceeded payouts on cases involving female officers by a ratio of 23:1. The numbers of male officers involved in or at the scene of an incident exceeded the numbers of female officers involved by a ratio of more than 9:1 (Spillar, Harrington, & Wood, 2000, p. 1).

Over the years police officials have made many attempts to more narrowly define and establish specific criteria for use of force, particularly as a result of the litigation process. Courts have often used the amount and types of training officers receive as a litmus test for good faith efforts to control use of force. Nonetheless, this topic is a contentious one in police community relations, and interpretations seem to be subjective and evolving with each new technology introduced. And, because each excessive force lawsuit against the LAPD averaged a payout of almost $1 million, we can be assured that such a gender gap in policing styles will not be ignored by administrators. In the same LAPD liability study, a sub-analysis of the cost of police brutality and misconduct found that:

> Male police officers disproportionately accounted for the excessive force lawsuit payouts involving killings and assault and battery: male officer payouts for killings exceeded female officer payouts by a ratio of 43:1 and male officer payouts exceeded female officer payouts for assault and battery by a ratio of 32:1.
>
> Often in cases where female officers were present at the scene of an excessive force incident, it appears they were not directly involved in the use of excessive force. Of the 27 female officers involved in or at the scene of an excessive force

---

[2] To read the entire report go to http://www.womenandpolicing.org/ExcessiveForce.asp?id=4516

incident, only 15 were alleged to be directly involved in the use of excessive force (Spillar, Harrington, & Wood, 2000, p. 1).

It appears that there is another significant difference between male and female officers who were named in lawsuits:

> [N]ot one female police officer was named in more than one lawsuit, while some male officers were defendants in more than one case, evidencing a pattern of use of excessive force among these male officers (Spillar, Harrington, & Wood, 2000, p. 1).

Another recent, and related, report in the *Houston Chronicle* (March 27, 2011) published a synopsis of the ten officers who have compiled the most complaints, and who appeared to have the highest records of sustained complaints as well as reprimands and suspensions. Of the ten, nine were male and one was female.

On another issue, studies that have analyzed stress, burnout, and job satisfaction commonly find that males and females experience satisfaction and confidence at similar levels. Overall, the satisfaction level seems fairly high with around 85% saying that they are happy and satisfied in their jobs (Snow, 2010). Men, however, report higher levels of externally induced job burnout (as from the pressures of dealing with others), while women report suffering more incidents of depression (Carlan & McMullan, 2009). Surveys of females working in law enforcement indicate that one of the most significant problems on the job is the negative feedback they receive from male colleagues. In one study of a large police department, 80% of the women reported that the men were openly hostile, threatening, and sexist, and frequently engaged in lewd personal interactions (Harrison, 2012). Research also indicates that when women perceive of sexual harassment as a problem in their agency, they report lower levels of job satisfaction (Harrison, 2012). Still, women appear to stay on the job for the same reasons that men do: the pay, the benefits, the challenges, and the opportunities to help in the community. In examining turnover, however, the reasons that women give for leaving are different from those of their male counterparts. Women cite stress, inflexible schedules, lack of promotions, gossip, poor training, and discriminatory work policies as the main reasons for terminating their employment.

Studies of women who work in the criminal justice field continually make reference to the idea that many females feel that they must overperform or that they are being held to a higher standard of performance than males in the system. In one study, almost half of the women surveyed believed that they had to work twice as hard, while only 9% of the men questioned admitted that. Women often note that they are isolated from the type of male networks that seem to buffer and support their colleagues. Men, they indicate, appear to receive more mentoring, information, and protection on the job. These feelings of isolation appear to be even greater for women of color working in law enforcement. As a result, women ultimately leave policing at higher rates than men, beginning at the academy and continuing into later career levels.

Management theorists would also be interested in the way the professional isolation of women in a male-dominated field like criminal justice might insulate them from corruption and codes of silence. By being treated as outsiders, they may not feel the same loyalty to colleagues who engage in scandals or cover-up schemes. In a post-9/11 investigation of homeland security information, two female FBI agents became the only agency whistle-blowers and testified about mistakes in the tracking and identification of suspected terrorists. Officials in Lima, Peru, also made the news when they proposed developing all-female police departments to reduce corruption and enhance the credibility of state law enforcement (Carlan & McMullan, 2009).

The Women Police Chiefs of Mexico

Reasons for the sudden rise in the number of female police chiefs in Mexico have little to do with the type of employment opportunities developing through legal and social reforms in the United States. Erika Gandara was a dispatcher in a small town, Guadalupe Distrito Bravos, just over the Texas border. When the police chief and male police officers were either killed or quit, she became chief by default. Gandara cut a brave and honorable figure as she pledged to maintain authority proclaiming that "I am not here to do social work or humanitarian labor" (Otis, 2011). Less than six months later, attackers' grabbed her from her home and burned it to the ground as they fled. She has not been seen since. Reportedly, there is no longer a police force there.

Erika's jurisdiction is not far from Praxedis G. Guerrero, where 20-year-old criminology student Marisol Valles Garcia took over as chief of police. She filled a position that had remained unfilled for more than a year, replacing a man who was murdered. Eight other officers had quit, and many residents fled the vast farming area near the U.S. border where there were already 2,500 drug-related killings before the end of 2010 (Otis & Venezia, 2010).

Valles Garcia had very definite ideas about establishing community policing with her small force of 13 officers, 9 of whom were women. Officers were to go door to door trying to connect with families and promote crime prevention (Torres, 2010). The chief did not see herself on a suicide mission; rather she felt compelled to stay focused on the challenges of keeping her beloved community safe. She was doing so with only four guns and one patrol car and a salary of $600 a month for which funds could not be guaranteed. In one media account she said donations are welcome (Otis and Venezia, 2010). Unfortunately, it was not long before the threat of death became too much pressure on the young wife and mother of a young son. Reportedly, she attempted to seek asylum while on a personal trip across the border to the United States. Because Valles Garcia's whereabouts are unknown and she did not return to her job, she has been dismissed from the position.

It should be obvious that gender equality or equal opportunity, or even liability concerns, are not part of the equation with these two Mexican examples. In addition, little here can be viewed as increased job opportunities or social reform. Ironically, a major reason espoused by both of these towns when hiring a female police chief was that the drug cartels would be less likely to harm a woman.

Toward Gender Equality in Policing

Overall, feminists argue that the strides that women have made in the policing occupation have more to do with court orders and legislative mandates than any real organizational change. Many feel that women are still victims of tokenism, social stereotyping, and role entrapment (Carlan & McMullan, 2009), meaning that they are still underrepresented on elite teams and in assignments that lead to promotions and leadership positions. Still, public surveys seem to indicate that there is support within the community for female officers and that many people believe they are as effective as men in the job. Analyses of these surveys also note that support for women police officers increases with the education level of the respondents.

Awareness of the success of women in the role of policing and the risks they assume to carry out the job are all part of changing public perceptions about female officers. By promoting the understanding that women face the same dangers and make the same sacrifices as their male colleagues, old stereotypes and biases may end. In his book, *True Heroines: Police Women Killed in the Line of Duty Throughout the United States, 1916-1999*, William Wilbanks (who also wrote *The Myth of a Racist Criminal Justice System*, 1986) provides a profile of all 138 female law enforcement officers killed in the line of duty between 1916 and 1999. Wilbanks has also updated this catalog with each of the female officers subsequently killed from 1999 to the present, which includes correctional officers, sheriff's deputies, and other law enforcement occupations.[3]

Women in Law and Courts

Courts

The U.S. Supreme Court, in *Bradwell v. Illinois* in 1872/3, upheld an Illinois law that banned female lawyers from appearing in state courts. The ruling read in part:

> Man is or should be women's protector and defender. The natural and proper timidity and delicacy which belong to the female sex evidently unfits it for many of the occupations of civil life. The constitution of the family organization, which is founded in the divine ordinance, as well as in the nature of things indicates the domestic sphere as that which belongs to the domain and functions of womanhood. The harmony of interests and views which belong or should belong to the family institutions, is repugnant to the idea of a woman

---

[3] For a look at this collection, go to http://www.drbillywilbanks.com/trueheroines/addendum.html

adopting a distinct and independent career from that of her husband . . . the paramount destiny and mission of woman are to fulfill the noble and benign offices of wife and mother (*Bradwell v. Illinois*, p. 130).

In words that would perhaps reflect more than just the disparate treatment of women, Justice Miller went on to say:

> I am not prepared to say that it is one of her fundamental rights and privileges to be admitted into every office and position including those which require high special qualifications and demanding social responsibilities. In the nature of things it is not every citizen of every age, sex, and condition that is qualified for every calling and position (*Bradwell v. Illinois*, p. 130).

Narratives from that time period reflect just how difficult it was for a woman to be taken seriously in the legal profession. Nellie Robinson was a female attorney in the 1890s in New York. She was referred to as a rising star in the field as she had won two cases in the Court of Special Sessions. When she was interviewed about the prospect of other young women becoming lawyers, she said that it was a hard life:

> The nervous strain of court practice is wearing even to men, and women are much less able to endure it. I would certainly advise girls to study law as part of a valuable practical education, but I would discourage them from attempting court practice unless it is necessary. It is useless to deny that there is a prejudice against woman lawyers. I mean among the men in the profession. When I first began to practice I had the feminine idea of the social courtesy extended by men to women, and I thought everything was going to be perfectly lovely; but I found out my mistake. If I wanted to win, I had to fight tooth and nail. I did it, but it isn't every woman who would be physically able to endure the strain (Willard, 1897, p. 374).

The progress of women in court-related occupations has been painfully slow. As Supreme Court Justice Ruth Bader Ginsburg relates, when she was a young student at Harvard Law School in the mid-1950s she was one of only nine women attending alongside 500 men. Imagine her dismay when the women were cornered in a room by a professor who demeaned them for occupying spaces in the class that could better be filled by men. She transferred not long after to Columbia where she graduated first in her class and had the distinction of being the first woman to serve on two major law reviews (Parker, 2012).

Today there are three female justices on the U.S. Supreme Court. Elena Kagan and Sonia Sotomayor were appointed by President Barak Obama, and Ruth Bader Ginsburg was appointed by President Bill Clinton. Observers have been quick to note the differences in the style of the two newest members of the court compared to their predecessors. According to one social psychologist, Lawrence Wrightsman (Biskupic, 2011), Kagan and Sotomayor are strategists and are oriented toward an in-depth analysis of details. Another assessment, this one from a political scientist, found them to be more direct in their questioning and intent on pinpointing issues. Interesting profiles emerge that will perhaps shape oral arguments before the Supreme Court in the future as Biskupic (2011, p. A9) explains, "Sotomayor and Kagan have caused a spike in that one-upmanship — although with distinctly different emphases and personal styles. Sotomayor . . . has a hard-charging style and exudes an urgency for answers — particularly on the facts of a case, not the wide legal framework that Kagan typically tests."

Although being a member of the U.S. Supreme Court is a high-profile position that draws attention to the achievements of women, critics argue that below that prestigious post, women are vastly underrepresented in the number of law clerks serving there. In 2006, Greenhouse reported, "Just under 50 percent of new law school graduates in 2005 were women. Yet women account for only seven of the 37 law clerkships for the new term, the first time the number has been in the single digits since 1994, when there were 4,000 fewer women among the country's new law school graduates" (Greenhouse, 2006, p. A22).

More so than with leadership positions in policing and corrections, judgeships are tightly controlled by partisan politics. This is evident in discussions of why there are disproportionately fewer women appointed as clerks to the U.S. Supreme Court. As Greenhouse (2006, p. A22) writes, "Some speculated that Justice Antonin Scalia, who hired only two women among 28 law clerks during the last seven years and who will have none this year, could not find enough conservative women to meet his test of ideological purity." Overall, women hold 22% of the federal judgeships, with the highest number coming from California (48), New York (37), and Texas (30). Examining state-level judicial seats, we find only a slightly higher percentage are held by women (26%) (Center for Women in Government and Civil Society, 2010).

Judges, of course, come from the ranks of lawyers in America, and feminists have long watched the rates at which women have been accepted into, as well as graduated from, law schools. In addition, women's law groups monitor performance on bar exams and on law school admissions tests. In a report issued by the American Bar Association's (ABA) Commission on Women, the following milestones were noted. In 1994, women represented 45% of those entering law school, and by 2002, that number had increased to 50%. A decade later the numbers are closer to 47% enrolled in law school, about 48% of graduates, and 45% of law firm associates (ABA, 2012; Center for Women in Government and Civil Society, 2010). Over the last 15 years, the percentage of female lawyers in this country increased from roughly 23 to 31% (ABA, 2011).

The ABA report also pointed out that as the number of billable hours starting attorneys are expected to compile at their firms has increased to an average of 2,300, it has been more difficult to balance work and home life. Billable hours are usually added to a regular 600 non-billable-hour-work-year, meaning that women must sacrifice more of their family time in order to compete for promotions within the more prestigious law firms. The report also noted that many professional women in the field are also "sandwiched" into caring for both children and elderly parents. Some forms of technology make it easier to work away from the office, but working at home also makes it difficult to be unavailable, leading to many more extended hours of work being conducted at home.

Ironically, it is often men who are most discouraged from seeking judgeships because the pay is much less than an experienced partner in a private law firm would earn. Supreme Court Justice Sonia Sotomayor relays that although her mother was somewhat dismayed that she would be taking a cut in pay to become the first Hispanic Federal District Court judge in New York, she was not deterred. Surviving a grueling 18-month confirmation process, she reflected that her whole life had been challenges and that as a minority woman facing a number of career barriers, she felt the struggle was a normal part of any new opportunity. And, even though she may have felt insecure and not totally comfortable with the new job, she was confident in her ability to develop mastery as she progressed (Sotomayor, 2013). Six years after her appointment to the federal bench in Manhattan, she was seated in the Second Circuit Court of Appeals where she spent 12 years before being nominated to the U.S. Supreme Court. Her reflections on that journey are bittersweet as she notes that the steps became "successively more difficult, the attacks more personal, the entire process faster, more brutally intense" (Sotomayor, 2013, p. 298).

In an interview long after her infamous courtroom battle as prosecutor of the O.J. Simpson murder trial, Marcia Clark reflected on the satisfaction of working in the District Attorney's Office before she became headline news. She acknowledged that she missed the days before Court TV and still thinks about the Simpson trial every day. She admits that women are more heavily scrutinized than their male counterparts and in many instances, it is a lose-lose proposition. "Don't show emotion and you're too tough . . . show emotion and you're a wimpy girl, not strong enough to handle the gig. Although I think we're making strides to get out of those binds, it's going to take awhile before women are judged with a fair measuring stick" (Carpenter, 2011, p. D1). Clark left government work and wrote a book about the Simpson trial, *Without a Doubt*. She admits she loves to write and wrote most of the state's motions and briefs herself during the Simpson trial. She is now a novelist with a best-selling mystery *Guilt by Association* on her resume. Clark also does some criminal appellate law on the side.

Another high-profile prosecutor, Kelly Siegler, also became a media sensation for her graphic "pushing-the-envelope" strategy in the murder trial of Susan Wright, who stabbed her husband nearly 200 times. Directly in front of the jury, she hauled in the crime scene's bloodstained bed mattress and directed her assistant to lay on it in a manner similar to the victim. Then, picking up the murder weapon, she straddled the prone body of her assistant and simulated stabbing him over and over before the horror-struck audience. Siegler also resigned after a long string of successful death penalty convictions and went to work as a special prosecutor in the retrial of death row inmate, Anthony Graves. In preparation for that case, Siegler became convinced of Graves' innocence and eventually worked for his exoneration (www.kellysieglerlaw,com; http://www.texasmonthly.com/story/innocence-found.[4]

---

[4] For a biography of Siegler, see http://www.kellysieglerlaw.com/bio.html

From Law to Politics

Susana Martinez, the first female governor of New Mexico, began her journey to the state capitol as a District Attorney in Las Cruces, New Mexico. Making anti-bullying and child abuse prevention two priorities for her administration, Governor Martinez quickly signed into legislation wide-sweeping measures on both. In keeping with April, as child-abuse prevention month, she ordered flags flown at half-mast and posted billboards around the state encouraging the reporting of child abuse. The bill instituted an instant-reporting hotline system that had both cell-phone and land-line contacts. Her legislation also mandated child-abuse incident training for all law enforcement officers (Simonich, 2011b).

The anti-bullying bill that Martinez signed was a bit more controversial. Annoying her own political party with the "feel-good" measure, the legislation requires every school in the state to implement a bullying-prevention program by 2012 (Simonich, 2011a). Given the opposition, which came exclusively from within her own party, one might question whether issues like child abuse and bullying are really viewed as women's causes, something that transcends party lines and agendas. Martinez has also championed a Native American Suicide Prevention bill and appointed the first female Secretary of Corrections for the state, Lupe Martinez (no relation) (http://corrections.state.nm.us/).

Perhaps one of the highest profile women to go from law to politics was Attorney General Janet Reno. Appointed during the administration of President Bill Clinton,[5] Reno impressed members of all parties with her tough image and no-nonsense style. According to Jeffreys-Jones (2007, p. 218), it seemed that Clinton appointed Reno in order to bring some high-profile gender balance to federal law enforcement. In his nomination speech he bragged, "she has a listed phone number."

Women in Corrections

There are over 430,000 employees in adult state and federal corrections facilities in this country. As of 2005, approximately one-third of them were female (Bureau of Justice Statistics, 2008). In jails across the country, about 20% of correctional officers who are direct line or custody personnel are female. When you consider staff positions other than corrections officers in jail, the percentage of female employees increases to the one-third figure that is the percentage found in most correctional employment sites.

The race and gender breakdowns are still different from those of the inmate population, though it is significantly more diverse than 20 to 30 years ago. Black males make up 11% of the workforce, Black females make up almost 10%. White females make up 20% and White males, 46%. Hispanic males constitute another

---

[5] We could also discuss Hillary Clinton's law-school-to-politics climb, but she held no office within the general justice system.

5% of the state personnel and Hispanic females, 2%. The remaining almost 7% are men and women of other racial groups. Approximately 36,000 persons are employed today in the Federal Bureau of Prisons (AllGov, 2013). In all jurisdictions, 63% of those working with the adult population are correctional officers, although the ratios of officers to inmates vary quite a bit. Other employees may be clerical and treatment staff, equipment and industry specialists, and administrators.

Data from 2000 indicate that about 34% of correctional officers are minority and about 22% are female. African Americans constitute 24% of officers and Hispanics approximately 8% (Camp, 2003). Information on salaries reveals that although pay for entry-level positions varies across the country, the averages range between $16,000 and $30,000. These salary figures do not include overtime pay, which often supplements an officer's pay by as much as 30%.

Of the roughly 262,000 direct custody officers employed in public state correctional institutions as of 2005 (Bureau of Justice Statistics, 2008, the latest available data), about 76,000 or 27% are women and only 14% of those are in supervisory positions. This figure is similar to the number of women who are in supervisory positions within the Federal Bureau of Prisons, whereas of 2010, only 17 of more than 100 head warden and associate warden positions are filled by women (Prisontalk, 2013).

In 1992, Kathleen Hawk was named as the first female head of the Federal Bureau of Prisons. Still, she was more than a decade behind the first woman director of the Department of Corrections in California, Ruth Rushen. Rushen was also the first African American female to direct a state prison system. Before taking over one of the country's largest correctional organizations in 1981, with 82 prisons, camps, and parole offices, Rushen built her career in the state's probation and parole systems.

In a 2003 study that surveyed prison wardens and superintendents nationwide, researchers analyzed 90 responses from females and compared them to their male counterparts. Although there were few significant differences between the groups in terms of philosophy and management style, women were more likely to accept suggestions from their line staff and more likely to emphasize rehabilitation, they were less likely to discuss professional job stresses with colleagues. Demographically, the group of female wardens was slightly younger than the men but more educated although they were less likely to have served in the military. Both groups were predominantly White (Kim, Devalve, Devalve, & Johnson, 2003).

Doing Corrections

Researchers often find that job satisfaction is a major factor distinguishing male and female employees in the correctional system. According to a recent study of correctional officers in the Midwest (Lambert & Hogan, 2010), gender was just one of the measures that appeared to influence job satisfaction, with men expressing lower levels of satisfaction than women. Still, there are a number of other variables including "position, tenure, job variety, job autonomy, perceived dangerousness of the job, and perceptions of organizational innovation" that affected job satisfaction. According to the authors, "those working in custody positions reported, on average, lower satisfaction with their jobs compared to staff working in noncustodial positions. Tenure and perceived dangerousness of the job had an inverse correlation. Job variety, job autonomy, and perceptions of organizational innovation each had a positive correlation with job satisfaction" (Lambert & Hogan, 2010, p. 172).

The history of women's leadership roles in federal corrections is similar to that of state corrections and law enforcement in general, as the milestones slowly crept up the chain of command until a woman was named Director of the Bureau of Prisons in 1992. Another woman, Helen Marberry, was the first female to be named a warden at the Federal Correctional Institution-Milan in Michigan. She took over the post in 2004 at the age of 45. Interviewed by *The Ann Arbor News* shortly after she began her tenure, she made the following comments about her career choices:

> My mother was probably the biggest role model . . . . When I was a teen, she worked at a halfway house in St. Louis. She cooked at a halfway house and I would hear her tell stories of inmates being in the system. Halfway in, halfway out. I went to Central Missouri State University, undergraduate in corrections and a master's in public administration. I've always seen myself as someone who wanted to give back, impact changes. I was a case manager, a social worker, a special agent and associate warden at FCI Oxford, Wis., and the U.S. Penitentiary at Leavenworth, Kan., prior to FCI Milan . . . . I don't know if I set out to be a warden, but as I got involved in this business (of corrections), opportunities presented themselves . . . . As a woman (warden), I bring the calming effect to this environment. Men tend to be more challenging a lot of times. Women tend to calm the environment (Pyen, 2005).

Women and Risks in Corrections Work

As in policing, employees are always aware of the dangers and risks inherent in the job. However, that said, people still seem to react with more concern and apprehension about women in these jobs than they appear to with men. For example, when Texas Department of Criminal Justice Officer Susan Canfield was killed in an escape attempt at a Huntsville prison unit, her husband was quoted as saying he always worried about the dangers in her taking this job. Even though all spouses of criminal justice personnel might feel that way, the reactions and quotes relative to danger and risk seem to appear more blatantly when it is a female who is killed or injured.

In analyzing the 2007 event in which Canfield was murdered, officials faulted the officer with whom she was assigned, Joe Jeffcoat, for not following policy which led to the ensuing escape. Jeffcoat subsequently resigned, but a number of other lapses in training and policy were also cited as contributory, and those were beyond a single employee's authority (Langford, 2007).

When a female correctional officer was taken hostage by two protesting inmates on death row in Texas, security cameras captured the event on tape. Fifty-seven-year-old Jeannette Bledsoe was treated with respect by the inmates, which may be more a testimony to her suitability for the job than a reason to avoid the risks of doing the job. The situation was resolved peacefully in about 13 hours after the inmates aired their grievances and complaints (Graczyk, 2000).

For Iowa Corrections Officer Kristine Sink, however, risk on the job seemed to be exacerbated by the sexually explicit and violent movies prisoners are allowed to watch. When Officer Sink complained or shut off the movies, she was reprimanded by her supervisors and threatened by the inmates. She alleged that "the movies played multiple times a day for a week on a television in a common area where 45 inmates could watch. Some inmates would openly masturbate and make sexually harassing comments to her" (Foley, 2013). Still, after ten years of frustration and retaliation, she finally filed a lawsuit in hopes of raising awareness of this type of easily rectified hostile work environment.

Raising the Profile of Women in Criminal Justice

Looking back at the struggles women faced, Balkin (1988) concludes that resistance to the gender-integrated workforce was not only the perception that criminal justice was not a suitable job but also the belief that women should not be working outside the home at all. Today a number of professional organizations exist to help women work together to achieve common goals for professional activity and recognition. The International Association of Women Police (IAWP, http://www.iawp.org/) holds meetings, publishes a magazine, presents awards, and provides mentoring, networking, and peer support. Founded in 1915, the group also provides opportunities for training and encourages the membership and participation of male officers. Its first and longest-serving president, Alice Stebbins Wells, is credited with being the first female police officer in Los Angeles, and someone who set the standard for hiring all around the country. As the LAPD website explains:

> After Wells successfully petitioned for a place on the LAPD, she was equipped with a telephone call box, a police rule book and first aid book, and the "Policewoman's Badge Number One." The need for her own badge arose when Wells, utilizing the free streetcar passage policy for law enforcement was accused of misappropriating her husband's credentials.
>
> Wells was assigned to work with the LAPDs first juvenile officer, and was quickly subject of an order issued by the force that ruled that young women could now only be questioned by female police officers. Wells began her career supervising skating rinks and dance halls, as well as interacting with female members of the public. Two years after Wells joined the force, two other female officers were sworn in, with all female officers now under the control of the Civil Service. Sixteen other cities had hired police officers as a direct result of Well's

activities (http://www.lapdonline.org/history_of_the_lapd/content_basic_view/833).

The legacy of Alice Stebbins Wells is therefore much more than just a notation in most criminal justice and policing textbooks. In addition to founding the IAWP she began the Women's Peace Officers Association of California in 1928. Paving the way for other women to embark on successful careers was her passion. In 1918, she even convinced the university that later became UCLA to offer a specific college course for women in policing.

There are a number of professional organizations that focus on women in law. The American Bar Association has a Commission on Women in the Profession. They list related national organizations as follows:

- Association of Black Women Lawyers
- Legal Momentum: Advancing Women's Rights
- Lex Mundi, Women in the Law
- National Asian Pacific Women's Forum
- National Association of Minority and Women Owned Law Firms
- National Association of Women Judges
- National Association of Women Lawyers
- National Bar Association Women's Division
- National Conference of Women's Bar Associations
- National Women's Law Center

In Texas, the Association of Women Attorneys (AWA), which is based in Houston, looks for ways to empower female attorneys in the state. Their website describes their mission as follows:

- Strengthen the image of women attorneys in the community.
- Work toward the elimination of all forms of discrimination against women attorneys.
- Promote a forum for the exchange of knowledge and experiences of women attorneys.
- Increase, expand, and improve job opportunities for women attorneys.
- Promote continuing legal education and professional growth.
- Promote active participation in Bar organizations.
- Encourage and assist the professional development of women attorneys.
- Encourage women to enter the legal profession and assist them during their legal education (http://www.awahouston.org).

As with women's organizations for police and law, the Association of Women Executives in Corrections offers awards, training, and regular meetings to promote the development of female leaders in corrections. Affiliated with both the American Correctional Association and the American Probation and Parole Association, this group has been active for about 15 years. You can access their website at http://www.awec.us/.

Critical Thinking Questions

1. What recruiting strategies would you use if you were tasked with increasing the number of female applicants to your criminal justice agency?

2. What do you think the court would rule in the case of correctional officer Sink who felt sexually harassed by inmates watching sexually explicit and violent shows? Considering that inmates pay for all television and movie access and equipment, what movies and shows would you put on the acceptable viewing list?

3. Do women bring special skills to the criminal justice workplace? If so, how do managers utilize those effectively while still being fair in assignments and on other personnel issues?

Books, Websites, and Media Resources

A female Mexican sheriff: http://www.nypost.com/p/news/international/baby_faced_mex_sheriff_we_can_live_umBi2wXG39U1I26xkEO9oM#ixzz1FS5aiz00

Clark, Marcia, & Carpenter, T. (1998). *Without a doubt.* New York: Penguin Books.

Giffords, G., Kelly, M., & Zaslow, J. (2012). *Gabby: A story of courage, love and resilience.* New York: Scribner.

Interview with Justice Ginsburg: http://supremecourt.c-span.org/Video/JusticeOwnWords/SC_Jus_Ginsburg.aspx

Prejean, H. (1993). *Dead man walking.* New York: Random House.

U.S. Justice System Employment: http://www.bjs.gov/index.cfm?ty=tp&tid=5

Popular Films

Silence of the Lambs (1991), Jodie Foster.
V. I. Warshawski (1991), Kathleen Turner.

References

AllGov. (2013). *Federal Bureau of Prisons.* Retrieved from http://www.allgov.com/departments/department-of-justice/federal-bureau-of-prisons-bop?agencyid=7204

American Bar Association. (2011). *A current glance at women in the law, 2011.* Chicago: ABA Commission on Women in the Profession.

American Bar Association. (2012). Enrollment and degrees awarded: 1963-2011 academic years. Retrieved from http://www.americanbar.org/content/dam/aba/administrative/legal_education_and_admissions_to_the_bar/statistics/enrollment_degreesawarded._authcheckdam.pdf

Balkin, J. (1988). Why policemen don't like policewomen. *Journal of Police Science and Administration, 16,* 29-36.

Barratt, C. L., Thompson, R. J., & Bergman, M. E. (2011). *Women in federal law enforcement: Why do non-supervisory sworn female officers seek promotion into supervisory roles and how did female supervisors get there?* Arlington, VA: Women in Federal Law Enforcement. Report abstracted online at http://www.wifle.org/pdf/WIFLE-TxAMCollaboration.pdf

Biskupic, J. (2011, March 4). Rookies on the bench may recast liberal wing. *USA Today*, p. 9A.

Bradwell v. Illinois 83 U.S. 130 (1872).

Bureau of Justice Statistics. (2008). *Census of State and Federal Correctional Facilities, 2005.* Washington, DC: U.S. Department of Justice.

Camp, C. G. (2003). *The 2002 Corrections Yearbook*, Middletown, CT: Criminal Justice Institute.

Carlan, P., & McMullan, E. (2009). A contemporary snapshot of policewomen attitudes. *Women and Criminal Justice*, 19, 60-79.

Carpenter, S. (April 18, 2011) Taking law into her own hands: Former prosecutor Marcia Clark metes out justice in a new murder-mystery. *Los Angeles Times*, p. D1.

Center for Women in Government and Civil Society. (2010). *Women in federal and state-level judgeships.* Albany: University at Albany, State University of New York.

Federal Bureau of Investigation. (2011). *Crime in the United States, 2010.* Retrieved from http://www.fbi.gov/about-us/cjis/ucr/crime-in-the-u.s/2010/crime-in-the-u.s.-2010

Foley, R. J. (2013, January 7). At Iowa prison, a lonely battle against sex movies. Associated Press in the NY Daily News. Retrieved from http://www.nydailynews.com/news/national/prison-inmates-watched-violent-sexually-explicit-movies-article-1.1234724

Graczyk, M. (2000, February 2). Death row standoff ends quietly. *Associated Press.* Retrieved online January 5, 2014 at http://www.apnewsarchive.com/2000/Death-Row-Standoff-Ends-Quietly/id-8c59b6ad79e6516a85e0f7227a8f8ed3

Greenhouse, L. (2006, September 1). Women scarce among law clerks. *Houston Chronicle*, p. A22.

Harrison, J. (2012). Women in law enforcement: Subverting sexual harassment with social bonds. *Women and Criminal Justice*, 22(3), 226-238.

Jeffreys-Jones, R. (2007). *The FBI: A history.* New Haven: Yale University Press.

Johnson, T. (1999). *A history of the Houston Police Department.* Eric Document 446013, Educational Resources Information Center.

Kim, A., Devalve, M., Devalve, E., & Johnson, W. (2003). Female wardens: Results from a national survey of state correctional executives. *The Prison Journal*, 83(4), 406-425.

Lambert, E. G., & Hogan, N. L. (2010). Wanting change: The relationship of perceptions of organizational innovation with correctional staff job stress, job satisfaction, and organizational commitment. *Criminal Justice Policy Review*, 21(2), 160-184.

Langford, T. (2007, December 5). TDCJ officer faulted in fatal prison break. *Houston Chronicle*, p. B1.

Langton, L. (2010, June). *Women in law enforcement.* Crime Data Brief, Bureau of Justice Statistics. Washington, DC: U.S. Department of Justice.

Martin, S. E. (1991). The effectiveness of affirmative action: The case of women in policing. *Justice Quarterly*, 8, 489-504.

Otis, G. A. (January 30, 2011). Las valientes of Mexico. *New York Post*, Retrieved online January 5, 2014 athttp://nypost.com/2011/01/30/las-valientes-of-mexico/

Otis, G. A., & Venezia, T. (2010, October 22). Baby-faced Mexican sheriff to take on world's worst drug gangs. *New York Post.* Retrieved from http://www.nypost.com/p/news/international/baby_faced_mex_sheriff_we_can_live_umBi2wXG39U1I26xkEO9oM#ixzz1FS5aiz00

Parker, K. (2012, September 30). New film plays homage to female trailblazers. *Houston Chronicle*, p. B10.

Prisontalk. (2013). *BOP wardens and administrators.* Retrieved from http://prisontalk.com/forums/showthread.php?t=519369

Pyen, C. W. (2005, July 3). First female warden strives for safe and orderly facility. *Ann Arbor News*, Retrieved online January 4, 2014 at http://www.prisontalk.com/forums/archive/index.php/t-134311.html

Reaves, B. A. (2010). *Local police departments, 2007* (NCJ 231174). Washington, DC: Bureau of Justice Statistics.

Schiller, D. (2008, December 2). DEA on lookout for savy women. *Houston Chronicle*, p. B1.

Simonich, M. (2011a, March 29). NM becomes ally in fight against bullying. *The Las Cruces Sun Times*, p. A8.

Simonich, M. (2011b, March 29). Martinez aims to increase abuse awareness. *The Las Cruces Sun Times*, p. A8.

Snow, R. L. (2010). *Policewomen who made history.* Lanham, MD: Rowman & Littlefield.

Sotomayor, S. (2013). *My beloved world.* New York: Knopf.

Spillar, K., Harrington, P., & Wood, M. (2005, September). *Gender differences in the cost of police brutality and misconduct: A content analysis of LAPD civil liability cases: 1990-1999.* The Feminist Majority Foundation and The National Center for Women & Policing. Retrieved from http://www.womenandpolicing.org/ExcessiveForce.asp?id=4516

Taylor, B., Kubu, B., Fridell, L., Rees, C., Jordan, T., & Cheney, J. (2005). *Cop crunch: Identifying strategies for dealing with the recruiting and hiring crisis in law enforcement* (NCJ 213800). Washington, DC: Police Executive Research Forum.

Torres, O. (2010, October 21). New chief in town: A lawless border community is turning to a 20-year old student. *Houston Chronicle*, p. A1.

Turner, A. (2010, September 1). She measured up to the job. *Houston Chronicle*, pp. B1, B3.

Wilbanks, W. (1986). *The myth of a racist criminal justice system.* Pacific Grove, CA: Brooks Cole.

Wilbanks, W. (2000). *True heroines: Police women killed in the line of duty.* New York: Turner.

Willard, F. (1897). *Occupations for women.* Coopers Union, NY: The Success Company.

Employment Issues and the Law

Introduction

A young Canadian couple kept their families informed every step of their normal pregnancy and delivery but confounded everyone when they decided not to reveal the gender of the newborn. Simply named "Storm," the parents felt that the child's interactions with others should not be controlled by gender roles and assumptions. Homeschooling two older sons, the couple believes that children should be able to choose aspects of gender identity that they are comfortable with and not the "tyranny" of imposed gender biases (Roth, 2011). The parents explained that "kids receive messages from society that encourage them to fit into existing boxes, including with regard to gender." They added their belief that "if we delayed sharing that information, in this case, hopefully, we might knock off a couple million of those messages." At the point the newspaper story appeared, the four-month-old's gender was still unknown to everyone but the parents, the brothers, and the two midwives present at the birth (Roth, 2011). Even the grandparents did not know, which at least means they don't have to change diapers!

The case of baby "Storm" illustrates just how much "gender matters." The parents are defying all social sensibilities with their provocative approach—which has to make us wonder, "Why IS it so important that we know that baby or any other baby's sex?" Theorists and practitioners agree that gender is a major factor in how we are socialized as children, but few parents go so far to attempt to thwart that process. In fact, across America, we start sending gender messages right at birth with blue stork signposts and tiny pierced earrings, bows, and plastic tool kits. If you were to go through a baby's clothing store right now, what images would you see on girls' clothes versus boys' clothes? If you were picking out clothing as a present, would you try to avoid a gender stereotype like a princess pink shirt or a dump-truck brown design?

In this chapter we look at how the law views gender and the impact of gender stereotypes in the workplace. Many traditions in employment are rooted in myths about gender-related skills and employment preferences. The development of a gender-neutral work environment has been a long and slow process, and many of the opportunities we take for granted were hard-fought efforts as the previous chapter demonstrated. Some of the assumptions that the law has had to address in the criminal justice arena have been related to the concept of risk and dangerousness.

Women and High-Risk Occupations/Assignments

A number of factors have been identified with an increased risk of occupationally related violence. These include any type of work that directly involves the public such as jobs in community-based settings, particularly law enforcement, nursing, social work, and other occupations requiring home visits. For example, child protective workers, process servers, police officers, and parole and probation officers would fall into this latter category. In addition, those who provide some type of service, care, advice, or education are also thought to be at higher risk. Other risk factors include being in close contact with unstable or volatile people and working in bars or restaurants or sporting events where alcoholic beverages are served.

In *Dothard v. Rawlinson* (1977), the state of Alabama took a desperate gamble when they attempted to argue that direct-contact positions within the prisons were too dangerous for women. Although they were attempting to hold on to the minimum height and weight requirements and their contention that being male was a necessary or *bona fide* occupational qualification, the U.S. Supreme Court was unimpressed. In fact, the justices ruled that if the prison was truly that dangerous, then it was too dangerous for men as well. The presence of such violence and peril, they reasoned, likely meant that conditions were cruel and unusual, a violation of the Eighth Amendment. The state was given a limited time to impose order and safety within the institutions or have them shut down. For women, the barriers to working in close custody, where employees built up experience necessary to promotion, were beginning to erode.

Current technologies have made working in correctional institutions considerably safer. Video surveillance, metal detectors, personal alarm systems, and radio frequency identification devices (RFIDs) all have been employed to decrease the rates of assaults on officers. Proper classification and housing assignments for inmates also reduce the risk that a violent inmate will be allowed in a less-secure environment, as does better training and equipment for personnel.

Although prisons, jails, and mental health facilities may be safer places to work than ever before, other occupations remain high risk for both men and women. For example, the recent revelation that a young female CBS News reporter, Lara Logan, had been brutally beaten and sexually assaulted by a frenzied mob while covering political events in Egypt shocked our country. The event and our processing of it reflected the many social changes that have taken place regarding women on the job. First, the fact that a female was on assignment in an unstable and potentially dangerous locale is characteristic of perhaps only the last 25 years. That what happened to her was acknowledged and reported is an even more recent breakthrough in our treatment of sexual assault. That the woman has spoken publicly and honestly about it tells us that we have reached a point in our response to victims where open dialogue about the experience can take place.

Having sexual victimization emerge from the shadows of the problem workplace is a first step in the reduction of abuse and stigmatization. When a company like KBR is accused of ignoring sexual harassment and assault of its female employees working overseas, the litigation exposes bad management practices and policies that place workers at risk. Likewise, when female staff working for a federal judge risk their jobs to complain about a sexually threatening work environment, it is an opportunity to formally unite and emphasize the values that a society holds, and the conduct that it will not tolerate.

The legal analysis of cases such as that of Texas Federal Judge Kent and KBR often brings to light that the organization had a history of such problems, and inappropriate, if not illegal, conduct had already been detected. What we need to stress at this point is that the tolerance or acceptance of these past behaviors is a substantial liability to an agency or company during litigation. It is the legal concept of "knowing" or that one "should have known" that exposes an entity to liability. In law the concept of *respondeat superior* means that a supervisor is responsible for the conduct that occurs within an organization, regardless of whether he or she knew about it or not simply based on the principle that, as a leader, he or she should have known. The legal language that you will often see in these cases is "knew or should have known," which means that you already did know of something going on and that makes you as liable as being in a position where you should have known, even if you didn't. It is assumed that not knowing what is going on in your company is no excuse. Supervisors, those who hire and retain employees, are under an obligation to vet records, encourage reporting, follow up on allegations, and be aware of any past suspicious or actionable conduct that may pose a threat to the current work environment.

One example is the case of a lawsuit filed by a female employee of KBR who was sexually attacked by David Breda Jr., another KBR employee. Records indicate that Breda, who pled guilty to the attack and was sentenced to two years in federal prison, was a "former U.S. Army recruiter who had previously been sanctioned for molesting an 18-year-old female recruit." Knowledge of such a record would, in most legal textbooks, constitute negligent hiring (Pinkerton, 2010).

Feminists argue that hostile work environments are often created because men may be more tolerant of the physical or sexual deviance of their colleagues and peers. Even formal charges do not seem to draw condemnation that may be proportionally fitting. For example, well-known and wealthy hand surgeon

Michael Brown had a long and violent history of spousal abuse and illegal drug use, both of which are not personal or arbitrary judgments of character — they are crimes. As Todd Ackerman reported (2010, p. A17), in 2002, Brown was "charged with and later convicted of beating his pregnant third wife with a broken bedpost and pulling her down the stairs by her hair. In 2006, the Texas Medical Board revoked his license after he tested positive for cocaine." According to public records from courts and medical boards, "He's been treated for narcissistic personality disorder, bi-polar disorder, and depression and spent time at an addiction rehab center and court-ordered anger management counseling" (Ackerman, 2010, p. A17). Still, his thriving surgical centers in Houston, Dallas, Austin, Phoenix, and Las Vegas earn about $45 million per year. "In 2008, he was awarded a Republican Congressional Medal of Distinction which included a lunch with Vice President Dick Cheney and a dinner with President George W. Bush. This year, he threw out the first pitch at an Astros game" (Ackerman, 2010, p. A17).

Sexual Harassment

Behavior theorists often explain that sexual harassment can be an issue of power, abuse of power, or an attempt to gain power over another employee. In the criminal justice system, feminist critics have pointed out that traditional patriarchal structures and paramilitary models lend themselves to male dominance. It would not be unusual to find, within such a system, that men cover for each other and protect a code of silence that would inhibit the discipline of predatory actions. Critics further complain that simply relying on the establishment of written policies is not an effective preventive mechanism for reducing sexually inappropriate behaviors. In reality, despite years of training and retraining on the issue, sexual harassment is alive and well in many workplaces, criminal justice system workplaces included. To those who have filed claims, agencies rarely resolve problems quickly or satisfactorily, and internal affairs offices have not been effective in handling such cases.

Identifying and Analyzing Sexual Harassment

Sexual harassment may take many forms from verbal comments meant to embarrass or belittle a co-worker to unwanted physical contact including patting, groping, and rubbing up against someone. Harassment may include derogatory comments about one's ability to do the job, sexualized jokes, and gestures or cartoons, as well as the presence or distribution of pornographic images. More serious allegations may involve threats of a sexual or assaultive nature and completed, as well as attempted, sexual assaults.

One of the more common misconceptions about sexual harassment is that once a woman engages in any sexual conduct with a perpetrator, that she would not be able to claim that her rights had been violated. The law instead recognizes that sometimes safety and defusing a potentially combative assailant must take priority. An employee then would be protected even if she complied with sexual demands, as long as the demands were unwelcome. And, as has been determined by the courts, just because a woman does not verbally protest does not mean that she welcomed the sexual behavior. In other words, silence cannot be interpreted as consent. The courts have also indicated that previous intimate behavior with her harasser does not preclude a victim from being able to file charges later if the conduct becomes unwelcome. However, under these circumstances, the person bringing charges must have clearly communicated that the conduct was now unwelcome.

Although men may be less likely to identify behavior they experience as sexual harassment, they account for about 12% of all sexual harassment victims who file charges. About 90% of all perpetrators filed upon are male. Studies have indicated that men who engage in sexual harassment are more authoritarian in their orientation toward women and are lower on empathy in their relationships with others. The psychological profile of a sexual harasser is of a person who holds more negative and traditional attitudes, sees gender relationships as adversarial, and is more likely to support hypermasculine stereotypes for acceptable behavior. One of the red flags on the job that may identify a potential perpetrator of sexual harassment is that someone pays more sexual attention to co-workers.

Data indicate that about 55% of women in the workforce today have experienced sexual harassment. That figure jumps to 72% when surveying women who work in policing, firefighting, or the military. The most common form of sexual harassment that respondents reported was inappropriate gender or sexual comments. Over 40% of those participating in one survey said that such comments were a daily occurrence at work. According to Harrison (2012), work groups supervised by males and employing a disproportionate number of males are more likely to tolerate higher levels of sexual harassment. Adding the discomfort of unwanted remarks to already stressful jobs seems unnecessarily oppressive and in some cases leads to depression and anxiety.

Research has indicated that for many victims, confronting or reporting sexual harassment does not end the behavior; in fact, in some cases it may result in escalation or even retaliation. It is no wonder that many victims feel that nothing will be done or that the negative way they will be labeled by their co-workers will outweigh any benefit of reporting. For example, in one study, only 21% of women who experienced an attempted or actual rape even reported it, and 19% quit their jobs. Statistically, then, women were as likely to quit as they were to report, which is a very troubling finding. It is also noted that women often just request transfers of shift or reassignment to other units within the agency. It also appears that there is considerable variation between women in how they will handle sexual harassment on the job. A 2009 survey by Chaiyavej and Morash found that policewomen who viewed sexual harassment as a violation of work policy and organizational regulations were more likely to take it more seriously and to respond more assertively. On the other hand, those who were more concerned about social reaction or who felt more alienated in the work environment responded more passively to the situation (Chaiyavej & Morash, 2009).

The effects suffered by victims of sexual harassment are well documented in the literature. They include both personal and professional losses. Many victims report depression, anxiety, eating and sleeping disorders, low self-esteem, anger, headaches, fatigue, nausea, and weight fluctuations. On the job, they acknowledge decreased productivity and job satisfaction, low morale, and increased time away from work such as use of vacation and sick time, as well as disruptions in their career paths.

Legal Concepts and Issues

It is important to remember that sexual harassment cases are most often civil suits and as such have different standards of evidence and levels of proof than criminal cases. Often, it can be determined that someone's rights have been violated simply by establishing a set of facts, such as that contact occurred or that the person alleged to have committed harassment was in a position of power over the subordinate employee. In litigation for sexual harassment, the key elements of an offense are evaluated in terms of how the plaintiff perceived the conduct, regardless of the intentions of the alleged harasser. Many men will contend that their actions were meant to convey flattery and that the content of their comments was harmless. Because there are often significant differences in the way workplace behaviors are interpreted, the court found it necessary to adopt a standard for evaluating sexual harassment based on what was reasonable to an average woman today. The judge would ask the jury to evaluate the comments or conduct as would the average, reasonable woman, so that they would be careful not to impose, in the case of a male juror, any gender bias in their deliberations.

The notion of a reasonable woman standard replaced the traditional concept of "a reasonable person" used in law. In *Ellison v. Brady*, the court explained that just because certain forms of teasing and flirting may be common, that does not make them right. The court felt that in adopting a victim's perspective on the conduct directed at her, they would also need to view it through the eyes of a woman who might be more fearful of her pursuer's intentions. The court concluded that:

> Conduct that many men consider unobjectionable may offend many women. . . . "A male supervisor might believe, for example, that it is legitimate for him to tell a female subordinate that she has a 'great figure' or 'nice legs.' The female subordinate, however, may find such comments offensive"; "men and women are vulnerable in different ways and offended by different behavior. . . . " men tend to view some forms of sexual harassment as "harmless social interactions to which only overly-sensitive women would object"; the characteristically male view depicts sexual harassment as comparatively harmless amusement . . . we believe that many women share common concerns which men do not necessarily share. For example, because women are disproportionately victims of rape and sexual assault, women have a stronger incentive to be concerned with sexual behavior. Women who are victims of mild forms of sexual harassment may understandably worry whether a harasser's conduct is

merely a prelude to violent sexual assault. Men, who are rarely victims of sexual assault, may view sexual conduct in a vacuum without a full appreciation of the social setting or the underlying threat of violence that a woman may perceive. (*Ellison v. Brady*, 924 F.2d 872; 1991).

For over 25 years, the U.S. Supreme Court has recognized that sexual harassment is a form of sexual discrimination. This was clarified in the decision of *Meritor Savings Bank v. Vinson*. In this case the court found ample evidence of a hostile work environment. Within its decision, the court identified two forms of harassment: quid pro quo and hostile work environment.

Quid Pro Quo

In Latin the phrase quid pro quo literally means "this for that." It reflects some form of arrangement where with a promise or threat, a tangible reward or payment will be made. In order to establish a claim of quid pro quo, the person offering the reward, a promotion, or a bonus must actually have the power to do so, such as a manager, supervisor, or agent of the employer. Under this type of claim the court would assume a strict liability position. This means that the organization is held liable regardless of whether or not it knew of the transgression. An organization is, in the eyes of the court, automatically liable for the actions of its supervisors. Still, a quid pro quo case is less frequently seen in litigation. Fewer than 10% of women surveyed on workplace sexual harassment indicated that they had been offered positions or favors for sex, and even fewer ever filed a formal complaint. The second type of claim, the creation of a hostile work environment is something you may see in a class action or multiple-plaintiff suit.

Hostile Work Environment

In a hostile work environment case, the allegations are that an employee is subjected to oppressive and intimidating conditions on a daily basis. This could mean that hazing or teasing is routine or areas display sexually offensive posters and pictures. In establishing that such an environment exists, the court focuses on the pattern of such actions and displays; a single incident would not qualify. In a clear-cut case, the conduct would be attributed to more than one perpetrator, would include verbal as well as physical conduct, would be repeated frequently, and would target several employees. In ruling on such a case, the trier of fact would need to find that the conduct is based on gender, is unwelcome, is condoned or overlooked by authorities, and interferes with the terms, conditions, and privileges of the job.

Supervisors must be very proactive in establishing the ground rules and parameters of collegial employee relations to avoid being charged with allowing a hostile work environment. A good defense for an organization has evolved through past litigation and is known as the *Faragher/Ellerth Affirmative Defense*. This standard has basically two parts. The first is that the organization took reasonable care to prevent sexual harassment. This would include having a comprehensive written policy against harassment or discrimination. The policy would be communicated clearly and regularly, and officials would respond quickly and appropriately to any complaints that are filed of this nature. Investigations should be thorough and fair. Steps should be taken to ensure that retaliatory actions are not launched against any alleged victims. Confidentiality should be maintained as appropriate, and corrective action should be taken. Administrators must build confidence and trust in employees so that they not only feel safe, but know that violators will be dealt with effectively.

The second part of the Faragher/Ellerth Affirmative Defense is that the plaintiff or victim did not take advantage (as a reasonable person would be expected to) of the employer's prevention mechanisms or the employer's attempts to correct and resolve the situation. This means that if an employer responds reasonably to the charges and proposes reasonable solutions, corrective actions, and so forth, then that should be considered as good faith efforts on the employer's part, and the employer should not be held liable. It further suggests that perhaps the plaintiff is bypassing feasible remedies by not trying to work with the employer's reasonable solutions.

One of the ways that employers might be unsuccessful with such an affirmative defense is if they design a policy where an employee has no choice but to report her claim of harassment to her direct supervisor, when under certain circumstances, it might be that supervisor who is the perpetrator. It is clear that a better (more defensible) policy would be one that gives the victim several different options for reporting.

Investigating Complaints of Sexual Harassment

When the courts go back and evaluate the standard of care an organization or agency used in investigating an allegation of sexual harassment, it will look at a number of criteria. One is that the investigation should be conducted by someone who is completely neutral on the case and is specifically trained in these types of complaints. The investigator should have interviewed the alleged victim and the accused as well as all relevant witnesses. The interviews should be similar in length and style. All pertinent documents should be reviewed, and all findings should be clearly documented. A formal written report should be written and filed, and it should be shared with all interested parties. Examples can be found in *Fuller v. City of Oakland* and *Silva v. Lucky Stores, Inc.*

Compensatory and Punitive Damages

In 1991 Congress amended Title VII of the Civil Rights Act in recognition of the difficulties plaintiffs faced once allegations of sexual harassment were formally processed and taken to court. Prior to this revision, women who quit their jobs or were fired in retaliation for their complaints were barely able to reclaim lost wages even if they prevailed in the end. This gave them little incentive to challenge offenders in court. Today, sexual harassment victims can recover not only compensatory damages related to pay but also costs associated with "future pecuniary losses, emotional pain, suffering, inconvenience, mental anguish, loss of enjoyment of life, and other nonpecuniary losses." In some instances the court may also award punitive damages where it can be shown that an employer acted with malice or with reckless or callous indifference.

Employment, Promotion, and Wage Differentials

Discrimination and Tokenism

Attempts to identify sexual discrimination in the workplace cannot be reduced to simple numbers or comparisons. Realistically, one must look closely at the rate at which both men and women meet the criteria for promotion, go up for promotion, and are willing to accept the assignments that allow for promotions. The decision to pursue advancement within an agency is a personal one that may involve consideration of many lifestyle and family-related options. For example, in one study, both male and female officers explained that going up for promotion would cause too much disruption within their current routines. For the men, the decision was most often tied to losing off-duty employment and the potential income that extra hours provide. For women, changes in shifts and assignments would jeopardize child-care arrangements that would not offset the incremental pay raise (Whetstone, 2001). That said, what we do need to examine is the rate at which qualified women are denied opportunities for leadership positions that they compete for relative to their male counterparts within an organization.

Sexual discrimination may include any number of unfair practices employed in testing for promotion or specialized assignments. It may also include being paid less for similar work. In some instances, women may be singled out for repeated and unnecessary "fitness for duty" evaluations. Retaliation for complaints of gender discrimination may further compound the problem with unwarranted discipline, demotion, or termination. In addition to being isolated and shunned, a woman may find that she is denied opportunities for the types of training that will advance her career, may be the target of constant criticism, or may even be subjected to unnecessary physical force during training exercises. In jobs that involve contact with offenders, not receiving emergency backup or assistance from fellow officers could be fatal. The psychological harm from being stalked at home or harassed at work can lead some employees to quit their jobs and sacrifice their careers.

Although a lesser form of discrimination, women in policing often report the use of "tokenism" within departments that demeans or misrepresents their contributions and their role. As one officer explained, "It seems like every time the news media want a statement from the police department, they call on me. Yes, I do have good speaking skills but I have also been told many times that they want a female representing the department. It makes me feel like I am 'window dressing' for the department. They want it to appear as though they are so progressive with diversity, yet there are so many things going on within the department that hinder female officers from climbing the administrative ladder" (Archbold & Schulz, 2008, p. 62). Another female officer commented that "The attention I have received from my supervisors prevented me from testing this past time because there is a stigma for females who test for the position of sergeant. The idea is that if you are a woman, you will get it [promotion] no matter what your qualifications are" (Archbold & Schulz, 2008, p. 66). And finally, a third respondent confided that "I would not participate in promotion if I still feel like they are just looking for a female to promote and not the most qualified person for the position. . . . I would want people to know that I got promoted because I am a good cop, not because I am a woman or to become a piece of window dressing for the organization" (Archbold & Schulz, 2008, p. 66).

Disparate or Adverse Impact

Ironically, many plaintiffs' attorneys do not uncover wage discrimination until they are investigating other workplace problems, primarily sexual harassment and hostile work environment cases. Many women do not realize that the unwanted sexual advances are part of a more complex network of illegal and discriminatory practices within a workplace. One of the tests that the court uses for determining if a screening device or elimination criterion is constitutionally viable is whether or not it has a disparate impact or adverse impact. By that, the law attempts to identify any policy or practice that serves to disadvantage members of a protected class — for our discussion here, that would be gender. In most analyses, the court would use a formula to determine if the specific criteria used are responsible for differential results that have this negative impact. The Federal Civil Rights Enforcement Formula is a 4/5 or 80% rule. This means that if the success rate for women on this measure or criterion is less than 4/5 or 80% of the success rate for men, then a disparate impact exists. Still, disparate impact does not necessarily mean that a criterion is invalid or cannot be enforced. If the agency can demonstrate that the criterion is a *bona fide* occupational qualification (BFOQ), essential to carrying out the job effectively, then disparate impact may be overcome. However, the courts still would challenge agencies to find ways to recruit more women who could meet the criterion, train more women to be able to succeed on that criterion, or reassess how the job is done, perhaps to lessen the reliance on that particular mode of performance.

To illustrate the way the concepts of disparate impact and bona fide job qualification are related, we will use the example of women challenging a state's hiring process for juvenile correctional officers. In this particular case, the women claimed that they were being screened out of the applicant pool because of a physical agility test that required a certain number of push-ups and chin-ups. The women argued that these two tests, focusing on upper-body strength, had a disparate impact on women applicants. Data substantiated that less than 80% of women were able to pass this phase of the physical agility test. Clearly, the tests had a disparate impact. The question now shifted to whether this upper-body strength component was an essential feature of the job.

In order to determine what traits are BFOQs, a number of approaches can be used, and the courts consider all of these. An assessment could be done by having a neutral observer follow officers on duty and note the number of times during the course of a shift, or a week, or a month, upper-body strength is called upon in order to accomplish a task. Other assessments may challenge the notion that chin-ups and push-ups are a valid proxy for strength or the ability to perform certain on-the-job maneuvers such as scaling a backyard wall or a playground fence. The point of some of these challenges is to suggest alternatives like using an obstacle course, a more real-life scenario for agility, rather than repetitious exercises. Often, departments were caught in the hypocrisy of their more experienced officers being unable to complete these same exercises after only a few years on the job. Other requirements like not being color blind would be considered a *bona fide* occupational job qualification. And, data would indicate that although almost entirely male, only a small percentage of candidates are eliminated on color-blindness. In addition, it is important to note that race is never considered a legitimate BFOQ.

We are all familiar with businesses that appear to hire only men or women because the nature of their service is a specific form of entertainment or service. The courts have upheld such restrictive hiring as a legitimate BFOQ when they reflect a single or primary function of the business. As Bandsuch (2009, p. 1029) explains:

> An immodest example is that sex (being female) is a BFOQ for Playboy Clubs because their primary purpose is entertainment for men, while sex is not a BFOQ for Hooters Restaurants since their central function is the serving of food, and its entertainment is considered secondary.

Business attempts to restrict hiring to the most attractive employees are argued as profit driven, but what is more legally perplexing are recent cases that involve firings based on a beauty bias, in particular, where physical attractiveness is the basis for an individual's termination. Incidents like the one involving banker Deborahlee Lorenzana, who was fired from her position because she was "too hot," have garnered media attention for the controversy surrounding job criteria that punish someone for being too attractive or too much of a distraction for males in the workplace. Experts in employment discrimination conclude that the elusiveness of appearance discrimination, and the lack of specificity about it in existing legislation, will make it difficult to regulate under existing anti-discrimination statutes (Corbett, 2011).

On the other hand, more specific aspects of appearance such as uniforms and clothing are more easily analyzed under the law. In these incidences, the validity or BFOQ of differential clothing or uniform standards is evaluated:

> Southwest Airlines also failed in its bid to convince the courts that its attempt to market and provide "heterosexual titillation [to] male customers" lifted its female hiring practices to that of a BFOQ. . . . United Airlines imposition of different weight requirements for men (large-frame standard) and women

(medium-frame standard) flight attendants had no BFOQ to justify it. Nor did the Seventh Circuit find a BFOQ to support a company rule requiring "women to wear uniforms and men to wear customary business attire." A similar office rule that required women clerks to wear smocks while male clerks could wear shirts was ruled an invalid dress code requirement with no supporting BFOQ. In another case, a dress code mandating that a female lobby attendant wear an openly provocative uniform was also found to violate Title VII due to the sexualized nature of the unequal burden imposed on women without any justifiable BFOQ (Bandsuch, 2009, p. 1029).

In evaluating cases such as those mentioned above, the courts rely on Title VII of the Civil Rights Act and its amendments to ensure that employers protect individuals against discrimination and to promote equal opportunities in our society. What the courts appear to focus on, historically, is whether the actions of the employer reinforce sexual stereotypes and, if this is so, they are likely to rule in favor of the plaintiff. This concept is clearly demonstrated in the way the court has examined cases of transsexual police officers. In these lawsuits, the court appears to distinguish between circumstances that individuals are protected against (the use of sexual stereotypes) and those that are less likely to be afforded protection (bias against sexual orientation). As Bandsuch explains:

> In Smith v. City of Salem, for instance, the court held that the suspension of a transsexual police officer for being too effeminate violated Title VII. . . . In two similar cases, the respective circuit courts found Title VII to protect a transsexual police officer who was refused promotion and another who was denied a job because of their respective feminine demeanors. Both the Fifth and Sixth Circuits believed gender-stereotyping was the motivating factor behind such treatment, not the transsexualism (2009, p. 1001).

The Wage Gap and the Equal Pay Act

The discrepancy between the wages of males and females has been called the "wage gap." According to experts, women currently earn 77 cents for every $1 that males earn (Saxenian, 2011). The difference, that 23 cents on the dollar, represents the wage gap. In some fields, such as financial services, that rate is even lower (women earn 65 cents to every dollar earned by men) (Malveaux, 2011). Guidelines for employer policies on wages can be found under the *Equal Pay Act* passed in 1963 which modified the *Fair Labor Standards Act*. This legislation mandates that men and women receive equal pay for equal work. This is usually taken to mean that the skills, efforts, and responsibilities are basically the same and are carried out under comparable working conditions.

When analyzing challenges under the *Equal Pay Act*, arbiters would be less concerned about whether employees of one sex possess additional training or related skills, rather they would only need to know whether the tasks associated with a specific job actually requires those skills. Thus, even though men in this field might have other experience and training, if it is not essential for the specific job advertised or filled, then they cannot be compensated with additional pay. Even so, differences in wages are permissible as long as they are not gender based. Thus, what you may see operating is a seniority system, a merit system, or a system that provides bonuses for a certain rate or quality of production. And, although unions are more common in policing than they are in corrections, under the terms of the *Equal Pay Act*, labor unions cannot cause or attempt to cause an employer to discriminate on the basis of sex when setting or advancing wages.

To remedy some of the weaknesses that have been identified over the years in the *Equal Pay Act*, legislation has been consistently proposed to tighten loopholes allowing discriminatory pay practices to continue. That bill, the *Paycheck Fairness Act*, has been blocked each time by partisan conservatives who do not want any government constraints or regulation of free-market industry. In effect, they claim, such a measure would impose costs on big companies that have traditionally saved money and boosted profits by paying women less.

The Paycheck Fairness Act (PFA)

The main thrust of the PFA is to change the way the courts evaluate gender discrimination lawsuits resulting from disparate wages. Writing a position paper for the conservative and pro-business Heritage Foundation, Sherk (2011) explains:

- Currently, under the Equal Pay Act, once employees have provided *prima facie* evidence of sex discrimination in compensation, the burden of proof shifts to the employer to show that the difference in wages results from "any factor other than sex."
- The PFA would eliminate the "any factor other than sex" defense and replace it with a "bona fide factor other than sex" defense. Employers can use this "bona fide factor" defense only if they demonstrate that business necessity demands it.
- However, if the employee demonstrates that an alternative employment practice exists that would serve the same business purpose without producing a gender differential and that the employer has refused to adopt this alternative practice, then employers may not use this defense.
- The PFA would make employers liable for unlimited punitive damages in addition to compensatory damages in cases of sex discrimination in compensation.
- The PFA would make it easier to bring class-action lawsuits in such cases.

Advocates, however, argue that the Paycheck Fairness Act will close loopholes in the *Equal Pay Act*. One advantage is that it would bar employers from retaliating against workers for simply talking about their salaries to each other. They also claim that the threat of compensatory and punitive damages is necessary to deter employers who engage in gender discrimination in wages. For those interested in tracking the progress of this measure, it is also referred to as H.R. 1519.

Pregnancy, Light Duty, and Maternity Leave

Under federal law, which includes Workers' Compensation policy, the Pregnancy Discrimination Act, and the Americans with Disabilities Act (ADA), employers must treat pregnancy like any other medical condition or temporary medical condition in terms of policies, requirements, or benefits. That means that the treatment of pregnancy cannot be more restrictive or limiting than any other temporary disability that the agency or business makes allowances for — such as offering reassignments or leaves or making demands such as having medical clearance or doctor's authorizations.

In most police departments, the practice of "light duty" has been a cost-effective way to avoid workers' compensation claims for on-duty accidents and injuries but has been more controversial when used with off-duty injuries and with pregnant patrolwomen (Rabe-Hemp, 2011). In the past, light-duty status allowed trained and experienced officers injured on the job to recuperate and return to their positions which would prevent the department from having to hire and develop new recruits. As Rabe-Hemp (2011, p. 125) explains, "light duty policies for off-duty, injury and pregnancy are predicated on maintaining the morale of the officers and preserving a trained and capable force." Still, critics often complain that it is difficult to assign and rotate a larger number of pregnant officers through a "light duty" schedule, especially when coupled with maternity leave. Together, it is argued, these represent a significant period of time during which to redeploy other officers and to attempt to maintain minimum strength levels. Some of these cases have been litigated and have resulted in demands on departments to clarify their light-duty policies.

Of the expectations for light duty when pregnant, the courts have reasoned that the standard for a pregnant women is to be treated like any other "comparable" temporarily disabled person in that workplace (see Tysinger v. Police Department of the City of Zanesville, 2006). Thus, if other temporarily disabled persons do not ask for light duty, than the pregnant female would be held to that standard. If the workplace does not arrange light duty for anyone, than someone who is pregnant could not expect a more favorable treatment. The difficulty in these situations is that a pregnant woman is compared to any person recuperating from anything. As an example, let us use another officer who is recovering from carpal tunnel surgery. The person with an immobilized wrist may feel that he or she can still perform undercover operation or investigation of illegal guns at pawn shops, but a pregnant woman may believe that her regular tasks place her baby at risk. The question is really whether pregnancy is comparable to other injuries or medical conditions.

Under the Pregnancy Discrimination Act, it is unlawful to deny a woman a job because she is pregnant or will possibly become pregnant. Women must be allowed to perform their jobs as long as they can do so, and they cannot be required to stay off the job until the baby is born. However, as Barnard and Rapp (2009) explain, equal treatment does not always mean that employers have no options when it comes to pregnant employees:

> Pregnancy, unlike, for example, skin color in a race discrimination case, directly affects a woman's ability to perform her job. Thus, in certain circumstances, the

PDA does not prohibit terminating the employment of a pregnant woman based on her inability to perform her job. For example, the PDA's promise of equal treatment does not mean that an employer must:

1. Create a special, "light duty" assignment (or similar accommodation) for a woman to perform during her pregnancy, if the employer does not offer light duty assignments or similar accommodations to other temporarily disabled employees.
2. Hire a pregnant woman if the applicant would require a leave of absence immediately after starting work, if the employer would not hire anyone who required a similar leave.
3. Modify its leave policy to provide special accommodations to pregnant employees, "if a company's business necessitates the adoption of particular leave policies."
4. Continue to employ a pregnant employee when her requested leave coincides with the busiest time of the year for that employer (Barnard & Rapp, 2009, p. 212).

In a recent interview, P. David Lopez, general counsel for the Equal Employment Opportunity Commission (EEOC), remarked that he was still surprised to see pregnancy discrimination cases in the workplace today. He related the account of a woman who drove a shuttle at a car lot who was fired for being pregnant. Her boss "was concerned she'd be a health and safety hazard because at any moment she could cramp up and get nauseous" (Sixel, 2011). Employment discrimination, experts like Lopez tell us, is often about stereotypes, so proactive training and education initiatives are important for ensuring that women's health issues and needs are well understood in the workplace.

Legal Standards in Workplace Discrimination Litigation

There are many areas of gender discrimination litigation that remain unclear. For example, there is some debate over whether cases should be decided by attempting to set forth what a "reasonable employer" would do in any given circumstance. The defendant in cases such as this would be subject to assessment concerning the rationality of his or her choice of who to promote or hire. Much like the concept used by jurors in deciding if a defendant's actions were reasonable, this would hold the employer to a standard in promotions and hiring that assumes that some choices are easy to objectively assess. What the jury would attempt to decide is whether the average reasonable or rational boss would make the same choices. The more irrational an employer's decisions appear, the more likely it is that the jury may find discrimination.

Another area in which law continues to evolve is in clarifying what criteria make one person comparable to another when attempting to determine that one employee was discriminated against. The idea of a "comparable" person could mean anything from similar credentials or similar skills and experience to perhaps a veritable twin or clone of another. What attorneys want to avoid is a situation in which the jury does not feel that the plaintiff is as similarly situated as the person who is alleged to have gotten the promotion or job in a discriminatory process. This means that the goal is to show that the plaintiff is as qualified as a specific and real "comparable" person actually acting in that promoted role. Thus, it may be possible to infer that discrimination is the only reasonable explanation for why she was not chosen.

Conclusions

Successful managers today are those who proactively ensure that the workplace environment not only protects its employees but also nurtures them. The courts have identified problem agencies as those that do not write formal policies on issues such as sexual harassment, fail to enforce the policies they have, and disregard employee concerns or complaints. When supervisors treat an allegation of sexual harassment as a personal problem, one that the employee should handle on his or her own, they are setting the organization up for an unnecessary lawsuit. Sexual harassment is not difficult to detect, and attempting to sweep it under the carpet will only complicate the problem.

With all the emphasis today on "best practices" in government and on accountability for meeting goals, everyone will need to work together, not in factions. The workplace of tomorrow is diverse, and respect for that diversity is essential in building cohesive and collaborative teams in the criminal justice system. Women will make up at least half of the professional criminal justice workforce on the line, as well as in leadership positions. Assisting with these goals for the future, the National Organization for Women maintains a website that lists some of the companies and corporations deemed most harmful and unresponsive to women. They provide a number of resources for training and for the development of a more women-friendly work environment. In addition, they work to support legislation that they believe is conducive to improving the lives of women and their families, including the Family Medical Leave Act; Don't Ask, Don't Tell; and Paid Parental Leave (http://www.now .org/issues/wfw/index.html). Take a minute now and look at the website noted here for additional information that might help clarify and further define issues raised in this chapter. For example, look at the companies that the National Organization for Women identifies as their "Merchants of Shame." What criteria seem to identify these corporations as harmful to women?

Today women make up only 3% of the executives of the Fortune 500 and only 10% of the Forbes 400 Richest Americans (Wilkins, 2012). It is not unexpected, then, to find that women make up only 14% of SuperPAC donors, those who have political power and influence through donations to major candidates. Women may prefer donating to charities over politics, and the impact of that can be seen in the failure to pass critical legislative measures that would benefit women across the country (Wilkins, 2012).

For the last 15 years women have been receiving more bachelor's degrees then men and, in the last few years, more masters and doctoral degrees as well (Yen, 2011). These figures are consistent with admissions data indicating women currently make up 57% of those entering college (American Council on Education). Despite increases in education, lower rates of unemployment (almost 1%) for women are no doubt attributable to the stability of low-paying service industry jobs. There are other trade-offs as well. As Malveaux (2011) explains, "In the African-American community, women's higher educational attainment is often associated with lower marriage rates and less childbearing." In the next chapter we look more specifically at the effects race and economic status have on women in the criminal justice system.

Critical Thinking Questions

1. What can you do as a supervisor to maintain healthy gender relations between your employees in a criminal justice agency?

2. Is the climate of the criminal justice workplace better today than years ago in terms of the prevalence of sexual harassment? Why or why not?

3. Some critics argue that women prefer less travel, fewer transfers, and less overtime which are used as benchmarks toward promotions and raises. Is this accurate, and are these reasonable criteria for success?

Books, Websites, and Media Resources

Howard, L. G. (2007). *The sexual harassment handbook.* Franklin Lakes, NJ: Career Press.
Pay equity statistics: http://www.aauw.org/files/2013/02/Behind-the-Pay-Gap.pdf http://www.pay-equity.org/

Popular Films

Erin Brockovich (2000), Julia Roberts.
Norma Rae (1979), Sally Field.
Silkwood (1984), Cher.

References

Ackerman, T. (2010, September 5). Troubles contradict former surgeon's persona. *Houston Chronicle*, pp. A1, A17.
Archbold, C., & Schulz, D. (2008). Making rank the lingering effects of tokenism on female police officers' promotion aspirations. *Police Quarterly, 11*, 50-73.

Bandsuch, S. J. (2009). Ten troubles with Title VII and trait discrimination plus one simple solution (A totality of the circumstances framework). *Capital University Law Review, 37,* 965-1115.

Barnard, T., & Rapp, A. (2009). Pregnant employees, working mothers and the workplace– Legislation, social change and where we are today. *Journal of Law & Health, 22,* 197-239.

Chaiyavej, S., & Morash, M. (2009). Reasons for policewomen's assertive and passive reactions to sexual harassment. *Police Quarterly, 12,* 63-85.

Corbett, W. R. (2011). Hotness discrimination: Appearance discrimination as a mirror for reflecting on the body of employment-discrimination law. *Catholic University Law Review, 60,* 615-660.

Dothard v. Rawlinson, 433 U. S. 321 (1977).

Ellison v. Brady, 924 F.2d 872 (1991).

Harrison, J. (2012). Women in law enforcement: Subverting sexual harassment with social bonds. *Women and Criminal Justice, 22,* 226-238.

Malveaux, J. (2011, May 13). More female grades, but what about pay? *USA Today,* p. A11.

Meritor Savings Bank v. Vinson, 477 U. S. 57, 91 L. Ed. 2D 49, 106 S. Ct. 2399 (1986).

Pinkerton, J. (2010, October 10). Woman sues KBR, claiming it's at fault for sexual assault. *Houston Chronicle,* p. B2.

Rabe-Hemp, C. (2011). Exploring administrators' perceptions of light-duty assignments. *Police Quarterly, 14,* 124-141.

Roth, Z. (2011, May 24). *Parents keep child's gender under wraps.* Yahoo! News. Retrieved from http://news.yahoo.com/blogs/lookout/parents-keep-child-gender-under-wraps-170824245.html

Saxenian, C. (2011, April 9). It's time to close the wage gap between women, men. *Houston Chronicle,* p. B7.

Sherk, J. (2011, February 22). *The Paycheck Fairness Act.* WebMemo #3159. The Heritage Foundation. Retrieved from http://www.heritage.org/research/reports/2011/02/paycheck-fairness-act

Sixel, L. M. (2011, April 9). Q&A: EEOC cautions about criminal checks. *Houston Chronicle,* Business Page 1.

Tysinger v. Police Department of City of Zanesville, 463 F. 3d 569 (2006).

Whetstone, T. S. (2001). Copping out: Why police officers decline to participate in the sergeant's promotion process. *American Journal of Criminal Justice, 25,* 147-159.

Wilkins, E. (2012, April 1). SuperPACs on the rise, but not with women. *Houston Chronicle,* p. A8.

Yen, H. (2011, April 27). Women make bigger gains in education. *Houston Chronicle,* pp. A1, A6.

Race, Class, and Gender: Separating the Effects

Introduction

In Harriet Beecher Stowe's literary classic, *Uncle Tom's Cabin*, she introduces the reader to the sexually abused slave Cassy, whose two young children are torn from her arms and sold off. When her next child is two weeks old she slips him the powerful drug laudanum that passes him, she believes, safely into the gentle sleep of death. In her mind, Cassy has made the only choice she felt possible, to save him from the unbearable life of slavery in early America. As she intended, Stowe's work troubled women readers, and stirred the passions of mothers everywhere as she pushed her audiences uncomfortably into her abolitionist framework (Ammons, 1977).

Today, issues of power and influence in the United States are shaped in the context of gender, race, economics, and politics. Women make up more than half of the population of the United States and roughly half of the employed in this country, but they represent only 10% of the Forbes 400 richest citizens, only 3% of Fortune 500 executives, and only 14% of Super PAC donors (Wilkins, 2012). Examining these data, Wilkins (2012) explains that "academics believe there is a link between the underrepresentation of women in the political money chase and the underrepresentation of women in U.S. elected office" (p. A8). Wilkins goes on to explain that women are often more interested in social change than in gaining access in political venues and are consequently more likely to donate to charities and causes than political candidates' campaigns. As we conclude our study of women and the criminal justice system, we emphasize the need to pay attention to the broader social context in which the images of women are shaped.

Studying the Intersection of Race, Class, and Gender

In this chapter we look at the many and varied ways that race, gender, and socioeconomic status come together to explain female criminality and victimization. The interaction of other, additional demographic factors such as income, age, and education also plays a role in many of the criminological and victimization theories that we previously discussed. For example, Resko (2010) argues that when race and ethnicity are examined in the context of domestic violence, it is important to control for economic status which is a more significant predictor of risk. Otherwise, race might mask the true differences caused by income if victims are only analyzed according to one feature or trait. Having multiple measures of income and financial status is also important as the intersection of race, ethnicity, and socioeconomic status is often a complex set of variables.

Some recent examples from the media demonstrate this complexity. In New York City, a powerful French politician was accused of sexually assaulting a maid in an expensive hotel. The African-born worker, Rodriguez (2011) explains, like the Latina housekeeper, Mildred Patricia Baena, impregnated by movie star ex-California governor Schwarzenegger, represent less-powerful women in low-income jobs who are easily exploited and forgotten. Charges are rarely filed in cases such as those described above, and convictions are even less likely. Rodriguez refers to these revelations as the "dark side of the global melting pot" where we see the negative effects that have been historically associated with global migration, social stratification, labor segregation, and interracial sex.

The ability to study victimizations in greater detail cannot only help us refine theories of crime but also design more effective crime-prevention strategies. Rational theories, as you may remember, developed at a time when disciplines such as public administration and urban planning employed geographic profiling and spatial analysis to more accurately define community areas and places as part of the crime event context. Sophisticated computers, able to analyze large data sets with new variables collected in expanded versions of the UCR and National Crime Victimization Survey, gave us more dimensions of crime to study than just the criminal. And, a wider range of topics have also been entered into the National Crime Victims' Survey that allows research to be done on an expanded array of issues related to a specific criminal event. Items include whether the offender appeared to be drunk or high, what the victim was doing at the time of the incident, any previous contact with the criminal justice system the victim might have had, crimes that may have been committed by friends and family members of the respondent, and any defensive or self-protective measures the victim may have taken during the offense.

Effectiveness, in this case, may be tied to being able to take a more specific look at gender and race differences in attitudes, behaviors, and lifestyles. In addition, scientific analysis and rigorous research can be used to address continuing concerns about sexism, discrimination, racial profiling, and disproportionate minority confinement.

Tracking more pieces of information about crimes allows us to get a bigger picture of what takes place in a crime event. Interviews with victims tell us about interactions in time and place that contribute to the risk of a crime taking place. The implications for the criminal justice system in preventing and intervening in crime were numerous, particularly in designing safer living, working, and recreational spaces.

Research studies as well as case histories will be used to better understand the complexity of the relationship between all of these factors. As we discussed in the first chapter of this book, the overlapping disadvantages that many women face, not only from their backgrounds but in their current circumstances, make understanding the separate effects of any one problem, such as drug use or domestic violence, difficult. Improving opportunities within our society, particularly for disadvantaged groups, will allow us to reduce the effects of poverty, underachieving schools, and health problems within communities. Developing effective treatments, interventions, policies, and laws is also challenging in the context of these gender-based disadvantages.

The Changing Complexion of America

The minority population in this country is currently the largest growing sector. Changes in demographics mean shifts in power as political representation based on voter districts is central to our form of government. Demographers estimate that White males now represent only 15% of new employees entering the workforce in this country. Undoubtedly, the Hispanic population is where the most growth has occurred. Early results from the 2010 Census indicate the following trends according to an article by Hope Yen (2011). Over the past decade, the number of multiracial Americans rose nearly 20%. Currently, there are over 5 million persons in this country who identify themselves as multiracial. Texas, California, and New York are states that claim a high number of multiracial residents. In addition:

> Some 40 states now show population losses of white children since 2000 because of declining birth rates. Minorities represented all of the increases in the under-18 population in Texas and Florida and most of the gains in the child population in Nevada and Arizona. In all, non-Hispanic whites make up roughly 65 percent of the U.S. population, down from 69 percent in 2000. Hispanics had a 16 percent share, compared with 13 percent a decade ago. Blacks represent about 12 percent and Asians roughly 5 percent (Yen, 2011, p. A19).

Based on the national data, one of these growing minority-population states, Texas, will gain four seats in the U.S. House of Representatives, more than any other state's projected increase. Consequently, key votes in the coming years on issues such as an Equal Rights Amendment and the *Paycheck Fairness Act* may be impacted by changes in legislators who will be elected by this growing population base. In addition, funding for health care, child support enforcement, and domestic violence victims services will all be influenced by new voter demographics.

A group of researchers analyzed population trends across the country and made the following predictions regarding the effect of an increasingly diverse population on economic welfare:

> The results show that the diversification of the population could increase the number of children in poverty in the United States by nearly 1.8 million more than would occur with the lower levels of diversification evident in 2008. In addition, poverty would become increasingly concentrated among minority children with minority children accounting for 76.2 percent of all children in poverty by 2040 and with Hispanic children accounting for nearly half of the children in poverty by 2040 (Murdock, Zey, Cline, & Klineberg, 2010, p. 1).

The study also indicated that lower levels of education would be disproportionately found in poorer minority households and that over the next 25 years "85.2 percent of the increase in the number of children in poverty would be in households with a householder with less than a high school level of education" (Murdock, Zey, Cline, & Klineberg, 2010, p. 1).

Social feminists argue that gender stratification and structural inequality present in today's society mean that women continue to face disadvantages increasing their exposures to both victimization and criminalization. As Mona Danner (1999, p. 30) explains, "most women live with fewer advantages than do most men within their class and ethnic group. Poor and ethnic minority women are especially vulnerable because they may experience domination by men of their own class and ethnic group as well as by elite persons who may exercise their domination with impunity." This is particularly evident in domestic violence data and in statistics relative to property crime in low-income areas. It is also seen in predatory violent crimes such as the incident in Dunbar Village, Florida, where a group of young males from a housing project in a poverty-stricken area known for violence broke into a neighboring apartment, attacking an immigrant mother and her nine-year-old son. As the story was reported:

> For three hours, the pair says they endured sheer terror as the 35-year-old Haitian immigrant was raped and sodomized by up to 10 masked teenagers and her 12-year-old son was beaten in another room. Then, mother and son were reunited to endure the unspeakable: At gunpoint, the woman was forced to perform oral sex on the boy, she later told a TV station. Afterward, they were doused with household cleansers, perhaps in a haphazard attempt to scrub the crime scene, or maybe simply to torture the victims even more. The solutions burned the boy's eyes. The thugs then fled, taking with them a couple of hundred dollars' worth of cash, jewelry and cell phones . . . the mother

described how she and her son sobbed in the bathroom, too shocked to move. Then, in the dark of night, they walked a mile to the hospital because they had no phone to call for help (Associated Press, July 10, 2007).

The Degenerative Effects of Discrimination

In controversial debates that center on social justice and epidemiology, some researchers have argued that the cumulative negative effects of racial discrimination and poverty, over time, shorten the life span and degrade its quality (Blitstein, 2009). Various health statistics have been used to illustrate this point. For example, Blitstein notes that "Black residents of high-poverty areas, for instance, are as likely to die by the age of 45 as American whites are to die by 65. The disability rates of black 55-year-olds approach the rates of 75-year-old whites" (2009, pp. 49-50). Theorists add that neither genetics nor socioeconomic status alone seem to account for the significant differences in mortality norms between the groups.

In essence, what interpretations of these data seem to indicate is that social disorganization and its inherent health and safety risks increase the chances that women of color will face life-threatening illnesses and premature death. Joblessness has been linked with depression as have perceptions of job and wage discrimination. If one were to use welfare as an indicator of unemployment, lack of access to health care, and exposure to poverty, then studies indicate that family violence may also be a risk factor for many women. For example, Meloy and Miller explain that:

> In community-based samples that include both women who receive welfare and other low-income women, the rate of low-income battered women welfare recipients is higher than the rate found in samples of low-income women who are not on welfare. Severity of violence is also more strongly associated with women who receive welfare. In addition, battered women on welfare are more likely to experience adverse physical health, increased levels of drug and alcohol abuse and mental health problems than low-income women who never received welfare (2010, p. 118).

These problems appear in disproportionate rates in public housing projects. Meloy and Miller point out that:

> Of the over 5 million people living in public housing in the United States, most are minorities, and most of the households are female-headed. In 2002, the U.S. Supreme Court upheld a federal housing law, the Anti-Drug Abuse Act of 1988 (revised 1994), designed to evict public housing tenants for any resident or guest arrested for drug-related or violent crimes. This law unintentionally puts battered women at risk of losing their homes if they call police to report violence, essentially holding battered women responsible for their partner's abuse. Ironically, if they do not report the violence, they risk more beating but can remain in public housing (2010, p. 123).

Another stress factor that is particularly significant in women of color living in low-income urban areas is fear of crime. In her study of African Americans from five inner-city neighborhoods, Yolanda Scott (2001) found that women were more afraid of personal crime than were men but that fear of property crime was more gender balanced. As she explains, fear of property crime among the poor is often related to the difficulties anticipated if one were to lose or attempt to replace essential household items. The awareness of one's vulnerability seems related to the overwhelming burden of the costs of repairing or repurchasing life's necessities.

Another related phenomenon in research on women from poor neighborhoods is that fear often manifests itself as fear of what might happen to their loved ones. And, as minority males face much higher rates of violent victimization, women's fears of what is likely to befall the men in their lives are legitimate. For women surveyed, fear of crime is not just what might affect them directly, as Madriz (1997) notes, but what might happen to their sons, brothers, fathers, uncles, and cousins. In many cases, Madriz goes on to explain, they also worry about their men being falsely arrested or abused by police as well as treated unfairly once in the criminal justice system. In fact, police presence in the community appeared to be something that the middle class felt safer with, but minority women interviewed by Madriz were less comfortable and felt less safe with police around.

Some Theoretical Applications of Poverty, Race, and Gender

Differential opportunity theories, constructed during the Great Depression and influenced by the development of inner-city slum areas, argue that by lacking access to legitimate means to earn a living, people will adopt deviant or illegitimate survival mechanisms. Various coping strategies and their desirability are reinterpreted as options become more limited and pressures to meet their needs increase. In socially disorganized areas, drugs, gangs, and other forms of violent and property crime compete with traditional means of earning a living and running a home. A mother who needs diapers and baby formula may believe that she has no option but to take money from a relative who is a gang member, even if that money is tied to drugs or burglaries.

In a deregulated, or more anomic society, as sociologist Robert Merton would explain, deviant adaptations, like innovating new ways to provide food and clothing, will be explored. People who become disenfranchised from traditional norms by their loss of opportunities are more likely to see law breaking as not only viable, but necessary. Even using a rational theoretical framework, one could argue that rationality is relative. From different cultural and gender perspectives, even from different socioeconomic positions, what constitutes the best decision or course of action will vary. For example, in Alex Kotlowitz's (1991) book, There Are No Children Here, he shares with readers the life of a single mother of five in a housing project in Chicago. Surviving on various forms of public assistance as she tried to find work, LaJoe was notified by authorities that her benefits would be drastically cut. A former boyfriend had used her address for his driver's license and unemployment checks as well as on his paperwork when he was arrested on drug charges. Although he had never formally lived there or supplied her any income, the evidence implicated her in a type of scheme to defraud the welfare system that she felt powerless to fight. In an effort to provide for her children, she played where "a friend's mother ran an all-night card game for women" (p. 102). As Kotlowitz (1991) explains:

> The game was pitty-pat; players won by accumulating pairs. Now, she played almost nightly, winning $35 one night, $20 another. . . . Many weekends and some weekdays, LaJoe spent her nights away from home playing cards. She'd leave after putting the children to sleep and not come home until morning, usually early enough to help prepare the kids for school. . . . Though there was always an adult in the house . . . the children worried about their mother. It was while she'd been away one night that she'd been mugged and her fingers sliced (p. 102).

Young Women Associating with Gangs

In a study of young Mexican American girls, researchers attempted to describe the different roles that could be seen in associations with male gang members (Cepeda & Valdez, 2003). They found four types or groups of young women and explained the relationships that they had with the gangs. The first was the "girl-friend" who was described as a steady partner and one with whom the gang member would often have children. Becoming a mother seemed to give the girlfriend more status and respect around the gang. Even so, this young woman had the least actual gang contact of the four types.

The second type of gang associate identified by the researchers was a young woman called a "hoodrat." This was a negative image that involved sexual promiscuity, partying with extensive drug and alcohol use, and more involvement in the criminal activity of the gang. The hoodrat was the least respected and most disparaged of the girls with whom the male gang members associated.

The third type was the "good girl," who is someone who had been a childhood or long-term friend of a gang member. She may have gone to school with the gang member or grown up nearby in the neighborhood. This is close to the fourth type, the "relative," who is a girl who is actually related to a gang member with whom she continues to have a close personal relationship. This could be sisters or cousins of the gang members. Both types, girls who are acquaintances and the relatives, will be more respected by gang members, and like girlfriends, they will have less involvement with gang activity and will be considered to be less streetwise (Cepeda & Valdez, 2003).

Data from the National Longitudinal Study of Adolescent Health seem to support the idea that young women who are deeper in poverty and facing limited opportunities are also more likely to join gangs themselves. This relationship between deprivation and gang membership appears to be stronger for girls than for boys (Bell, 2009). As one national survey found, female gang members were younger, less likely to be immigrants, and more often Hispanic than male gang members. Cepeda and Valdez (2003) conclude that the risky behaviors associated with gang membership and gang associations take place in a social-cultural environment where they are "modeled, practiced, and reinforced similar to Moore's (1991) concept of choloization." From interviews with a number of young women associated with gangs in San Antonio, Texas, the authors concluded that "sexual activity, reproduction strategies, and excessive use of drugs and alcohol may be recognized as normative within this population given their perceived limited opportunities. Moreover, the street culture and lifestyle of these gangs creates a symbiotic relationship with these male gang members that encourages a withdrawal from societal norms" (2003, p. 103). They further suggest that these behaviors are similar for young African American females.

Data and research on young females associated with gangs have implications not only for offending but for victimization as well. As we will see in the next section, young females in Mexico face the same pressures as described above and often engage in deadly risks to provide for their families.

Young Female Victims in Mexico

The rape, torture, kidnapping, and killing of hundreds of young women across the Mexican border area near Juarez constitute what the literature refers to as "femicide," the systematic murder of women, with underlying motives based on gender. Experts believe that explanations for this phenomenon must include recent changes in business models that brought large American corporations into the border areas. Here the economy benefits from flexible trade policies like the North American Free Trade Agreement (NAFTA). Under its provisions, manufacturing costs are lower because raw materials and parts are shipped to Mexico where wages and environmental protections are weak so that goods may be assembled and exported cheaply. With a population of 1.5 million, Juarez has been a mecca for young people from poverty-stricken rural areas across Mexico to move to in order to find this new type of work. According to one news report, it attracts "tens of thousands of young women from small, poor towns with $55-a-week jobs in maquiladoras operated by such wealthy major corporations as General Electric, Alcoa, and DuPont" (Sarria, 2009).

As the workplace becomes deregulated, lower-wage workers, who are more tolerant of changing shifts and schedules, are preferred — which means women. As Nidya Sarria explains, "The young women of Juarez are also favored by the maquila bosses for their nimble fingers and obedience" (2009). However, by 2005, these maquiladoras were also places from where more than 800 young female workers have been murdered and another 3,000 vanished.

> According to the Organization of American States's Inter-American Commission on Human Rights: "The victims of these crimes have preponderantly been young women, between 12- and 22-years-of-age. Many were students . . . relative newcomers . . . reported missing by their families, with their bodies found days or months later abandoned in vacant lots, outlying areas or in the desert.

In most of these cases there were signs of sexual violence, abuse, torture or in some cases mutilation." . . . These women share some similar characteristics: pretty and slender, with dark, shoulder-length hair, at least nine of them vanished while shopping downtown or looking for work (Sarria, August 3, 2009).

A number of conflicting theories have been offered to explain these killings. Some suggest that drug cartels, police, and even military officials have been responsible for these deaths and disappearances. Although turnover among the members of all of these suspect groups has been exceptionally high, the saga of victimization continues. To date, most of the cases remain unsolved.

Prioritizing Gender and Considering Sameness

When theorizing about gender and its influence on the criminal justice system, one must wonder whether men and women should be treated alike. The "sameness" argument, while it sounds more defensible and legalistic, has been criticized because its actual implementation is fraught with discrepancies. For example, if more equal treatment means that more women will be sentenced to prison and for longer periods of time, wouldn't it be wasteful if their risks of recidivism or committing serious or violent crimes were lower? Also, without the provision of the same range of facilities, programs, and access to treatment that men are afforded, is it really fair to keep women incarcerated longer? This is particularly true where states do not have less-secure and thus less-expensive facilities to assign women to serve their time.

Judges are also faced with dilemmas when dealing with cases that involve both gender and cultural implications. Many have been criticized for not prioritizing gender over culture when, for example, they allow Native American men accused of battering, incest, or rape to participate in various tribal healing programs that do not involve incarceration (Zatz, 2000). Another example that has been a "flashpoint" for feminist critics is when judges do not impose serious punishments on fathers who engage in the genital mutilation of their daughters in this country, or when pediatricians suggest that minor or partial mutilations done under a doctor's care might represent a culturally sensitive compromise.

Although motive isn't always considered relevant in a criminal case, research still seems to indicate that women and men may commit the same crimes for different reasons. As Piquero and Benson (2004) explain, women appear to engage in white-collar crime after some type of family misfortune or economic emergency threatens the stability of the home or way of life. Would explanations such as this influence you as a juror? Should they?

Research on Differences in Sentencing

The question of gender-neutral sentencing has been examined in research studies over the past few decades with mixed results. First, research generally seems to indicate that the gender and race of the judge have little if any impact on sentences handed down. According to Zatz (2000), this is most likely because of sentencing guidelines used in federal and state courts which do not allow for any significant deviations or discretion.

In a 1995 analysis of 50 different court data sets used in research, the results seemed to show that in half of the studies, women seemed to receive more lenient sentences, particularly in felony cases in larger cities. However, the bias did not seem to be as much about the sentence length, as was evidenced in the decision not to incarcerate. For example, in a study of Texas offenders by Curry, Lee, and Rodriguez (2004), it appeared that judges viewed women as less blameworthy, less dangerous, and as having greater family responsibilities, as well as having greater potential for reform. In this study, neither the relationship between the victim and the offender, nor the race or age differences appeared to have any effect on the chances that a female offender would be incarcerated.

Several criminologists have suggested that incarceration may not be as important for regulating the behavior of women as it is for men (Zatz, 2000). They contend that women's closer connections to their families and economic dependence on family members may provide more informal social control. Judges' attitudes about this may have a significant impact on the sentencing of female offenders if the law permits such discretion. In Daly's (1989a) research, the fact that women appeared to receive more lenient sentences seemed to be related to having family ties. The support of family is often viewed as essential to success in the community which may explain why these women received shorter prison terms or sentences of probation. Daly (1989b) also found that judges placed considerable weight on what they perceived to be in the best interests of the offenders' children. Many justices seem to feel that preserving the family unit was an obligation to consider in weighing sentencing options. However, research also suggests that this may be a more direct advantage for White women. Black women, it seems, must not only have children, but be deemed good or fit mothers before they benefit from any special consideration. African American women do seem to benefit in sentencing from being married. Other findings indicate that White women appear to some degree to be disadvantaged in sentencing if they are living alone. Again, Zatz (2000, p. 513) would argue this may be because they do not fit the gender stereotypes or expectations about familial roles. She explains that "the courts are making decisions not solely based on women's family status but also on prosecutors' and judges' assumptions about black and while families and about black and white women's relationships with their children" (Zatz, 2000, p. 513).

In other studies, researchers have found that judges seemed to take into consideration, in terms of offering more leniency, whether women had mental health problems, demonstrated remorse, or played a more minor part in the offense itself (Zatz, 2000). One might argue that even though the law may allow accomplices to be charged with the same offense as the perpetrator, judges may mitigate that in actually pronouncing a sentence. Thus, the offenses are really not the "same," and treating someone with "sameness" is not really at issue. There is also some indication that judges are influenced by the "blurred boundaries" that are often seen where women are both victims and offenders. Even so, researchers stress that "the color of chivalry" is White (Zatz, 2000). Women of color, particularly younger women and those who may not be as deferential to authority, are more likely to be viewed as worthy of harsh prosecution.

In 2002, dentist Clara Harris from Clear Lake, Texas, stood trial on murder charges for running over her husband in a fit of jealousy after finding him in a hotel with his mistress. Her attorney (the same man who defended Andrea Yates for the drowning of her children) faced a dilemma about whether to put her on the stand. This decision was an extremely controversial point in the trial. Some speculated that among other things, her "lilting" Colombian accent, as the media called it, would enforce cultural stereotypes about "hot-headed" rage and vengeance. (The same stereotypical role is played by Sofia Vergara in the television series *Modern Family*.) This strategy would be consistent with that of theorists who argue that women must fit a rather narrow and "ideal" image of the wronged or battered woman in order to effectively use some defenses. The fact that she had known for some time about her husband's affair with their receptionist may have diminished her ability to successfully project the more spontaneous "crime of passion" image. Still, the jury of nine women and three men determined that there was a level of "sudden passion" as they found the former Miss Colombia-Houston guilty and recommended a sentence of 20 years. Although Harris left behind twin sons, it may have been thought that the boys would do well with his parents.

The task of considering the complex family dynamics in the Harris case is similar to another controversial Houston trial of a boy who was 10 years of age at the time he shot and killed his father, Dr. Rick Lohstroh. The minor was found to be delinquent in juvenile court and sentenced to 10 years in the Texas Youth Commission. The jury specifically asked the judge if such a verdict would keep the child away from the negative influences of his mother which were readily apparent at trial. His sentence was later overturned by the Fourteenth Court of Appeals.

As discussed earlier in the section on women and drugs, the constraints of mandatory sentences often make it difficult for the courts to consider any special family needs or arrangements in these cases. Even so, Farrell (2001) found that White female defendants were more likely to receive downward departures (from the sentencing guidelines) and disproportionate decreases in the lengths of their sentences. Those decreases were notably for providing "substantial assistance" in the court, which may simply mean that White females were more likely to provide evidence against co-defendants than women of color. In a further examination of this issue, Spohn and Brennan (2011) reported no difference in the scale of benefit White males and females of all races received in the context of providing substantial assistance to the state. In fact, the authors suggest that judges might use their discretion under the assistance provision to manipulate federal sentencing guidelines toward what they consider to be more appropriate sentences. Offenders deemed worthy of such consideration, the researchers conclude, appear less likely to be Black and Hispanic males.

Overall, Black women are incarcerated at a rate that is eight times that of White women, and the rate for Hispanic women is four times that of Whites (Joseph, 2006, p. 303). Still, women in general tend to have less criminal history than men, and fewer of the more serious, violent offenses in their histories, which may explain why they are less likely to receive the most severe sanctions. Aggravating factors used in sentencing, such as in capital punishment cases, are more likely to impact men as "women arrested for murder are more likely to be first offenders than women who are arrested for other crimes" (Streib, 2000, p. 875).

Many of the trends seen in the criminal justice processing of adult women also occur with female juveniles. As data from the American Bar Association (2001) indicate, African American girls are much less likely to have the charges against them dismissed than are their peers who are White. Overall, young women of color have had the highest increases in the detention population, and African American teens make up almost 50% of those in secure confinement. Young Hispanic women make up almost 15% more (ABA, 2001).

As in other areas of criminal justice, media images and the way women are portrayed in popular culture have always had significant influence on our views on appropriate behaviors. Movies like Mi Vida Loca (1993) and Set It Off (1996) seem to play off racial, cultural, and gender stereotypes. As Chesney-Lind and Eliason explain:

> One could argue that media constructions of girls' and women's crime serve a variety of purposes in a patriarchal society. First, these constructions of women's crime serve as "cautionary tales" to girls and women that their demands for economic and political equality could have serious consequences. Moreover, the construction of some women as "bad," particularly African American girls and women, supports racist notions that are arguably at the core of US culture. . . . Finally, the academic silence about the sexual orientation of criminalized girls and women, coupled with the notion that their behavior is a product of "masculinization" sets the stage for the demonization of another group — lesbian women, all the while "celebrating" the "good" (i.e. white, heterosexual, and passive) woman as a cultural ideal (2006, p. 37).

Gender, Race, and Incarceration: Some Historical Observations

Historically, race, income, and immigrant status have been associated with the increased likelihood of being sent to prison for an offense. As Harris uncovers in her exploration of the history of Bedford Hills Correctional Facility in New York:

> Crimes for which a girl or woman could be sent here included petty larceny, habitual drunkenness, being a "common and disorderly person, violating the tenement house law, endangering the morals of children, frequenting chop suey houses of bad repute, or any other misdemeanor or felony except murder, manslaughter, burglary or arson" (1988, pp. 47-48).

As a rule, the more serious criminal offenders were sent to Auburn Penitentiary, as were most minority women. Harris remarks that by 1913, the female population at Auburn was 50% Black, and the female reformatory was only 5% Black. She adds that "A large proportion of Auburn was also foreign-born, especially Irish and German." It is also recognized that women who appeared more masculine were more likely to be treated as serious offenders. Judges displayed stereotypical values when faced with less conventional women who did not meet traditional standards for appearance, hygiene, and style.

Along the same lines as discussed above, juvenile offenders who were sexually active were considered promiscuous, and those suspected of not being virgins, were considered "incorrigible" and in need of institutional controls. It was not until the deinstitutionalization of status offenders took place throughout the country during the 1970s, that the system was able to refocus attention on more serious offenders. As a result, a number of training schools or reformatory-type facilities were closed.

Current figures indicate that about 15% of incarcerated women who are mothers have had their parental rights terminated. Often terminations are conducted whenever a parent has been convicted of child abuse or neglect. Proceedings are also commonly initiated if the mother has a record of certain types of drug offenses (Faris & Miller, 2010). In fact, in one sample population of female prisoners with drug-related offenses, the rate of termination was over 30%. According to Grella and Greenwell (2006, p. 89), this group was more likely to be made up of young minority women and those who "had more children, were less likely to have ever worked or been married, initiated regular drug use at a younger age, and were more likely to have been in foster care or adopted themselves and to have engaged in sex work." Besides the many high-risk factors that these inmates have for poor parenting, legislation, like the *Adoption and Safe Families Act*, has increased the likelihood that they will have their rights terminated. Intended to speed up and streamline adoptions, these laws have required the terminations of parental rights as a precursor to seeking more permanent placements for children left behind when mothers face incarcerations periods of two years or longer.

The Politics of Issues of Race, Class, and Gender

What constitutes "the best interests" of women has been debated over a number of sensitive and political issues from the treatment of victims and the sentencing of offenders to pay issues and the legal regulation of vice. For example, on the topic of prostitution, Weitzer (2005) argues that the government's redefining of prostitution into human trafficking has allowed it to craft new stricter laws to control low-income and marginalized women in this country, as well as to force other countries, dependent on American aid, to rewrite tougher laws as well. The consequence of poorer countries being coerced into adopting tough laws is that they may not be able to enforce them or garner any public support for them; therefore, any use of those laws is likely to be especially discriminatory. In addition, Weitzer contends, feminist groups have taken a similar position that prostitution is always a violent and exploitative violation of women's rights that creates victims who are not helped by legalization or decriminalization. Although the motives and agendas of these two groups, governments and feminists, may be vastly different, they have, Weitzer argues, served to skew data and misinterpret research that do not allow us to accurately assess or address prostitution.

One way to deal with the problems of biased information is that we, as educated professionals in this field, must study and critique the research and data ourselves with an eye to academic rigor and high standards of empirical analysis. By closely "decoding" definitions and populations sampled, we can see more accuracy in the issues. As Weitzer implies, just because it is on a Fact Sheet, that does not make it a fact. Being more guarded and questioning consumers of Internet information and talk-show propaganda are important parts of intellectual life.

In his article "Telling the truth about damn lies and statistics," Joel Best (2001, p. B7) explains that he once read a graduate dissertation that used the following quote: "Every year since 1950, the number of American children gunned down has doubled." At first he thought it was the student's error, so he went to the library and found that the student had quoted the source accurately. Professor Best calls this the worst statistic ever. He explains:

> Just for the sake of argument, let's assume that "the number of American children gunned down" in 1950 was one. If the number doubled each year, there must have been two children gunned down in 1951, four in 1952, eight in 1953, and so on. By 1960, the number would have been 1,024. By 1965, it would have been 32,768 (in 1965, the F.B.I. identified only 9,960 criminal homicides in the entire country, including adult as well as child victims). By 1970, the number would have passed one million; by 1980, one billion (more than four times the total U.S. population in that year). Only three years later, in 1983, the number of American children gunned down would have been 8.6 billion (nearly twice the earth's population at the time). Another milestone would have been passed in 1987, when the number of gunned-down American children (137 billion) would have surpassed the best estimates for the total human population throughout history (110 billion) (Best, 2001, B7).

To get to the point of the story, Dr. Best traced the quote from each outlet that used it back to the original source. It turns out that it was much like the childhood game where you whisper something to someone and it is continually passed along until at the end you have a totally different statement. The original statement that was misinterpreted by the next user was this:

> "The number of American children killed each year by guns has doubled since 1950."

Go back and read that sentence over a couple of times, slowly and carefully. As you can see this is a simple comparison between two years, say, for example, 1950 and 2005. That would mean if there were 200 deaths in 1950 it would be 400 in 2005. That is a far cry from the exponential increases under the first statement. Joel Best calls what happened in this example a "mutant statistic," something perhaps we might all be guilty of creating when we try to rephrase research findings in our own words in our papers.

An example of a mutant statistic was when White Supremacist David Duke, former Ku Klux Klan Grand Wizard campaigning for Governor of Louisiana, told an audience that Blacks were responsible for seven times the amount of crimes committed by Whites. This outrageous distortion, intentional or not, was traced back to an official statistic that showed a 7% difference in the crime rates of Blacks and Whites in a certain area over a certain period of time. Seven percent is not seven times. Think about it, would you even go to a sale if they said "7% off"? In most places, 7% is not even a sales tax. The potential damage from spreading statistical fallacies is something that we must be constantly vigilant about, particularly during elections. And, though it is required that we try to avoid plagiarism and rephrase the work of others into our own explanation, we must strive for accuracy and avoid the evils of "mutant" statistics. The use of careful language and accurate data is important because we never really escape the political environment in which we operate.

Policy for the Future

Unfortunately, the overlapping problems of race, class, and gender affecting young women in the criminal justice system seem to propel them into complex cycles of victimization and offending. Joseph (2006, p. 305) argues that the influences of race, class, and gender place women of color at greater risk for rape victimization and that "homicide now ranks as the major cause of death of young black women." She argues that better monitoring and investigating of discrimination charges as well as culturally sensitive government services would improve conditions for those historically excluded from education and employment opportunities in impoverished communities. Only through realistic and meaningful opportunities will low-income women and women of color be able to independently provide for themselves and their families.

In terms of reducing crime in poverty-stricken areas, Scott (2001) contends that communities must be assisted in developing their own problem-solving initiatives from within. Historical cultural differences between the community and their police as well as the traditions of order-maintenance policing styles have made it difficult to develop trust between law enforcers and the residents of troubled neighborhoods. She suggests:

> Social policy then should concentrate on developing intra-community neighborhood clean-up programs, and social organizations that encourage residents to actively participate in these efforts in order to reduce their fear of victimization. . . . Social policy directed at increasing feelings of safety in the neighborhood then, might focus on public efforts toward increasing positive views of local police, and confidence in the criminal justice institution more generally (Scott, 2001, p, 128).

For female offenders, researchers often argue for interventions that would allow more restorative approaches to justice and more therapeutically oriented resources. Alternative homes and residential treatment centers appear to be suggested by findings that not only do young women express relief at being removed from turbulent or abusive homes (Gaarder & Belknap, 2002), but also that parents are more likely to seek out-of-home placement for delinquent girls than boys (Krause & McShane, 1994). Access to environments where young women feel safe and respected are important, particularly in providing alternatives to gangs or street life.

Karina Rodriguez (2010) explains that young women, particularly Latinas, need mentors, tutors, and counseling. Those in poor neighborhoods without legitimate social networks need after-school programs "where mentors can help them learn to deal with their problems in positive ways." She adds that early childhood development programs and parenting education seminars as well as drug and alcohol treatment programs for parents would improve dynamics within families that are often violent and disruptive.

As we have stressed throughout this book, the criminal justice system must continually engage in a critical process of introspection and self-analysis. Only by carefully monitoring our motives, outcomes, and perhaps even the unintended consequences of our well-meaning laws and policies can we hope to provide services free of sexism, racism, or ageism. We must also be skilled in assessing and managing the most current resources for combatting the social problems that have been the focus of this chapter. As cyber-technologies and streaming Internet communications make it possible to spread messages of hate and racial propaganda more quickly and over greater areas than ever before, we must use these same instruments for positive change. Issues of race, class, and gender are often highly charged and emotionally laden for victims, offenders, and personnel working in the criminal justice system. Sensitivity and respect are keys to promoting healthy relationships in our communities. As Joseph (2006, p. 308) reminds us, "The future challenge is for the scales of justice to be rebalanced so that there will be justice for all, irrespective of a person's race, ethnicity, class or gender."

Critical Thinking Questions

1. How do race, gender, and poverty intersect to produce victimization and criminality?

2. Will traditional gang intervention strategies work for girls? What alternatives would be effective?

3. What role does politics play in the plight of young minority women caught up in the cycle of crime and victimization? How is the media involved in the "politics" of blame and accountability for disproportionate rates of victimization and offending?

Books, Websites, and Media Resources

Institute on Domestic Violence in the African American Community: http://www
   .dvinstitute.org/

Johnson, S. (2010). I'm still standing: From captive U.S. soldier to free citizen — My journey home. Austin,
   TX: Touchstone.

Rodriguez, T., Montane, D., & Pulitzer, L. (2008). The daughters of Juarez: A true story of serial murder
   south of the border. New York: Atria Books.

Popular Films

Set It Off (1996), Jada Pinkett-Smith and Queen Latifah.
What's Love Got to Do with It (1993), Angela Bassett.

References

American Bar Association and the National Bar Association. (2001). Justice by gender: The lack of
   appropriate prevention, diversion and treatment alternatives for girls in the justice system. Retrieved from
   http://www.abanet.org/crimjust/juvjus/justicebygenderweb.pdf

Ammons, E. (1977). Heroines in Uncle Tom's Cabin. American Literature, 49(2), 161-179.

Associated Press. (2007, July 10). At Fla. housing project, rape just another crime. Retrieved
   from http://www.msnbc.msn.com/id/19698132/ns/us_news-crime_and_courts/t/
   fla-housing-project-rape-just-another-crime/

Bell, K. (2009). Gender and gangs: A quantitative comparison. Crime & Delinquency, 55, 363-387.

Best, J. (2001, May 4). Telling the truth about damned lies and statistics. Chronicle of Higher
   Education, 47(34), B7, B9.

Blitstein, R. (2009, July–August). Weathering the storm. Miller-McCune, 2, 48-57.

Cepeda, A., & Valdez, A. (2003). Risk behaviors among young Mexican-American gang-
   associated females: Sexual relations, partying, substance use, and crime. Journal of Adolescent
   Research, 18(1), 90-106.

Chesney-Lind, M., & Eliason, M. (2006). From invisible to incorrigible: The demonization of
   marginalized women and girls. Crime Media Culture, 2(1), 29-47.

Curry, T. R., Lee, G., & Rodriguez, S. (2004). Does victim gender increase sentence severity?
   Further explorations of gender dynamics and sentencing outcomes. Crime & Delinquency,
   50(3), 319-343.

Daly, K. (1989a). Criminal justice ideologies and practices in different voices: Some feminist
   questions about justice. International Journal of the Sociology of Law, 17, 1-18.

Daly, K. (1989b). Neither conflict nor labeling nor paternalism will suffice: Intersections of race,
   ethnicity, gender and family in criminal court decisions. Crime & Delinquency, 35, 136-168.

Danner, M. (1999). Gender inequality and criminalization: A socialist feminist perspective on
   the legal social control of women. In D. Milovanovic & M. Schwartz (Eds.), Race, gender, and
   class in criminology: The intersections (Chap. 2, pp. 29-48). New York: Garland.

Faris, J., & Miller, J. (2010). Family matters: Perceptions of fairness among incarcerated women.
   Prison Journal, 90(2), 139-160.

Farrell, A. S. (2001). Effect of gender and family status on downward departures in federal criminal sentences.
   Washington, DC: National Institute of Justice.

Gaarder, E., & Belknap, J. (2002). Tenuous borders: Girls transferred to adult court. Criminology,
   40, 481-517.

Grella, C., & Greenwell, L. (2006), Correlates of parental status and attitudes toward parenting
   among substance-abusing women offenders. Prison Journal, 86(1), 89-113.

Harris, J. (1988). They always call us ladies: Stories from prison. New York: Scribners.

Joseph, J. (2006). Intersectionality of race/ethnicity, class, and justice: Women of color. In A. Merlo & J. Pollock (Eds.), *Women, law and social control* (Chap. 15, pp. 292-312). Boston: Allyn & Bacon.

Kotlowitz, A. (1991). *There are no children here.* New York: Anchor Books.

Krause, W., & McShane, M. (1994). A deinstitutionalization retrospective: Relabeling the status offender. *Journal of Crime and Justice, 17,* 45-67.

Madriz, E. (1997). *Nothing bad happens to good girls: Fear of crime in women's lives.* Berkeley, CA: University of California Press.

Meloy, M., & Miller, S. L. (2010). *The victimization of women: Law, policies, & politics.* New York: Oxford University Press.

Moore, J. W. (1991). *Going down to the barrio: Homeboys and homegirls in change.* Philadelphia: Temple University Press.

Murdock, S., Zey, M., Cline, M., & Klineberg, S. (2010). Poverty, educational attainment and health among America's children: Current and future effects of population diversification and associated socio-economic change. *Journal of Applied Research on Children: Informing Policy for Children at Risk,* 1(1), Art. 2, 1-33.

Piquero, N. L., & Benson, M. (2004). White-collar crime and criminal careers: Specifying a trajectory of punctuated situational offending. *Journal of Contemporary Criminal Justice,* 20, 148-165.

Resko, S. M. (2010). *Intimate partner violence and women's economic insecurity.* El Paso, TX: LFB Scholarly Publishing.

Rodriguez, G. (2011, May 23). The old taboos, back in the news. *Los Angeles Times,* p. A13.

Rodriguez, K. (2010). *Latina gang members.* Unpublished master's thesis. Houston, TX: University of Houston, Downtown.

Scott, Y. (2001). *Fear of crime among inner-city African Americans.* New York: LFB Scholarly Publishing.

Spohn, C., & Brennan, P. (2011). The joint effects of offender race/ethnicity and gender on substantial assistance departures in federal courts. *Race and Justice,* 1(1), 49-78.

Sarria, N. (2009, August 3). *Femicides of Juarez: Violence against women in Mexico.* Council on Hemispheric Affairs. Retrieved online January 7, 2014 at https://www.commondreams .org/view/2009/08/03-8

Streib, V. (2000). Death penalty for female offenders. *University of Cincinnati Law Review,* 58, 845-880.

Weitzer, R. (2005, September/October). The growing moral panic over prostitution and sex trafficking. *Criminologist,* 30(5), 1, 3-5.

Wilkins, E. (2012, April 1). Super PACS on rise, but not with women. *Houston Chronicle,* p. A8.

Yen, H. (2011, February 4). Hispanics lead minorities showing big census gains. *Houston Chronicle,* p. A19.

Zatz, M. (2000). The convergence of race, ethnicity, gender, and class on court decision making: Looking toward the 21st century. *Criminal Justice 2000 Volume 3: Policies, Processes and Decisions of the Criminal Justice System.* Washington, DC: U.S. Department of Justice.

Index